[JUVENILE JUSTICE IN THE MAKING]

DAVID S. TANENHAUS

Juvenile Justice
IN THE MAKING

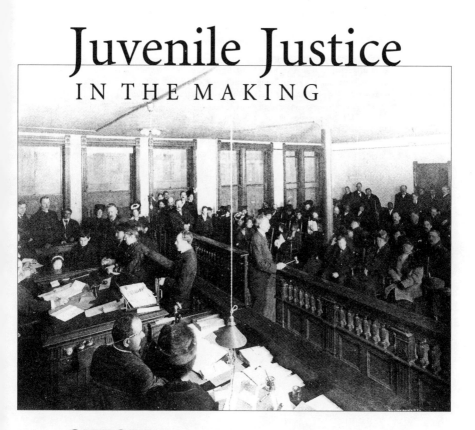

OXFORD
UNIVERSITY PRESS

2004

OXFORD
UNIVERSITY PRESS

Oxford   New York
Auckland   Bangkok   Buenos Aires   Cape Town   Chennai
Dar es Salaam   Delhi   Hong Kong   Istanbul   Karachi   Kolkata
Kuala Lumpur   Madrid   Melbourne   Mexico City   Mumbai   Nairobi
São Paulo   Shanghai   Taipei   Tokyo   Toronto

Copyright © 2004 by Oxford University Press, Inc.,

Published by Oxford University Press, Inc.
198 Madison Avenue, New York, New York 10016
www.oup.com

Oxford is a registered trademark of Oxford University Press

Library of Congress Cataloging-in-Publication Data
Tanenhaus, David Spinoza.
Juvenile justice in the making / by David S. Tanenhaus.
p.   cm.—(Studies in crime and public policy)
ISBN 0-19-516045-2
1. Juvenile courts—United States—History. 2. Juvenile justice,
Administration of—United States—History. I. Title. II. Series.
KF9794.T36 2004
345.73'08—dc21   2003008470

Title page photo: "Juvenile Court in Session," from Cook County Board of
Commissioners, *Charity Service Reports*. Chicago 1904/1905 (HV87.C4C5 Gen).
Courtesy of the University of Chicago Library.

9 8 7 6 5 4 3 2 1

Printed in the United States of America
on acid-free paper

For Jenifer L. Stenfors

(1970–1999)

[FOREWORD]

How does society deal with its young miscreants in ways that are fair, humane, and recognizable just? At the turn of the millennium and just after the first centennial of the invention of the world's first juvenile court, a brilliant young historian here illuminates the manifold ways in which the past can provide a beacon to the future for children in conflict with the law. Writing with a sharpness and dynamism that reveals the ethical paradoxes, social conflicts, and intellectual enterprise embedded in the transformative process of juvenile justice, David S. Tanenhaus engages the anguishing dilemmas of crime and punishment, youthfulness and accountability, consequences and second chances. Tanenhaus, who uncovered a treasure trove of dusty juvenile court records—case files from the first 30 years of Chicago's juvenile court—sifts through the dry, judgmental, often self-justifying prose of the harried probation officers, to reconstitute the vibrant life of the early twentieth century delinquent and the pulsing, dynamic, adaptive institution that first enmeshed the then largely immigrant children and now today's children of color hauled before the court.

Justice for children, the recognition of children as persons, with both rights and special needs, is intrinsically bound to the abolition of slavery in the U.S. Twice in the past century, the reframing of justice for the child closely shadowed the lurching forward of social struggle and legal emancipation of the Negro. It was, as Tanenhaus notes, in the Reconstruction era immediately following the Emancipation, and then again in the civil rights crucible of the 60s, that U.S. courts first addressed and then revisited the issue of children's rights. For if an African American is a person under the Fourteenth Amendment to the Constitution, then what about immigrants, what about women, and what about the child? Property relationships between human beings were eroding, although children had been the exclusive legal property of adult males for centuries—subject to their physical terror, torture, exploitation, and sale. Agitation about the rights of incarcerated children developed momentum in the Reconstruction years, when legal arguments and court opinions in Illinois closely linked slavery concepts with a lively debate on the nature of childhood. And if children are indeed legal persons, what kind of persons are they? These fundamental constructs of humanness involve issues of Constitutional rights, civil rights, criminal justice, and human rights for the majority of the world's people: its children.

The invention of a distinctive court for children, a legal polity described by Professor Francis Allen as "the greatest legal institution invented in the United States," spread like a prairie fire across the U.S. and throughout the world. The birthing of the juvenile court involved a radical insistence that children not be crushed for their transgressions nor brutalized for lack of access and opportunity—that society not give up on its children. The juvenile court's birth was part and parcel of the ferment of urban, industrializing, immigrant America at the turn of the last century. The midwives were the militant, determined women of Hull House: Julia Lathrop, Lucy Flower, Florence Kelley, Mary Bartelme, and the unifying Jane Addams. The terrain of these social reformers included four decades of campaigns for compulsory education and an end to child labor, the removal of children from adult jails and poorhouses, and efforts to advance sanitation, literacy, labor rights, neighborhood democracy, women's rights, the expansion of the public space, and opposition to war.

The juvenile court, laced with tension and paradox, emerged as part of this philosophical mosaic.

Locating the institutional history of the juvenile court in the social turmoil and challenges of each decade is Tanenhaus's singular, creative contribution, for he reveals the children's court as a dynamic work in progress, not a frozen idea or institution limited forever by the constraints and biases of its founders. Much like the family, the school, or the workplace, the children's court becomes, under Tanenhaus's inventive scrutiny, a structure capable of growth and modification, adapting to fresh challenges, emerging norms, and cyclical constraints. Yet he never loses the consistent and core role of the juvenile court as an instrument of the crime control industry—controlling those who might produce unrest or disturb the social order (immigrants, the poor, children of color, wayward girls). Simultaneously, this book places the institutional legal history of juvenile court in a vivid contextual framework, and identifies the changing, flexible, adaptive growth of a remarkably elastic legal entity. This is history as fresh, interpretive storytelling, a reconceptualizing of tired formulas that brings new questions to the forefront today.

Today, hundreds of thousands of children appear in juvenile courts each day in the U.S. on critical matters affecting their liberty, their family, custody, identity, safety from abuse, rape, terror or harassment, health care, education, asylum, speech, privacy, immigration status, and protection from search and seizure. Children are subject to the death penalty and to life without possibility of parole, to indeterminate sentences in locked facilities far away from their families and counsel, and to widening circles of prosecutorial discretion in escalated charging and sentencing enhancements. Further, the accelerating rate of arrest of girls, the revival of status offenses (acts committed by youth that would not be crimes were they perpetrated by an adult, offenses with quaint names such as incorrigible, unruly, or ungovernable, truants, runaways, loitering, curfew laws, and liquor or cigarette law offenses), and the escalating rate of school arrests have vastly widened the net of delinquency involvement for youth, especially youth of color and young women.

It is this contemporary expansion of the punishment power of the juvenile court that provides such vibrant resonance to the history unraveled and marvelously interpreted by Tanenhaus. Those who proclaim that there is, today, a "new breed" of young people, qualitatively different from previous generations, will find themselves silenced by the history lesson rendered here. The contemporary inflammatory language of "superpredator," remorseless, violent, and raging "pre-feral beings" or wolfpacks attempts to make the moral case for a harsh criminal response; subsumed by this media tidal wave of "gang crime" or juvenile violence was the language of "children" or youthfulness and its structures for adolescent delinquents. In the name of public safety, a racially coded discourse about dangerousness means that it is the children of color who bear the brunt of this backlash of vilification and fear. Juxtaposed to this throughout the century is the radical insistence—still believed by a majority of Americans—that children not be crushed for their transgressions—that society not give up on children, even that tiny minority of children who commit violent crimes.

Everyone agrees that the juvenile court has not lived up to its most ambitious missions. But the fact remains that juvenile court continues to sanction the vast majority of juvenile offenders without "criminalizing" the youth. And most youngsters who are petitioned to the court never return. The juvenile court reworks itself over decades and discourses to acknowledge the different nature of adolescent competence, capacity, and culpability from that of adults.

That famous extremist, William Shakespeare, wrote in *The Winter's Tale*:

> I would that there were no age between ten and three-and-twenty, or that youth would sleep out the rest; for there is nothing in the between but getting wenches with child, wronging the ancestry, stealing, fighting.

Ironically, if all male children aged 10 to 18 were put to sleep or were incarcerated until their twenty-third birthday, there would still be 90 percent of the violent crime in America: the adult offenders. The intense concentration on youth crime is a social and political choice—and always has been—rather than a strategic response to the facts about crime and public safety.

Tanenhaus does not neglect the other major social institutions whose vitality directly impacts young people, families, and the juvenile court. Schools, child welfare systems, probation, youth agencies, parks, and health care services constrict or expand, are well-supported or neglected by society. Where do the young go for help, attention, development, socialization, survival, care, and attention—other than each other? Indeed the intimate relationships between the common school and the institutions of juvenile justice long assumed that if children were no longer engaged in labor nor incarcerated in adult prisons, they would be attending school. This core principle of literacy and education as the proper preparation for citizenship and productive work tied the early juvenile court to the public school through truancy, probation, and juvenile sanctions. Recently, however, children are increasingly policed in schools, barricaded in schools, arrested in and excluded from schools (through expulsions, suspensions, high-stakes testing, and drop-outs), and petitioned to juvenile court for behaviors previously sanctioned within schools themselves—and in ways that are grossly racially disproportionate.

As fiscal priorities shift from education, scholarships, access to jobs, and cultural expression to prison construction, law enforcement growth, and expanded mechanisms for the social control and exile of sectors of youth, so the landscape of the young is transformed. When their minor offenses are no longer dealt with in stride by retail stores, teachers, sports coaches, neighbors, parents, mental health professionals, or youth workers, but rather police are called, arrests are made, and petitions are filed, we are all at peril. The institution of the juvenile court thus functions as a gateway for the failures of the other youth institutions; overcrowded juvenile correctional institutions, deficient youth facilities, and disproportionate racial and economic confinement are among the consequences.

The youth themselves, being the intelligent and observant people they are, are vividly alert to issues of fairness that lie at the heart of justice. They are sensitive to adult hypocrisies—particularly to society harshly holding the young alone accountable for protracted adult social failures. We would do well to support and welcome their voices, their opinions, and their best interests, as required by developing international human rights law. History schools us in the powerful role of children themselves, who have changed the world by their collective actions in Little Rock, Birmingham, Soweto, and Tien An Mien. We know, too, of the possibilities of adult, mobilized civic will to invest in our common future: all our children.

The idea and the institution of the juvenile court spread across the world a century ago; today, it is global human rights law that has created a unique body of children's law. Now, sadly and ironically, international law has codified and is developing children's rights with the tumultuous and elastic participation of virtually every nation in the world *except* the United States. The Convention on the Rights of the Child and its associated protocols and case law embody the innovations of the juvenile court founders, and the rights revolution of the sixties, with the new notion of the right to participation by children.

At the dawn of the new millennium, the issues clarified one hundred years ago are in full contention. This early history allows us to revisit first principles and emerge more enlightened to face the dilemmas of today.

Bernardine Dohrn

A lthough I misspent a great deal of my own youth, I did not end up in juvenile court until graduate school. In my case, an abiding interest in youth and legal history, not truancy, incorrigibility, or larceny landed me in the Cook County (Chicago) Juvenile Court. I soon learned that it had been the world's first such court and due to celebrate its centennial in 1999. As I researched the court's origins and reconstructed its early operations, I learned that the Illinois Secretary of State Archives held the case files for a perplexing Illinois Supreme Court decision, *The People v. Turner*, 55 Illinois 280 (1870). Justice Anthony Thornton, who had just joined the high court and served as a Republican representative for Illinois in the famous 39th Congress that had passed the Fourteenth Amendment, authored its unanimous opinion in *Turner*. It declared that under Illinois's brand-new constitution, children were entitled to the due process of law, and freed Daniel O'Connell, a fourteen-year-old Irish-Catholic boy, from incarceration in the Chicago Reform School. *Turner* has long puzzled scholars of juvenile justice, for a decision that treated a child like an adult with personal rights and privileges seemed to belong to the rights revolution of the 1960s. This apparent historical anachronism intrigued me.

I traveled to Springfield, the burial place of Abraham Lincoln, to learn more about Daniel O'Connell, who shared the name of the famous leader of the Irish liberation movement of the 1820s and 1830s. As I entered the state archive, one of its staffers was positioning miniature soldiers on a large map spread across a table. When I asked what he was doing, he explained that he was recreating the Battle of Gettsyburg to figure out a way for Pickett's Charge to have succeeded, so that "our side" could have won the war. That week I realized how Southern central Illinois really was, and, in the case files for *Turner*, I learned the significance of the Union's victory for Daniel's fate.

Although since the 1980s scholars have revealed that the Civil War, by abolishing chattel slavery, had launched a revolutionary era in which Americans debated what liberty, dependency, and governance would mean in the new nation, they have not explored how these debates raised new questions about "dependent children."[1] These were children who had been abused, neglected, or considered to be at risk of becoming juvenile delinquents, but who had not been charged with or convicted of committing a criminal offense. Whether the state, without a criminal trial, could incarcerate these children, such as Daniel, in reformatories in order to prevent them from turning into juvenile delinquents raised fundamental questions about whether children, like the freed people, now had civil rights that had to be protected. If not, would children become the new slaves in a society that supposedly had abolished slavery?

The imprisonment of Daniel raised fundamental questions about the legal status of children at a critical moment in American constitutional history when Americans began constructing a modern liberal state that privileged the constitutional rights of autonomous individuals.[2] His case also occurred at a transitional stage in the history of American childhood. Increasing numbers of Americans supported the idea that children should be in school, not at work in the factories, mills, and mines of the industrializing nation. But before 1870 few states had passed compulsory school attendance laws or restricted child labor, and the laws that did exist generally applied to children under twelve or fourteen years of age.[3] In urban America, almost one out of every three children between the ages of ten and fifteen worked to help support their families.[4] It is thus not surprising that the Chicago Reform School recorded the "occupations" of the children it received, or that "attending school" was listed as the occupation for only 178 out of the 1,121 boys committed to the institution between 1856 and 1869.[5] In fact Daniel had worked in a tobacco factory for eighteen months prior to his arrest.[6]

Daniel O'Connell's case thus posed profound questions about how American law should treat children in a formative era for not only law but also for childhood. The jurisprudence of youth that developed in response to this question of whether children were autonomous beings or the property of either their parents or the state set the stage for the subject of this book: the emergence and development of the American juvenile court. Through a detailed historical-institutional analysis of the trial-and-error development of America's first juvenile court, this book addresses one of the fundamental and recurring problems in the history of law—how to treat the young. Through its analysis of a revolutionary institution, it explores the early history of juvenile justice in order to help the reader think more clearly about what its future should be.

Since beginning this project, I have had the opportunity to work with judges, children's advocates, scholars, juvenile justice practitioners, archivists, and graduates of the juvenile court to engage its storied and controversial past. It is a pleasure to have the opportunity to thank all those who have made this book possible. I am indebted to Barry Karl for sending me to juvenile court, and to Bernardine Dohrn, Bill Novak, Peggy Rosenheim, and Frank Zimring for helping me to appreciate its political, legal, and social significance. Their passion for history and social policy have all shaped this book in countless ways. I also owe special debts to Jenifer Stenfors, Frank Zimring, Bill Novak, Michael Willrich, Andy Fry, Steve Schlossman, Mary Wammack, Tom Green, Chris Tomlins, Art McEvoy, Dirk Hartog, Steve Drizin, Elizabeth Dale, Andrew Cohen, Jeff Fagan, an anonymous reader for Oxford University Press, and my wonderful editor at

Oxford, Dedi Felman. At important stages, they all provided invaluable readings of the manuscript.

Like many of the children described in this book, I spent time at a number of institutions. The History Department at the University of Nevada, Las Vegas (UNLV), has been my academic home since 1997, and I could not have asked for more supportive colleagues, especially the members of our Faculty Enrichment Seminar who read parts of the manuscript. They include Andrew Bell, Greg Brown, Raquel Casas, Andy Fry, Jo Goodwin, Colin Loader, Chris Rasmussen, Willard Rollings, Hal Rothman, Michelle Tusan, Barbara Wallace, Mary Wammack, Paul Werth, Elizabeth White, and David Wrobel. I am also appreciative of my newer colleagues in the William S. Boyd School of Law for making a historian feel so welcome as part of a law faculty. Special thanks to Annette Appell, Mary Berkheiser, Chris Bryant, Lynne Henderson, Bob Lawless, Tom McAffee, Carl Tobias, and our remarkable dean, Dick Morgan, and his splendid executive assistant Dianne Fouret. I was also extremely fortunate to have spent 2000–2001 as a Mellon Postdoctoral Research Fellow at the Newberry Library in Chicago. It is a pleasure to thank Jim Grossman, the Newberry staff (especially Sara Austin), my fellow fellows, my friends at Coffee Expressions, and Dean Jim Frey of the College of Liberal Arts at UNLV for providing salary support that allowed me to spend such a stimulating year among humanists.

I would also like to express gratitude to the Rockefeller Archive Center, the Andrew W. Mellon Foundation, the Harry Barnard Family, the University of Chicago, and the James E. Rogers Research Grant Foundation at the William S. Boyd School of Law for providing the necessary financial assistance for completing this book. I also appreciate the help that I received from Archie Motley at the Chicago Historical Society, and from the archivists and staff of the Joseph Regenstein Library, the Newberry Library, the Illinois Secretary of State Archives, the Arthur and Elizabeth Schlesinger Library on the History of Women in America, the Department of Special Collections at the University of Illinois Library, and the Lied Library (and Law Library) at

UNLV. I am especially indebted to Phil Costello, the Archivist at the Circuit Court of Cook County, and his staff for locating the lost case files of the Cook County Juvenile Court and to the Honorable Sophia Hall, who granted me permission to work with them.

Earlier versions of parts of this book appeared as "Justice for the Child: The Beginning of the Juvenile Court in Chicago," *Chicago History* 27 (winter 1998–1999): 4–19; "The Evolution of Transfer out of the Juvenile Court," in *The Changing Borders of Juvenile Justice: The Transfer of Adolescents to the Criminal Court*, edited by Jeffrey Fagan and Franklin E. Zimring (Chicago: University of Chicago Press, 2000), 13–43; "Growing Up Dependent: Family Preservation in Early Twentieth-Century Chicago," *Law and History Review* 19 (fall 2001): 547–582; "The Evolution of Juvenile Courts in the Early Twentieth Century: Beyond the Myth of Immaculate Construction," in *A Century of Juvenile Justice*, edited by Margaret K. Rosenheim, Franklin E. Zimring, David S. Tanenhaus and Bernardine Dohrn (Chicago: University of Chicago Press, 2002), 42–73; and as "'Owing to the Extreme Youth of the Accused': The Changing Legal Response to Juvenile Homicide," *Journal of Criminal Law and Criminology* 92 (Spring & Summer 2002): 641–706. I am grateful for permission to incorporate this material into this book.

As this is a book about beginnings, it is also fitting to thank my parents, Gussie and Joe Tanenhaus, for their love and nurturing. I also thank my siblings, Beth, Sam, and Michael, and their spouses (Bill, Kathy, and Becca), and my nieces Annie, Stefanie, and Lydia, and my nephew Max, for their love and support. Growing up in a family that cared about ideas (thanks to Gussie, we had a portrait of Henry James over the mantel) ensured that they all would play active roles in this project. I especially want to thank Beth and Gussie for sending me newspaper clippings about children's cases, and Sam for discussing narrative strategies with me.

The writing of this book has spanned two lifetimes. Jenifer Stenfors, my first wife, after a heroic struggle against breast cancer, passed away on September 9, 1999. Jen's spirit inspires everyone who knew her, and this book is lovingly dedicated to her. My wife Virginia Tanenhaus has made life joyous once again, and I am delighted to thank Ginger and our delinquent dogs, Nigella and Oz, for their enduring love and support.

[CONTENTS]

If we don't want to throw out the baby with the bath water,
treat all youngsters more harshly, and perhaps even abolish
the juvenile court and return to the days of the Industrial
Revolution where we had one criminal court for both
children and adults, we must do better with the thousands
of juveniles we see every day in our juvenile courts.
—Judge Eugene A. Moore, January 13, 2000

Introduction

In 1999, in Oakland County, Michigan, the trial of Nathaniel Abraham, a thirteen-year-old, for first-degree murder focused international attention on the state of American juvenile justice during its centennial year.[1] When Nathaniel was only eleven, he had stolen a .22-caliber rifle and on October 29, 1997, shot Ronnie Greene Jr., whom he did not know, in the head. Nathaniel had fired the fatal shot from a hilltop more than two hundred feet from Greene. Two days later, after receiving a tip from a neighbor that Nathaniel had been seen firing a rifle, the police took the boy, who was in his Halloween costume, from his grammar school and questioned him in the presence of his mother at the station. At the time of his arrest, Nathaniel was no stranger to the Pontiac police; the sixth-grader was a suspect in more than twenty crimes, including burglaries, home invasions, and assaults.[2] Although Nathaniel confessed to firing the rifle, he denied aiming it at anyone.

Oakland County prosecutors rejected Nathaniel's contention that the shooting was accidental. The neighbor who had told the police about Nathaniel also alleged that the boy had fired the rifle at him. The prosecutors found other witnesses who said that Nathaniel had vowed to shoot someone and had bragged about killing a person shortly after Greene's death. Under a collection of new laws that went into effect in Michigan in 1997, they prosecuted the eleven-year-old as an adult.[3] They charged him with first-degree murder, two firearm violations, and two counts of assault with intent to murder. If convicted of first-degree murder, Nathaniel would receive a sentence of life imprisonment without the possibility of parole.

Nathaniel's attorney, Geoffrey Fieger, argued that Greene's death was an accident, the result of "child's play" with a gun. "This is a little boy. We're not disputing the fact that he's guilty of something. It's the way he's treated that's at issue. We're not saying he should walk the streets. He should be treated like a sick 11-year-old, not a murdering 25-year-old."[4] He used a version of the infancy defense, which had been an important part of Anglo-American law from at least the fourteenth century until the spread of the juvenile court movement in the early twentieth century. Under the common law, children below the age of seven were immune from prosecution in capital cases (a category that the British Parliament expanded in the eighteenth century to cover increasing numbers of property offenses) because they were considered incapable by nature of having "felonious discretion."[5] This meant that they were not able to form the "necessary intent" to commit a crime. Children from seven to fourteen were presumed to be incapable of having the necessary intent, but the state could rebut this presumption and, if successful, prosecute the child. Children fourteen and older were tried as adults. Fieger argued that Nathaniel, as a mildly retarded child who functioned intellectually at the level of a six- to an eight-year-old, could not form the necessary intent to kill. Thus, he could not be guilty of murder.[6]

The prosecutors depicted the boy as a premeditated killer who knew what he was doing. They argued that he discussed killing someone and then followed through with his plans. After four days of deliberation, the jury reached its verdict. Nathaniel was acquitted of first-degree murder but convicted of second-degree murder. This meant that the jurors found that he either intended to kill or injure Greene or knew that his actions created a high risk of death or injury but could not find that he plotted to kill Greene.[7] As the foreman of the jury Daniel J. Stotlz explained, "we felt that he knew the firearm was dangerous."[8]

The trial, which Court TV broadcast in its entirety, made Nathaniel Abraham into a poster child for the troubled state of American juvenile justice. Amnesty International reprinted an AP photo of the African-American child in the Oakland County courtroom on the cover of its report entitled "Betraying the Young: Human Rights Violations against Children in the US Justice System." The report criticized the United States for violating treaties that it had ratified, including the International Covenant on Civil and Political Rights and the Convention against Torture, as well as ones, such as the 1989 United Nations Convention on the Rights of the Child, that it had not adopted. At the time of the Abraham trial, 192 nations, including all the members of the United Nations, except for the United States and Somalia, had ratified this landmark human rights treaty. As Amnesty International pointed out, American juvenile justice systems, which had processed over 1.7 million delinquency cases in 1995 alone, were overcrowded, relied on excessive incarceration, inflicted cruel and unusual punishments, failed to provide adequate mental health services, and processed a disproportionate number of cases of racial and ethnic minorities. All of these practices, according to the watchdog agency, violated international human rights law.[9]

Even more disturbing than the state of American juvenile justice was the trend toward transferring adolescents from juvenile court to the adult criminal justice system. In the 1990s, for instance, in response to mounting concerns about youth violence, more than forty states passed laws that made it easier to try children as adults.[10] This practice led to more children being imprisoned with adult inmates, where they are more likely to be sexually abused and less likely to have adequate educational opportunities. Moreover, children in the criminal justice system also faced severe sentences, including life imprisonment without the possibility of parole and the death penalty.[11] During the 1990s the United States was one of only six nations, including Iran, Nigeria, Pakistan, Saudi Arabia, and Yemen, known to have executed persons for crimes that they committed as juveniles. As the law professor

Victor Streib observed, "the death penalty for juvenile offenders has become essentially a uniquely American practice, in that it has been abandoned legally by nations everywhere else, due to the express provisions of the United Nations Convention on the Rights of the Child and of several other international treaties and agreements."[12] The United States, once the leader in the international crusade to secure justice for children, had become a rogue nation.

Faith in childhood, and its corollary that separate courts are required for children because they are developmentally different from adults, appeared to be vanishing. The United States, as the sociologist David Garland has shown, developed a "crime complex" in the late twentieth century. Americans accepted high crime rates as normal, politicized and presented crime in emotional ways, focused on victims' rights and public safety, distrusted the effectiveness of justice systems, discounted the authority of criminologists, and increasingly turned to the private sector for personal security. As Garland contends, "once established, this view of the world does not change rapidly." Instead, "our attitudes to crime—our fears and resentments, but also our common sense narratives and understandings—become settled cultural facts that are sustained and reproduced by cultural scripts and not by criminological research or official data."[13] People living in such a society tend to ignore falling crime and victimization rates, while questioning the effectiveness of justice systems and the relevance of the experts who study them. Thus, even as juvenile offending rates in the United States declined dramatically after 1994, states continued to pass more punitive laws, and three states executed men for crimes that they had committed as juveniles.[14]

Almost forgotten in this highly crime-conscious climate, during which a *New York Times* headline boldly announced "Fear of Crime Trumps the Fear of Lost Youth," was the fact that the juvenile court has been one of America's most influential legal inventions. The first juvenile court, which was established in Cook County, Illinois, in 1899, became a model within a generation for policy-makers in European, South American, and Asian nations. These child savers looked to this American creation to learn how to divert children from the criminal justice system and to handle their cases in a less punitive fashion. By the end of the twentieth century, as the criminologist Franklin Zimring noted, "no legal institution in Anglo-American legal history [had] achieved such universal acceptance among the diverse legal systems of the industrial democracies."[15] Yet the future of the juvenile court in the United States remained in doubt. Even some children's advocates, including the highly respected law professor Barry Feld, called for its abolition.[16]

With the world watching, including protesters at the courthouse led by the Reverend Al Sharpton, who charged that the prosecution of Nathaniel Abraham was racially motivated, Judge Eugene Moore had to sentence the thirteen-year-old. Moore had served as a juvenile court judge for more than thirty years and was a former president of the National Council of Juvenile and Family Court Judges. Due to the peculiarities of Michigan law, he had three options. First, he could sentence Nathaniel to a juvenile sentence and commit him to a maximum-security juvenile detention center, but he would have to be released before he turned twenty-one, even if he had not been rehabilitated and still posed a serious threat to public safety. Second, he could sentence Nathaniel as an adult and send him directly to adult prison for eight to twenty-five years. Third, he had the option of using a staggered sentence that would allow him to commit the boy initially to a juvenile detention center but retain the possibility of imposing an adult sentence. The prosecutors recommended that the judge exercise this third option.

Judge Moore began his much-anticipated sentencing of Nathaniel Abraham with a history lesson. He declared:

> In 1999 we celebrated the 100th anniversary of the founding of the Juvenile Court in America. It started in 1899 in Cook County, Chicago. Its roots were in England during the Industrial Revolution. During the Industrial Revolution, two groups of people joined hands to fight the abuse of children. One group opposed the criminal justice system treating children the same as adults when

punishing those convicted of a crime. Adults and children were punished alike. The second group was concerned about using children as chattels as a form of very cheap labor. Little food—no school—large dormitories, and working 18 hours a day was a common abuse of children.

The protection of children from these abuses brought about the Cook County (Chicago) Juvenile Court in America.

Moore highlighted the centennial of the juvenile court in order to reemphasize the foundational principles of American juvenile justice. The founders of the juvenile court, he explained, believed in *individualized justice* because they "recognized that children were different from adults. They were still young, immature and not fully developed. Thus character and behavior could still be molded and they could be rehabilitated. *Rehabilitation* became the byword of the juvenile court. Few wanted to lock up children for life." He added: "There was a recognition that if we were going to protect society from future criminal behavior by the child we had better do something to rehabilitate the child so that when released by the juvenile court, the child was changed. Only by doing this would you and I be protected from further criminal activity by the child." Yet, he lamented, juvenile courts from the beginning had not been given adequate resources. Consequently, "our Juvenile Courts failed in changing many delinquents' behavior." This failure had led reformers "to advocate that our Juvenile Courts not 'try to change a child' unless *we were even more certain that the child was 'guilty.'*"[17] The United States Supreme Court had agreed, and in its landmark 1967 decision *In Re Gault* had held that children in juvenile court were entitled to most of the due process safeguards that adults had in the criminal justice system, including the right to counsel.

Judge Moore's excursion into the history of the juvenile court appeared eccentric to many commentators, but this book is an argument that a thorough understanding of the history and institutions of American juvenile justice can be of substantial and specific help in confronting the policy choices of the twenty-first century. Indeed, I would argue that deciding the Nathaniel Abraham case without a deep understanding of history would be folly, for we would be discarding a usable past that can help us to think more clearly about the future of juvenile justice. Accordingly, this book revisits this past in order to answer three inter-related questions about the rise of the juvenile court. First, how was it possible to imagine and build a juvenile court? Second, how did these early courts actually work? And third, how did the juvenile court achieve legitimacy (i.e., when did it seem "natural" that a city or county must have one of these specialized courts)? The answers to these questions can be found in the history of the Chicago Juvenile Court, for not only did it serve as a model court but its creators, staff, clients, and commentators all helped to shape the administration of juvenile justice more generally. In addition, the first generation of juvenile justice practitioners addressed many of the issues that we still face. Although studying history cannot provide definitive answers to present questions, it can help us to frame more carefully the hard choices we must make and to remember why we established a separate system of justice for juveniles in the first place.

This book makes two important contributions to the existing literature about juvenile justice. First, it provides a set of findings that are far removed from the standard account of the juvenile court that describes it as an immaculate construction born fully formed, like Athena, in Chicago in 1899 and marched forward without any major changes until *Gault*.[18] Instead, as every chapter in this study shows, significant changes in the structure, rules, and self-conception of juvenile justice have been a part of its history from the beginning. Juvenile justice grew by accretion, and its experiential growth was largely fueled by local politics. This discovery should not come as a surprise to historians, for it is much less surprising than the creation myth it replaces. More important, the recovery of this history forces us to reexamine the critical question of whether the juvenile court is conceptually flawed because its architects combined elements of social welfare with crime control. The mixture, according to Barry Feld, produced "an inherently unstable organization that inevitably subordinated social welfare to penal concerns."[19] This book, however, reveals a much more complicated and less predetermined history, in which social welfare considerations often outweighed penal concerns. Thus, this book provides a corrected frame of reference for twenty-first-century policy-makers seeking to find the proper balance between social welfare and crime control.

Second, this book is an extended argument for institutional legal history. It offers a brand of analysis reminiscent of legal realism and the institutional studies of governance conducted in the early twentieth century, which argued that legal institutions and forms were more important than the words used in judicial opinions. Although this method appears more suited for 1934 than 2004, the history of juvenile justice (and of American law in general) has too often failed to examine institutional development in its social context. The result has been numerous studies of the rhetoric of juvenile justice and representations of juvenile delinquents but no thorough examination of the everyday workings of a juvenile justice system that revealed its trial-and-error development.[20] This book provides such a perspective on the evolution of America's first juvenile court. In doing so, it exposes the inherent tensions in establishing the precise line between the state's role as a guardian and the rights of children and their parents. It also reveals the beginnings of the contemporary battles over how to combat juvenile delinquency, including the question of whether it is better to target individuals and families for adjustment or communities for reorganization.

The historical journey begins in late nineteenth century with the crusade led by Lucy Flower and Julia Lathrop to establish the world's first juvenile court in Chicago. Chapter 1 reveals how lawmakers carved the jurisdiction over juvenile delinquents out of the state's preexisting child welfare system. The juvenile court was thus established with the dual goals of addressing social welfare and crime control, issues that remain interconnected in juvenile justice.

As the next chapters demonstrate, American juvenile justice has been a work in progress. Central to its development has been determining which children belonged in this separate system and, equally important, who should have the power to make decisions about the court's clientele. In the early twentieth century, legislators, machine politicians, philanthropists, reformers, reporters, judges, prosecutors, the police, probation officers, religious leaders, social workers, teachers, principals, mental health experts, parents and family members, community residents, and children themselves all played important roles in this struggle to define the appropriate role for the juvenile court in American self-government. The borders of juvenile justice then, much as they are today, were in flux.

Chapter 2 reveals what a promising but inchoate beginning the world's first juvenile court had in 1899. It describes how the "defining features" of progressive juvenile justice, such as private hearings, were additions that only later became standard practices in urban juvenile courts during the 1910s and 1920s. Chapter 3 reconstructs the handling of dependency cases in the Chicago Juvenile Court, including comparing how institutional and home-based welfare programs for dependent children operated in the early twentieth century. It also explores why mothers' pensions programs, the precursor to the federal welfare programs Aid to Dependent Children and Aid to Families with Dependent Children, were gradually removed from juvenile courts and did not ultimately become a "defining feature" of progressive juvenile justice. Chapter 4 focuses on the political and legal battles waged over the Chicago Juvenile Court in the early twentieth century. Although supporters of the juvenile court used these struggles to legitimate the new institution, these periodic battles also help to explain why many components of the progressive vision for juvenile justice did not coalesce until after World War I.

Chapter 5 examines the operations of the Juvenile Psychopathic Institute, which opened in 1909 and was the nation's first such institution. It focuses on William Healy, the first director of the institute, and his contributions to understanding adolescent development and the causes of juvenile delinquency. His research helped to make psychological testing into a "defining feature" of progressive juvenile justice, even though clinical work with children and adolescents was promoted more than it was actually practiced. The chapter concludes with an analysis of how Healy's studies deflected attention from juvenile justice, raised new concerns about its efficacy in the 1920s, and ironically contributed to the parents of the baby boomers adopting a medical model as part of their child-rearing practices.

Chapter 6 describes simultaneous movements in the 1930s that sought to remove children from the juvenile court. The first, led by the sociologist and social activist Clifford Shaw and his associates at the Institute for Juvenile Research, worked with residents of high-crime areas to develop their own delinquency prevention programs. The second, led by Denis Sullivan, the chief justice of the Cook County Criminal Court, attempted to restrict the juvenile court's jurisdiction over children charged with committing serious and violent crimes. Thus, during the Great Depression, when the nation experienced its first "crime complex" of the twentieth century, a new form of child saving that emphasized innovative, community-based delinquency prevention programs took root. Yet at the same time the Illinois Supreme Court stripped the Chicago Juvenile Court of its original and exclusive jurisdiction over children older than ten who were accused of committing felonies.

The conclusion returns to Judge Moore's sentencing of Nathaniel Abraham and analyzes his use of history in deciding the boy's fate. This book, much like Judge Moore's sentencing opinion, aims to provide a historical framework for thinking about the future of juvenile justice in the United States. It offers a new perspective for considering the proper role of the state as a guardian, the rights of children and their parents, and how to balance social welfare with crime control in the twenty-first century. Although history cannot provide us with specific answers, it can at least help us to ask better policy questions.

[JUVENILE JUSTICE IN THE MAKING]

ONE

We ought to have a "children's court" in Chicago, and
we ought to have a "children's judge," who should attend to
no other business.
—Frederick Wines, Secretary of the Illinois State Board
    of Charities, 1898

Imagining a Children's Court

At the Third Annual Illinois Conference on Charities, whose theme was "The Children of the State," Frederick Wines declared: "What we should have, in our system of criminal justice, is an entirely separate system of courts for children, in large cities, who commit offenses which could be criminal in adults."[1] The organizers of the conference—Lucy Flower, a philanthropist, and Julia Lathrop, the first woman to serve on the State Board of Charities—used this two-day event to help make the passage of a juvenile court law into a legislative priority for the upcoming session of the Illinois General Assembly.[2] The conference, held in November 1898 at the Eastern Hospital for the Insane in Kankakee, brought together the past and future of child saving in Illinois. Reformers like Wines, who had served on the State Board of Charities since its inception in 1870, conferred with relative newcomers like Mary Bartelme, a recent graduate of Northwestern Law School, who, a quarter of a century later, would become the first woman to preside over the Cook County Juvenile Court.

The attendees at the conference, it is important to remember, were discussing a legal institution that did not yet exist. It was not clear what a children's court would look like or how it might operate. In fact the proposed legislation that Flower and Lathrop wanted to promote at the conference had still not been drafted.

This chapter examines how it became possible to imagine a children's court, and how its supporters campaigned to translate their vision into an institutional reality. The moral crusade for justice for the child in Illinois, spearheaded by Lucy Flower and Julia Lathrop, took more than a decade and ultimately resulted in the passage in 1899 of the world's first juvenile court law, "an Act to Regulate the Treatment and Control of Dependent, Neglected and Delinquent Children."[3] This pioneering act, which had been significantly amended during the legislative process, asserted state responsibility for both dependent and delinquent children and thus merged concerns about child welfare with crime control. It served as a model law for most of the states in the union, and also for nations in Europe, South America, and Asia.[4]

In 1888, Lucy Flower, whom the social settlement leader Graham Taylor christened "the mother of the juvenile court," had first called for the creation of a "parental court" to hear the cases of all dependent, neglected, and delinquent children under sixteen years of age in Chicago.[5] Flower, a Bostonian by birth, had been orphaned and then adopted by a respectable Eastern family in the 1830s. She later taught school in Wisconsin to support herself until she married a prominent Madison attorney, James Monroe Flower, and moved with him to Chicago in 1873, two years after the Great Fire. While her husband established himself in the legal community, she turned her attentions to philanthropy and served on the Board of the Trustees of the Chicago Home for the Friendless and the Half-Orphan Asylum.[6] Once enmeshed in the city's culture of Protestant charities, including serving as the president of the influential Chicago Women's Club in 1890–1891, Flower learned about the dismal conditions for poor children in Chicago and forged important friendships, including one with Julia Lathrop.

The friendship of Flower and Lathrop symbolized the converging of two important female reform traditions and set the stage for close ties between Chicago's philanthropists and the evolving juvenile justice system. Flower was a member of the generation of female philanthropists whom the historian Kathleen

McCarthy has called the "Gilded Age patrons."[7] These were society women who generously supported the building of the city's charitable institutions, like the orphan asylums on whose boards Flower served. Lathrop, on the other hand, was twenty years younger than Flower and, as a graduate of Vassar College, belonged to the first generation of college-educated women in American history. Although she was certainly comfortable rubbing shoulders with Chicago's elite, Lathrop made her home at Jane Addams's Hull House, the famous social settlement on the city's Near West Side. Lathrop opted for social work as a full-time career, not the more traditional combination of marriage, homemaking, and part-time benevolent work. This powerful union of a philanthropist and a child welfare expert not only made the crusade for a children's court viable but also established the close relationship between the city's elite and the juvenile justice system that lasted well into the twentieth century. Without the support of the city's philanthropic community, the juvenile court, especially in its early years, would have had difficulties operating.

The Chicago crusade that Flower and Lathrop led represented a local manifestation of a transatlantic social movement in the 1880s and 1890s to solve the problems of crime and poverty, which were often conceived of and discussed in similar terms.[8] This concern with the social lives of urban populations developed as a response to the expansion of the wage economy, the spread of market processes, and the rise of large-scale industrialization.[9] These reformers did not believe that individual responsibility was an adequate explanation for the existence of widespread disorder in the modern city and questioned the concept of free will on which the liberal state was being built. They challenged the notion that individuals make all the choices that fundamentally shape their lives. Instead, they redescribed crime and poverty as environmental problems that required thorough investigation in order to discover and eradicate their root causes.[10]

The young male and his world, including the penal system, often became a subject for these late-nineteenth-century inquiries into the "dark places."[11] Partly this resulted from earlier studies like Henry Mayhew and John Binny's book *The Criminal Prisons of London and Scenes of Prison Life* (1862), which had revealed that the "greater number of criminals are found between the ages of 15 and 25."[12] As Mayhew and Binny explained, "[this period] when human beings begin to assert themselves is the most trying time for every form of government—whether it be parental, political, or social; and those indomitable natures who cannot or will not brook ruling, then become heedless of all authority, and respect no law but their own."[13] Concerns about older juveniles would lead to intensive study of these turbulent years, which in the early twentieth century the psychologist G. Stanley Hall labeled "adolescence."[14]

The new science of child development successfully made the case that adolescents were "more like infants in their nature and needs than they were like adults" and should be treated like children. Yet it was the presence of very young children in police stations and jails that outraged child savers and provoked them to question how the entire criminal justice system worked.[15] For instance, when John Altgeld, a lawyer with political aspirations, investigated Chicago's system of justice, he discovered in 1882 that 263 out of the 7,566 individuals (3.5 percent) incarcerated in the House of Corrections were fourteen years old or younger, including twenty children less than eleven years old.[16] According to Altgeld, the majority of these children had been arrested for being homeless or for wandering the streets and should never have been imprisoned.[17]

In a short book entitled *Our Penal Machinery and Its Victims*, Altgeld likened the criminal justice system to "a great mill which, in one way or another, supplies its own grist, a maelstrom which draws from the outside, and then keeps its victims moving in a circle until swallowed in the vortex."[18] This machinery made "criminals out of many that are not naturally so," including the children trapped inside, by subjecting them to "a criminal experience."[19]

The descent, according to Altgeld, began with an arrest. He asked his readers to imagine what this must feel like: "Stop right here, and for a moment imagine yourself forced to submit to being handcuffed, and see what kind of feelings will be aroused in you." He added: "Submission to that one act of degradation prepares many a young man for a career of crime."[20] Next, the offender was taken to the police station, where he would spend the night "with the vicious of every kind," literally an introduction to his future partners in crime.[21]

After the long night ended, the accused would appear before a police magistrate. At this stage, almost one third of the cases were discharged because of improper arrest. These individuals, although now free, had still suffered from the trauma of being arrested and spending a harrowing night in jail. The magistrate fined those charged with minor infractions—typically disorderly conduct—and if they were unable to pay the fine, he sentenced them to the House of Corrections to work off their debt to society, at the rate of 25 cents per day. This could take from a week to half a year and could devastate family members who depended on the incarcerated individual for financial support.[22]

Those charged with more serious crimes were bound over to the grand jury. If they could not pay the bond, they remained in jail until it next met. Since the grand jury was generally in session for only twelve days a month, with new members serving on each jury, the wait for one's case to be heard could be a few days, a couple of weeks, or even a few months.[23] If the grand jury issued a true bill (i.e., found that there was enough evidence to warrant prosecution), the accused began the waiting process again, this time for his or her trial.

By the late nineteenth century, according to a report by the members of the May 1898 Cook County Grand Jury, the grand jury generally devoted the first two days of its session to "boy cases," which were the "cases against boys of from ten to sixteen years of age, for various offenses, some of them serious, but most of them almost frivolous."[24] The prospect of sending the children involved in these "frivolous" cases through the criminal justice system upset these jurors as it had earlier ones.[25] Their report pointed out:

> Take the case of a boy of ten years, caught stealing a pair
> of shoes from the front of a store, where they were

temptingly displayed to attract customers. We find that he was locked up over night in the police station; sent from there to the justice court in the patrol wagon; tried in the justice court; bound over to the grand jury, and locked up in the county jail for twelve days, waiting for a session of the next grand jury. All of this time he was associated with adult criminals and drunkards, locked up in a cell, and generally subjected to treatment incompatible with his years or his offense.[26]

The problem, from their perspective, was that "the system—if it can be so called—recognizes no difference between the child offender and the most hardened criminals. All go the same route, and together."[27]

These concerns about the criminal justice system harming juveniles led grand juries to throw out many cases of children under sixteen years of age. As Judge Murray Floyd Tuley, "the Dean of the Chicago Bench," later explained, "before the Juvenile Court was established, all cases of boys detected in crime came to the Criminal court in the regular course of events. Not less than fifteen cases of boys under the age of sixteen years came before the Grand Jury every month."[28] He added: "Not less than seventy-five per cent of these cases were regularly thrown out by the Grand Jury because of the tender age of the boy. The deplorable fact must be admitted, however, that most of this seventy-five per cent turned loose by the Grand Jury eventually were returned and indicted later for repeated offenses." The reason for recidivism, he explained, was "not difficult to locate. The poisonous effect of the police station and jail experience clung to the boy after he was turned loose by the Grand Jury."[29] Thus, like Altgeld, Judge Tuley argued that the criminal justice system manufactured criminals.

By the early 1890s, a number of judges and the city's jailor publicly voiced their concerns about incarcerating young children with adults. On numerous occasions, for example, Judge Kersten, told police officers not to bring children under twelve years of age to his court. After discharging three such boys charged with larceny, he explained "I can't send them to the bridewell [i.e., the city jail] and I won't hold them to the criminal court."[30] Jailor Whitman also did not want young children sent to him. After Arthur Doyle, a seven-year-old boy, had been arrested for "stealing 30 cents worth of fruit" and sent to the bridewell to await the next session of the grand jury, Whitman worked "to secure his release."[31] During a meeting with Judge Baker, he explained, "It's a shame to keep that child in there among a lot of hardened criminals . . . he is too young to ever be convicted of anything, and he is only learning much that he ought not to know by staying there." The judge agreed to meet with the boy and then send him home.

What troubled many criminal justice practitioners and observers was that these children were not only housed with adults but that they received an education only in crime. Perhaps inspired by Altgeld's writings and his lectures on *Our Penal Machinery*, Adelaide Groves, who had cofounded the Chicago Young Woman's Christian Association in 1877, decided to tour the city's jail in 1886. She was shocked to see "quite small boys confined in the same quarters with murderers, anarchists and hardened criminals."[32] Groves decided that it was her mission to save these boys, both for this world and the next. In a letter to the editor of the *Chicago Inter-Ocean*, she asked her fellow citizens: "What is to be done with these lads as they leave the jail when their sentence there is served out?"[33] Without some proper education, she cautioned, they would become lost souls and a danger to society. Accordingly, she spent her Sundays instructing these boys in the Bible as well as teaching them how to read, write, and sing, and she continued to write letters to the editors of the local papers to publicize their plight. Groves also paid the salary of a teacher to educate the boys, and worked with the Chicago Woman's Club on a campaign to establish a manual training school for these incarcerated children.

Exposés in the press helped to build public support for the establishment of a school in the jail. In an article entitled "Boys Made Criminal by Confinement at the Bridewell," the *Chicago Herald* reported: "There are no healthful influences brought to bear on these youthful offenders, neither physically nor morally. . . . It is not a house of correction with them—it is a house of perversion, corruption and retrogression for them."[34] "The only thing," the article noted, "that to some slight extent is calculated to keep their minds awake is the prison library, an institution containing some 5,000 volumes." The boys, however, "refuse to read anything except the worst and most unwholesome fiction—the more sensational the better." The paper asked:

> Is it any wonder that the number of youthful yet
> depraved criminals in Chicago is rapidly on the increase,
> not only in point of numbers, but also in percentage and
> in the degree of crime? It is not a burning shame and a
> black disgrace for a city like this—flourishing, growing,
> enterprising—to let this state of things continue year after
> year, to let it become worse and worse and not make the
> slightest attempt at reform, when such reform could be
> accomplished at comparatively slight expense, and when
> the facts in the case have been laid bare and their hideous
> nakedness repeatedly and forcibly shown by the men best
> able to expose them?[35]

Espousing an environmental understanding of the roots causes of crime, the *Herald* determined that "these boys were really more sinned against than sinning. Victims of their surroundings, products of early impressions and associations, the city they call their home had capped the climax of the crime the community was committing against them by relegating them to such a hive of moral and physical rottenness as the bridewell."[36] Thus, the city itself, according to the paper, was responsible for the state of its young people.

The *Herald* noted that a religious awakening had begun to change this state of affairs. Superintendent Crawford of the bridewell had met with clergymen to point out that more than one thousand people under the age of 17 had been committed to his institution in 1891. These clergymen, the "spiritual guides of our city," then delivered sermons "on the wickedness of systematically depraving the young malefactors by inforced [sic] and continued contact with adult criminals." As a result of these sermons, "petitions were made up and signed over town by thousands of our best citizens asking the city council for the establishment and the adequate equipment of a manual training school for these young culprits." Although the city council supported the measure, its members claimed that "there were no funds applicable for the purpose, and thus the agitation came to naught for the time being."[37]

Finally, in 1897, once the city appropriated funds, the Board of Education opened the John Worthy Manual Training School to instruct these incarcerated children. And two years later, the completion of a boys' dormitory allowed children to be housed apart from the adult offenders.[38] These developments highlighted the need to separate children from adult offenders and to provide these children with a suitable education.

Yet children and adults still remained within the same justice system. The impassioned writings and lectures of people such as Altgeld and Groves and muckraking press coverage helped to focus attention on the problem of processing children's cases in the criminal justice system, but it was not until the final years of the nineteenth century that the crusade for a separate system of justice for juveniles coalesced.

During the 1890s, the Chicago Woman's Club emerged as the preeminent association advocating not only for the establishment of a school in the bridewell but also for the creation of a juvenile court.[39] Lucy Flower, who served as its president, worked closely with Julia Lathrop, who later became the first chief of the United States Children's Bureau in 1912, to find the political support and the legal means necessary to divert children from the criminal justice system.

In 1890, the possibility of establishing a children's court in Chicago seemed remote. A proposed bill introduced in the Illinois General Assembly the next year at least suggested that Catholic and Protestant child savers would be willing to work together. Timothy Hurley, the President of the (Catholic) Chicago Visitation and Aid Society, drafted the bill that would have given county courts the power to commit dependent children to any nonprofit child welfare agency incorporated under Illinois law.[40] Flower supported the measure because it would have given judges more flexibility in handling dependency cases. Under the existing subsidy system, judges had few options and could only commit children to a limited number of training or industrial schools. No public funds, for instance, were available to support dependent children placed in noninstitutional settings, such as a relative's home. Hurley's proposed bill, however, did not become law. This failure taught Flower that she would have to build a powerful coalition of associations to sponsor future child welfare legislation.[41]

In 1892 the election of John Altgeld to the governorship was a promising development. As one of his first acts, this reform-minded Democrat who had helped to expose problems in the criminal justice system appointed Julia Lathrop to serve on the State Board of Charities. As a state commissioner she cultivated important political connections and distinguished herself by visiting the jails and poorhouses in all 102 counties of Illinois. She drew on these experiences to make the case, first locally and later nationally, for a more humane approach to child welfare.

While Lathrop was making a name for herself as a state commissioner, Flower worked to ensure that women's organizations would support future legislation for a children's court. She established the Every Day Club, whose membership consisted of forty or so civic-minded society and professional women. They met over lunch and invited experts to join them to discuss their research.[42] Flower later used this club to gain the support of judges and clergymen at a critical moment in the campaign to pass the world's first juvenile court law.[43]

Flower also conducted research of her own into the handling of juvenile cases. In 1895 she visited Boston, her birthplace, to study its innovative system of child welfare and especially its use of probation in juvenile cases. This practice had begun in Massachusetts unofficially during the Civil War, when the police court in Boston released delinquent boys to Rufus Cook, an agent of the Children's Aid Society and the chaplain of the Suffolk County Jail, to place in suitable homes.[44] This system of probation and placement proved so successful that the state passed legislation in 1869 that enabled its Board of State Charities to place children in foster homes, and then in 1891 Massachusetts passed legislation requiring all criminal courts to appoint probation officers in all juvenile cases.[45]

After her return from Boston, Flower drafted a plan to transfer all children's cases in Chicago from the city's eleven police courts to a single, higher court. This consolidation of cases, she imagined, would assure the most consistent handling possible and also take local ward politics out of the process.[46] She presented the draft to her friend S. S. Gregory, a lawyer well versed in constitutional law and former president of the American Bar Association. Gregory told Flower, much to her chagrin, that the plan was unconstitutional. He explained that, according to the Illinois constitution, legal practice "must be uniform throughout the state and [that she] could not change it in Chicago without changing it in the rest of the state." Such a statewide law, he told her, "seemed impossible."[47]

The ongoing tensions between Chicago and downstate Illinois were probably Gregory's main concern. It was unlikely that rural counties would support a bill that changed their legal procedures to accommodate Chicago's needs. Discouraged, but still determined, Flower and Lathrop decided to consult Judge Harvey Hurd. In 1869, Governor John Palmer had appointed Hurd to rewrite Illinois's general statutes, a task that had taken him five years. Since then Hurd had periodically updated an authorized version of the state's laws and had also helped to draft important pieces of legislation, such as the 1879 Industrial Schools Act for Girls that allowed Illinois to develop a subsidy system for child welfare.[48] This privatized approach to caring for dependent children encouraged individuals to establish industrial schools under a state's incorporation laws.[49]

Hurd, not surprisingly, was reluctant to get involved in what looked like a time-consuming and potentially futile undertaking. Lathrop was eventually able to convince him to take the matter under consideration after describing to him the condition of the children she had seen in the jails and poorhouses across the state.[50] After struggling with the legal knot for days, Hurd finally cut through it. His solution was ingenious: if the legislation was *permissive*, not obligatory, then it might not violate the uniformity clause of the Illinois Constitution. This solution meant that a county might *choose* to have special hearings for children's cases but would not be required to do so under the proposed law. Thus, Cook County could establish a children's court without requiring any of the other counties to follow its lead. Hurd's solution made it possible to imagine that a children's court could be established in Chicago.

With Hurd's solution in hand, Flower and Lathrop met to devise a course of action. They realized that a children's bill "must not go to the Legislature as a woman's measure," so they would need to "get the Bar Association to handle it."[51] Accordingly, Lathrop asked Ephraim Banning, who served with her on the State Board of Charities and belonged to the Chicago Bar Association, to bring the matter before the association. At the its annual meeting on October 22, 1898, Banning introduced a resolution that called for President George Follansbee to appoint a five-member committee whose charge would be

> to investigate existing conditions relative to delinquent
> and dependent children, and to cooperate with
> committees of other organizations in formulating and
> securing such legislation as may be necessary to cure
> existing evils and bring the State of Illinois and the
> City of Chicago up [to] the standard of the leading
> states and cities of the union.

The resolution played to the civic pride of Chicagoans, who only five years earlier had hosted the Columbian exposition—a world's fair that not only showcased the famous shining "White City," a model city of the future, but also put Chicago on display for the millions of visitors who had come to town. The bar association adopted the resolution and named Banning, Hurd, Edwin Burritt Smith, John Ella, and Merritt Starr to serve on the investigation committee.

Hurd assumed responsibility for seeing that a bill would be drafted but realized that he had to act cautiously because the managers of the state's industrial schools feared that if Illinois adopted an antiinstitutional approach to child welfare, such as placing children in foster homes, they might be put out of business. The concerns of the industrial school lobby would shape the final form of the legislation.

Meanwhile, Flower and Lathrop worked to ensure that when a proposed juvenile court bill was ready it would be a legislative priority. Their conference, entitled "The Children of the State," the following month helped to galvanize support for the idea of a children's court. Reverend Jenkin Lloyd Jones, a Unitarian minister who preached at All Souls' Church in Chicago, served as the president of the conference and urged his fellow participants to reach a mutually acceptable agreement, because "whenever we have a consensus of opinion to present to the Legislature, it will give us what we ask for."[52] He asserted: "This conference is neither Republican nor Democratic; neither Protestant nor Catholic; neither rural, nor urban. It is not foreign nor native, and must never be." Thus, only by "coming together" could they succeed.[53] Following his call for unity, the participants agreed to appoint a committee to work with the Chicago Bar Association, women's organizations, and child welfare societies to garner support for a juvenile court bill.

The managers of industrial schools, such as Oscar Dudley, the superintendent of the Glenwood Industrial School, voiced concerns about the antiinstitutional tenor of the conference, especially Reverend Jones's keynote address, which had referred to industrial schools as an unnatural evil whose days were numbered.[54] Dudley agreed with Jones that a home was the best place for a child but believed that not all children were prepared to live in homes. "There is work for the industrial school that they must do," he explained, since "there is a class of children who can not be placed in homes until they are trained and fitted for them."[55] The following year, Dudley became a leader of the "industry school lobby" that fought to amend the proposed children's court bill.[56]

At the conclusion of this conference, a children's court bill still had to be drafted. It would be up to Judge Hurd and his committee to produce one, and they had only a little over a month before the January 1899 session of the Illinois General Assembly convened.[57] If Chicago were to have a children court before the turn of the twentieth century, they would have to act quickly. They would also have to act cautiously because of the suspicious industrial school lobby.

On December 10, 1898, in his Washington Street office in downtown Chicago, Judge Hurd met with representatives from the city's social settlements, women's clubs, charity organizations, schools, and the grand jury and the bar association to discuss how best to proceed.[58] John C. Newcomer, a Republican member of the general assembly from Chicago who had agreed to introduce the future bill, was also in attendance. The group chose Hastings Hart, the superintendent of the Illinois Children's Home and Aid Society, to try his hand at drafting the bill. He produced two drafts, which Hurd and the bar association committee spent the next three weeks expanding and rewriting.

After deciding that the proposed legislation—"An Act To Regulate the Treatment and Control of Dependent, Neglected and Delinquent Children"—should be known as the "Bar Association Bill," Hurd's committee presented a copy to the esteemed Judge Carter to examine.[59] Once the bill met his approval, Lucy Flower arranged for an Every Day Club luncheon on January 14, 1899, at which she presented the bill to the city's circuit court judges in order to gain their support for the measure. She also held a similar luncheon for clergymen, so that they could preach to their congregations about the necessity for a children's court in Chicago. The stage was now set. In February, Representative Newcomer and Senator Selon Case (also a Chicago Republican) introduced the bill to the General Assembly in Springfield, which referred it to the House and Senate judiciary committees.

Through the use of permissive language, the bill made it clear that its first objective was to establish a children's court in Cook County.[60] It said that in counties with more than five hundred thousand residents—at the time, only Cook County with its 1.6 million inhabitants met this criterion—circuit court judges may "designate one or more of their number . . . to hear all cases coming under this act." These cases, which included dependent, neglected, and delinquent children under sixteen years of age, were to be heard in "a special court room . . . designated as 'the juvenile court room' and all the findings were to be kept in a separate book known as the 'Juvenile Record.' Moreover, for convenience's sake, the court was to be referred to as the 'Juvenile Court.' "[61] Thus, what Flower had imagined to be a "parental court" and Wines had declared should be a "children's court" came to be known as a "juvenile court."

The juvenile court would not be a new court, but rather a branch of the circuit court that had "original jurisdiction" in children's cases. Justices of the peace and police magistrates would also be required to transfer children's cases to the juvenile court.[62] This consolidation of cases extended the logic of Illinois Supreme Court decisions that had addressed only the power of the state to act as a parent toward its dependent children to cover the cases of children who had broken a law.[63] Under the proposed legislation, the definitions of the "dependent" and "neglected" child were similar to those used in the state's industrial and training schools acts.[64] With regards to the definition of juvenile delinquency, the bill said: "The words delinquent child include any child under the age of 16 years who violates any law of this State or any city or village ordinance."[65] Thus, all children under sixteen years of age, if the legislation were enacted, would be treated as members of a single class in need of assistance, and all their cases would be handled in a manner that would "conform as nearly as may be to the practice in chancery," except in cases in which the child was charged with a criminal offense. In these more serious cases, the child would have "the right to a trial by jury."[66]

The bill also proposed that the juvenile court would be granted the "authority to appoint or designate one or more discreet persons of good character to serve as probation officers."[67] These officers would receive no public compensation, and their responsibilities would include investigating a child's home, representing the interests of the child in court, and taking "such charge of any child before and after trial as may be directed by the court."[68] As the historian Steven Schlossman has observed, "prominent advocates of the juvenile court conceded that its fate rested on the quality of probationary care," for "probation alone could transform the juvenile court into an education mission to impoverished children and adults."[69] Placing children on probation would offer the juvenile court judge an alternative to incarcerating them and opened up the possibility of devising *individualized* treatment plans to rehabilitate, instead of simply punishing, juvenile delinquents.[70]

Overall, the bill revealed how carefully its drafters were trying to fit the proposed children's court into the state's existing institutional structure for child welfare. As a concession to the industrial school lobby, for instance, the bill said:

> Nothing in this act shall be construed to repeal any
> portion of the act to aid industrial schools for girls,
> the act to provide for and aid training schools for boys,
> the act to establish the Illinois State Reformatory
> or the act to provide for a State Home for Juvenile
> Female Offenders. And in all commitments to said
> institutions the acts in reference to said institutions
> shall govern the same.[71]

This decision to overlay the juvenile court on this existing structure would lead to jurisdictional conflicts in the early twentieth century between the court and managers of institutions about who had custody and control over children in the juvenile justice system.

Although concessions were made to the industrial school lobby, its members and other opponents called into question the motives behind the Bar Association Bill. On the eve of the house hearings on the bill, the *Chicago Inter-Ocean* ran a sensational front-page story with the lead "Child Slaves."[72] The article declared that the establishment of a special court for children was "unobjectionable," supporting the diversion of children from the criminal justice system, but then announced that this was "only the least portion of the measure." The bill had been written, the article posited, with the "interests of two or three 'associations'" in mind.[73]

The opponents of the bill were playing to public concerns about "traffic in children" that dated back to the 1850s, when Charles Loring Brace's Children's Aid Society of New York had started rounding up and shipping street children from the congested ghettos of New York City to grow up on farms in the Midwest. Since then critics of child saving had questioned how carefully these private societies screened the applicants who requested children and worried that without proper followup visits to inspect their new homes these children might be exploited or abused. These critics feared that home-finding societies, whose original mission had been to search for homes for homeless children, would instead search for children for childless homes.[74]

A "prominent Chicago physician" quoted in the *Inter-Ocean* article alleged that private associations in Illinois were making money by selling dependent children to farmers in need of cheap laborers. The physician explained: "Some of these 'associations' make money on both ends of the proposition. They are paid by the county for 'disposing' of a child and paid by the person to whom the unfortunate child is sent, virtually a slave."[75] He was concerned that the representatives of these private associations would become the probation staff for the proposed court. In this capacity, they would gain greater access to state power, which would enable them to have poor children declared "dependent." Once gaining custody of these children, they could then sell them for a handsome profit.

Critics of the legislations cited section 8 of the bill, "Children Not to Be Kept in Poor Houses," as evidence for this sinister plot. The section read:

> When any child dependent upon the county for support
> is committed by the court to the care of an association,
> to be placed in a family home, the court may award a
> reasonable compensation for such services, to be paid by
> the county, including necessary expenses, provided that

the compensation so allowed shall not exceed the sum of fifty (50) dollars in the case of any one child.[76]

These cash payments, critics warned, would not only make child slaving more profitable but also legalize it.

The *Inter-Ocean* article also pointed out that the proposed legislation would allow private associations to impose their morality upon working-class Chicagoans. It quoted, for example, a "prominent" member of the general assembly who said: "The mother who permitted her little one to appear on the street not washed, curled, and combed to suit the critical inspection of an 'association' practicing philanthropy at $50 a head would be in danger of losing her child."[77] This critique played to the existing tensions among the city's ethnic groups and social classes over questions of public morality, such as Sunday-closing laws (i.e., laws that made it illegal to sell alcohol on Sundays) and compulsory attendance laws that required parents to send their children to school, instead of the labor market.[78]

As further evidence of conspiracy, the industrial school lobby seized on the fact that the bill's third section called for secret hearings of children's cases in the juvenile court. As they pointed out, it said: "when a case is being heard, all persons not officers of the court or witnesses, and those having a direct interest in the case being heard, shall be excluded from the court room."[79] This closing of the courtroom, they warned, would prevent the press from informing the public about "the anguish of a mother whose child was being taken from her by the 'association.' "[80] Secrecy also implied a new version of the infamous "gag" rule that had been used to silence opponents of chattel slavery during the antebellum era.

This article, warning of child slavery, put the supporters of the Bar Association Bill on the defensive and threatened its chances of passage. To save the bill, its most controversial feature would be removed and other sections amended to appease the industrial school lobby and its advocate, the *Chicago Inter-Ocean*. The language of child slavery had been effectively employed to challenge the legitimacy of state action.

The child savers salvaged their bill, although to win over the industrial school lobby they had to accept many changes, including the removal of the "secret" hearings clause and all of section 8. The latter excision, proposed by John Lane, a representative of the *Inter-Ocean* and most likely the author of "Child Slaves," prevented private associations from receiving cash payments for placing children in family homes. It also meant that children could still be confined in county almshouses, and this practice, much to the disgust of child savers like Lathrop, would not be banned until World War I.[81] In addition, by striking out proposed payments for foster care, the industrial school lobby ensured that private institutions would continue to play the leading role in caring for dependent children in Illinois.[82] As a result, the state had one of the highest rates of institutionalizing dependent children in the nation during the early twentieth century.[83]

The proposed jurisdiction of the juvenile court was also restricted. Oscar Dudley had the bill amended to exclude future inmates of industrial and training schools from the custody and control of the court. This meant that the court would lose jurisdiction over any child it committed to one of these schools. This lack of jurisdiction over children committed to institutions would become increasingly controversial in the early twentieth century and would prove difficult to amend. It also served as a reminder that in 1899 the child savers had to fit the juvenile court, like a piece of a puzzle, into an existing structure.

The power of the state to inspect children held in private institutions was also curtailed. Representative Dennis Sullivan, the only legislator to recommend a change, had the bill amended to prevent state officials from visiting "institutions where children are supported by voluntary or public charity."[84] This change was most likely an attempt to protect Catholic institutions from scrutiny by Protestant state officials.

Along similar lines, safeguards were inserted to prevent Catholic children from being stolen from the faith. Hurley, the representative of the Catholic charities, and Hastings Hart, who represented the Protestant ones, worked together to rewrite the bill so that it said: "The court in committing children shall place them as far as practicable in the care and custody of some individual holding the same religious belief as the parents of said child, or with some association which is controlled by persons of like religious faith."[85] This language helped to shore up Catholic as well as Jewish support for the measure.

The amended legislation pleased its supporters—including the *Chicago Tribune*, which endorsed the measure—and satisfied its critics.[86] The *Inter-Ocean* rejoiced that the bill had been corrected "in nearly every particular in accordance with the criticisms" expressed by the paper.[87] On March 23, the senate passed the bill by a vote of thirty-two to one.[88] The house, however, delayed voting on the measure. As Julia Lathrop, who had been sent by the Chicago Woman's Club as a delegate to monitor the bill's progress, later recalled, "Mr. Newcomer, the legislator in charge of the bill, became greatly alarmed."[89] Finally, on April 14, 1899, the last day of the last legislative session of the nineteenth century, the house unanimously passed the bill.

After a decade of concerted work, Flower and Lathrop could now breathe a temporary sigh of relief. They had finally succeeded in writing their ideals about childhood innocence and public responsibility into law. Through vesting state responsibility for both dependent and delinquent children in a juvenile court, they had merged the goals of promoting child welfare and controlling crime. In Chicago, the nation's second largest and fastest growing city, the cases of dependent and neglected children, as well as ones accused of committing crimes, could now be processed in a separate justice system. A sympathetic judge could use his discretion to apply individualized treatments to rehabilitate children, instead of punishing them. Yet, as Flower and Lathrop understood perfectly well, especially after the long struggle to pass the legislation and the amending of the Bar Association Bill, their efforts to secure justice for the child had only begun. It would require even more work, including the continued support of private associations and philanthropists, to build and legitimate the nation's first juvenile court and to ensure that child protection remained part of its ongoing mission.

TWO

*The real history of the juvenile court does not date from
scattered provisions on the statute books of the States,
or even from any codification of them, but rather from the
embodiment and organization of a new spirit and a new
method in actual practice.*
—Samuel J. Barrows, Commissioner for the United States
    on the International Prison Commission, 1904

Building a Model Court

On July 3, 1899, Lucy Flower's vision of a "parental court" for
Chicago became a reality when the Honorable Richard
Tuthill, a Civil War veteran and respected jurist who had sat on
the circuit court for more than a decade, ushered in the modern
era for juvenile justice by informally adjudicating the case of
eleven-year-old Henry Campbell.[1] The boy and his parents were
the first family to appear before the juvenile court, which promised to revolutionize the treatment and control of the city's
dependent, neglected, and delinquent children by following the
principle "that a child should be treated as a child."[2] As the
court's first chief probation officer, Timothy Hurley, explained,
"Instead of reformation, the thought and idea in the judge's
mind should always be formation. No child should be punished
for the purpose of making an example of him, and he certainly
can not be reformed by punishing him. The parental authority of
the State should be exercised instead of the criminal power."[3]

The Campbell case, which was heard in a courtroom on the
third floor of the County Building in downtown Chicago, was a
public event because the privacy provision of the Bar Association
Bill that would have limited access to juvenile hearings had been
removed to ensure its passage. As a result, the courtroom was
packed with spectators, including reporters. They described for

their readers how a misty-eyed Lena Campbell, who had had her son arrested for larceny, told Judge Tuthill that Henry was not a "bad boy at heart" but had been "led into trouble by others." She and her husband Frank did not want Henry "sent to any of the institutions" and informed the judge that the boy's "grandmother who lives at Rome, N.Y., will take him and keep him."[4] According to the *Chicago Daily News*, "Judge Tuthill questioned the parents closely, and finally agreed that the boy should be sent to his grandmother in the hope that he would thereby escape the surroundings which have caused the mischief."[5]

Judge Tuthill concluded the historic first day by inviting the "officials of the various charitable and reformatory institutions affected by the scope of the new court, people prominent in the work of juvenile reformation, police captains and interested citizens gathered in great numbers in the courtroom" into his chambers. They discussed practical matters, such as where to keep children awaiting their hearings, whether the city or county would pay for the care of these detained children, and how the judge and his makeshift collection of probation officers should administer the new law.[6] Tuthill explained: "Kindness and love for the children must be used in this work if we would hope to receive the benefits from which so much is expected. The burden will rest mainly upon you who will gather the cases for the court. I especially desire that in making your report to me you should go into detail and give all the information possible."[7] He finally stressed that "the bringing of the child before the court should be used only as a last resort."[8]

The inaugural day of the Cook County Juvenile Court captured both the sense of possibilities for the new juvenile law as well as its practical limitations. Henry Campbell's case had been an ideal one with which to begin, for it revealed that the juvenile court law provided Tuthill with the judicial discretion to focus on what was in Henry's best interests. The judge could order that the boy be placed in the custody and control of his grandmother rather than committing him to a juvenile reformatory as a punishment for his crime. On the other hand, as the subsequent meeting in the judge's chambers revealed, Tuthill had almost no public resources with which to operate the new court. Most of the features that later became the hallmarks of progressive juvenile justice—private hearings, confidential records, a detention home, and a professional probation staff—were not present at creation. As a result, the world's first juvenile court opened with a public hearing and a public record, but without public funds to pay for either the salaries of probation officers or to maintain a detention home for children. It took more than eight years before the city's first juvenile court building was constructed. Thus, the world's first juvenile court had a promising but rather inchoate beginning.

The juvenile court had such a tentative start partly because its invention raised fundamental questions about the role of the state in the increasingly interdependent world of the late nineteenth century.[9] In Europe and America, progressive reformers questioned classical legal conceptions of free will, the due process of law, and the benefits of limited state intervention into social relations. As Eric Foner has pointed out, progressives sought to "redefine the venerable term 'liberalism,' previously shorthand for limited government and laissez-faire economics, to describe belief in an activist, socially conscious state."[10] They envisioned that the state would provide for the positive rights of social citizenship to ensure that its citizens, especially children, would be able to achieve freedom through living in a society that provided the necessary "social conditions for full human development."[11]

The progressive efforts to extend the reach of the state into the everyday lives of predominantly working-class urban dwellers raised troubling questions about the proper relationship of new institutions, such as the juvenile court, to "the public." The inventors of the juvenile court intended it not only to remove children from the harsh criminal justice system but also to shield them from stigmatizing publicity. In the juvenile court, they imagined that hearings would be closed to spectators and the press, a juvenile's record would remain confidential, and no private lawyers or juries would play a role. The process, however, of making the juvenile court into a sheltered place to protect children, especially during the storms of adolescence, would take more than two decades.[12]

R ichard Tuthill realized that in order to build a model court he would have to be not only a wise judge but also a booster and fund-raiser for the fledgling institution. As an Episcopalian and thirty-second-degree Mason, whose ancestors had arrived in Massachusetts Bay in the 1630s, Tuthill belonged to the city's elite. A Republican lawyer, he had joined the Chicago bar in 1873 and become the city attorney two years later, and in 1880 President Chester Arthur appointed him to serve as the district attorney for the Northern District of Illinois. In 1887 he was elevated to the Circuit Court of Cook County, a position he would be reelected to through World War I.[13]

In his efforts to win approval as well as funding for the juvenile court, Tuthill already had the support of the coalition of Catholic and Protestant charity organizations, the Chicago Bar Association, and the city's women's clubs, all of whom had lobbied for the Bar Association Bill earlier that year. In addition, the mayor appointed Timothy Hurley to serve as Tuthill's chief probation officer. The president of the Visitation and Aid Society and an assistant in the city's law department, Hurley worked with the judge to educate the city's justices of the peace about the new law that allowed but did not require them to transfer children's cases to the new court. In the days leading up the court's opening, Hurley and Tuthill met with these justices to convince them that transferring cases was sound policy.[14]

Although the legislative failure to close juvenile hearings to members of the press had allowed for the juvenile court to become a much more public space than its inventors would have liked, Tuthill used this free publicity to champion an environmental interpretation of the causes of juvenile delinquency. In "Juvenile Law Is Good," a Sunday feature on the court that the *Chicago Tribune* ran less than two weeks after its opening, Judge Tuthill angrily rejected the idea that there were born criminals: "Born criminals? Stuff! There are no born criminals. If I believed that, I should lose my faith in God. Society makes criminals; environment and education make criminals, but they are not born so."[15] If the environment made criminals, he reasoned that society, through institutions such as foster homes, schools, and the juvenile court, could help steer children away (or even rescue them) from this downward path.

The *Tribune* article focused on Tuthill's handling of the case of Thomas Majcheski, a fourteen-year-old Polish boy, to highlight the judge's faith in environmentalism. Thomas had been arrested for stealing grain from a freight car in the railroad yards of South Chicago, a common offense that landed boys like Thomas in juvenile court during the early twentieth century. More than 50 percent of the boys who appeared before the juvenile court in its first decade of operations had committed some kind of theft, with perhaps as many as 1,656 (14.2 percent) of the 11,641 total cases of boy delinquency from this period involving stealing grain, coal, or merchandise from freight cars.[16] Numerous children were also arrested for other railroad-related offenses, such as "loitering on the railroad tracks, throwing stones at trains, setting fire to freight cars, breaking into cars, putting cartridges on the tracks, breaking signal lights, tearing down a fence in a railroad yard, loafing in the railroad station, 'flipping trains,' and a few other similar charges."[17] Both boys and girls participated in "flipping trains," which involved jumping onto and off of moving trains.

Judge Tuthill began his examination of Thomas with a question about the boy's cleanliness: "How long since you washed your hands?" According to the reporter, "the youthful delinquent thoughtfully regards the designated members, then steals a look at the Judge's immaculate digits. The contrast is great and in confusion the dirty fists seek cover underneath the owner's coat. The query might pertinently have included the rest of the young prisoner's anatomy."[18] The image of the well-groomed judge working to restore innocence to this "filthy" juvenile, who had literally been tarnished by his surroundings, revealed that the two lived in very different social worlds.

The juvenile court, as the article suggested, was carrying the "unwashed" into the city's business district. A few years later, the Chicago Open Board of Trade even vacated its premises on Clark Street after the juvenile court temporarily relocated to its building. In a subsequent lawsuit over the board's breaking of its lease, the board claimed that the court had brought "undesirables" into the building, rendering the space "unfit" for business, and had in effect "evicted" them. "Wicked, depraved and addicted to lewd and vicious practices, filthy in habits, afflicted with diseases and emitting foul and offensive odor," these undesirables crowded the building's elevator, halls, and stairways. In addition, patrol wagons and police officers congregated in front of the building, "leading the public to believe that the place is being raided as a gambling resort."[19] The board did not want to associate with (or be associated with) the juvenile court's largely immigrant, working-class clientele.

The police officer who had arrested Thomas informed the judge that the boy's father was dead and that his mother, a washerwoman, was trying to support her nine children. She could not afford to take time off from her work to appear in court. The officer noted that Thomas had stolen coal and grain from trains previously but had eluded arrest. Tuthill then placed his "immaculate hand . . . reassuringly upon the [boy's] ragged shoulders" and said, "Look up, my boy." The touch, as reported, had a magical effect: "By some sort of telepathy, this waif picked up by the strong arm of the law from out of the vastness of the city, knows that he is looking into the eyes of a friend; and he shifts his position, much as a friendless dog wags his tail upon hearing a kind voice." As a result of this touch, Thomas admitted his guilt: "Yes-y-yes, I took it."[20]

The judge asked if anyone in the crowded court had anything to add. Typically, during the court's early years, from 150 to 300 people would be in the courtroom, which stretched nearly sixty feet in length, was forty-five feet across, and had a twenty-five-foot ceiling. The crowd, as one commentator noted, would be "occupying every seat and window sill and massed inside the outer railing. The children whose cases were to be heard were kept in a clerk's room in the rear and brought one by one by an officer through this seething, restless group of exited, anxious fathers and mothers up before the judge."[21] Judge Tuthill's question was met with silence. " 'Then'—the words come slow and reluctant—'I think the best thing will be to send this boy to Pontiac," he announced. At the state reformatory, Tuthill explained, the boy would "have the benefit of schooling and—..." At this tense moment, "a young man with a strong face step[ped] from the knob of listeners" to deliver a rousing oration on the environmental causes of juvenile delinquency and to protest the judge's impending sentence.[22]

The young man, described as a lawyer with a "rising practice," informed the judge that he did not know Thomas, but that he did know "the class of people from which he comes." He explained that the men from these immigrant families were unskilled laborers, who often could not find work. He added: "Their families are uniformly large, eight or even ten children being not at all unusual. They are crowded into two or three small rooms. Here they live, eat, and sleep. The poverty of these places, miscalled homes, is beyond belief with one not acquainted with the actual facts. Driven by sharpest want, the children are sent out to pick up what they can." He asked the judge if he knew what these families did with the grain, but without pausing for an answer, he continued: "It is consumed, ravenously eaten, sometimes without even a pretense of cooking or parching. It is their sustenance Judge. They steal, or starve. I do not believe this boy is a criminal, only as his environment tends to make him one."[23] This speech, which ripped a page from the period's realist literature, offered a bleak assessment of urban poverty.[24]

Tuthill responded to the lawyer's outburst by offering him a deal. If he would agree to "take charge of the boy [and] assist him in becoming a self-respecting, honorable citizen," the judge would suspend Thomas's sentence.[25] It was an offer that the idealistic young lawyer could not refuse. When asked by a reporter what he was going to do with the boy, he replied, "Clean him up and get him some clothes and then take him to my mother. She'll know what to do with him."[26]

This newspaper account reflected the radical potential for the new court to redistribute the social responsibility for rearing indigent children. Yet important players, especially the women involved, were missing from the story. Thomas's mother, for example, plays no part in this courtroom drama. What would have happened if she had objected to this deal between the judge and lawyer? It is also unclear who now had custody of the boy. What if the judge in his haste to resolve the case had just placed a Catholic boy under the control of a Protestant family? Opponents of the Bar Association Bill had feared that such situations might arise and had amended the bill to help ensure that children would be placed in families of their own faith and that juvenile court proceedings would, at least, be open to the press.

Although articles like "Juvenile Law Is Good" glossed over many critical legal questions, they did help to publicize the mission of the new court. Over the course of the early twentieth century, Chicago newspapers educated their readers about how the juvenile court worked and what an improvement it was over the earlier system of processing children's cases in the adult criminal justice system. Tuthill and his successors who presided over the juvenile court learned how to use this free press coverage to make the case for appropriations from the city and county, as well as to defend the court against periodic attacks.

At the end of October 1899, the Chicago Bar Association released its report on the condition of the city's children, which praised the juvenile law and announced that Tuthill was "an exceedingly happy selection" for presiding judge. It also called for public officials and the press to spread the news about the benefits of the new court. In its conclusion, the report quoted from a speech delivered by the assistant state's attorney for Cook County, Albert C. Barnes, to the Illinois Association of States' Attorneys. Barnes declared that the juvenile court "unless thwarted by persistent and unnatural forces, by niggardly means for carrying out its provisions, or by the assaults of those who seek to defeat rather than promote beneficial legislation, will prove the dawn of a new era in our criminal history, and of a brighter day for the people of Illinois."[27] Barnes's argument that the juvenile law had enhanced Illinois's reputation became a common rhetorical device used by supporters of the court to boast about how their state had pioneered this advancement in child welfare.

Supporters of the court displayed it as a symbol of civilization and a badge of pride for Chicagoans, much like the city's Art

Institute or Field Museum of Natural History.[28] As Tuthill proudly observed,

> the good women of the State, always quick and earnest in everything which tends to the proper care of children, were leaders in the movement, laboring in season and out of season to induce the representatives of the people by the passage of this [juvenile] bill to place Illinois *primus inter pares* in respect to provisions made for the exercise of this highest duty of a State, —a civilized State, —to stand *in loco parentis*, to be a parent to all the neglected and delinquent children of the State.[29]

It was appropriate that Tuthill acknowledged the role that the "good women of the State" had played in the court's creation, since they also continued to be its leading supporters.

Lucy Flower, for instance, raised the funds necessary for the new court to begin its pioneering work and proposed that the Chicago Woman's Club establish a separate organization, to be known as the Juvenile Court Committee (JCC), which would pay the salaries of fifteen probation officers and run a detention home. Flower, however, stayed involved with the court's operations only until 1902, when her husband fell ill and the couple moved to California. As her daughter later wrote, "there she cheerfully lived for the rest of her life far from the home she was used to, the friends that she loved, the life that stimulated her, and the interests that had so long been peculiarly her own."[30] Flower's retirement from child saving symbolized the passing of her generation of Gilded Age patrons from the political scene. It would be up to Julia Lathrop, who became the first president of the JCC in 1903, and her fellow progressives to build a model court.

Since no public monies were available to establish a detention home for detained children, the JCC managed one located at 625 West Adams Street, more than two miles from the County Building in downtown Chicago, where the court held its first sessions. Years later, Emily Washburn Dean, the secretary of the JCC, recalled how frustrating this early work could be. Cook

County had donated an old omnibus and two horses to the JCC to transport the children to the twice-weekly sessions of the court (the court would not hear cases five days a week until 1907). The bus, however, began to fall apart, and the driver grew concerned about the safety of the children. The county officials told Dean that this was a city matter and that she should see the chief of police. He, in turn, referred her to the city's construction department, who referred her to the mayor. The mayor then told her it was, after all, a county matter. After six weeks of going around in circles, the JCC finally decided to buy the new bus itself.[31]

The bus, however, turned out to be too heavy for the association's smaller horse. The JCC was, after much effort, able to get from the city a bigger horse, which had belonged to the fire department and was now retired. "His legs," according to Dean, "were so long and he traveled so fast that he nearly dragged the small horse to an untimely end."[32] Apparently, he would also gallop at the sound of the fire alarm to the nearest blaze. The JCC, once again, spent its own money to buy two new horses and convinced the city to donate a barn for their use. Fittingly, Dean noted, "the stalls proved to be so small that the horses could not lie down day or night, so finding that there was nothing else to do the Committee rented a barn and the feed!"[33]

Anecdotes like Dean's remind us how haphazard the administration of juvenile justice was during these early years and also reveal what a critical role the JCC played in keeping it going. But how did the JCC manage to raise the money to pay the salaries of probation officers, buy horses and omnibuses, and rent barns? In part, philanthropists, such as Louise de Koven Bowen, made large donations. Bowen was the granddaughter of Edward Hiram Hadduck, who had made his vast fortune through investing in the land that became the heart of Chicago's Loop.[34] At the urging of Lathrop, the well-connected Louise Bowen assumed the presidency of the JCC to help the association raise money.

Bowen became the Lucy Flower of the twentieth century, a dedicated philanthropist who led the city's crusade for child welfare.[35] Under Bowen's leadership, the JCC sponsored cultural events to raise money, such as a Shakespeare Song Cycle performed at the Chicago Auditorium on February 3, 1904. The hosts of this gala read like a *Who's Who* of Chicago society, including Mrs. Marshall Field Jr., Mrs. Cyrus McCormick, Mrs. Potter Palmer, and Mrs. Julius Rosenwald.[36] Such events not only raised revenue but also helped to link the court in the public mind with the city's leading citizens, even if the members of the Chicago Open Board of Trade could not stand to share a building with its clientele.

The JCC did not intend to fund a juvenile detention home indefinitely. It was a costly endeavor, and the association was having difficulty raising the necessary revenue. The members also believed that the court provided a vital public service and should be publicly financed. After years of lobbying, the Illinois General Assembly finally passed legislation authorizing the county commissioners to establish and maintain a detention home, which was located in the juvenile court building that opened in August 1907.[37]

Significantly, the detention home, with the support of the Chicago Board of Education and the JCC, provided schooling for its wards. Florence Scully, who had previously taught at the John Worthy Manual Training School for delinquent boys, instructed the children. It was a challenging task, "for some of the boys were there two days, some two weeks and some only two hours." Moreover, "they were of all ages and all stages of common school education and no education." Accordingly, Scully had to work individually with each child. She also introduced "a great deal of hand work, such as clay modeling, raffia work, weaving, designing and drawing," which she used "as incentives to the harder tasks in arithmetic, reading, and spelling in which most of the boys were sadly deficient." Based on the success of her work, the Board of Education provided a teacher for the delinquent girls and a kindergarten teacher for the dependent children at the home.[38]

Due to overcrowding, however, the court itself was moved back to the County Building in 1913, and the juvenile court building "was given over to the uses of the detention home," which included not only housing and schooling the children but also providing physical and medical examinations and care.[39] The separation of the court from the detention home continued until the construction in the early 1920s of a new juvenile court and juvenile detention home on the city's West Side. These adjourning buildings opened in November 1923, but the detention home—a three-story building that partially enclosed a three-and-a-half-acre playground, remained under the jurisdiction of the county commissioners, not the administrative authority of the juvenile court.[40] Although administratively separate from the juvenile court, the proximity of the detention home to the court reflected the expert opinion that these interrelated parts of the juvenile justice system should be in the same place.

Other cities did not always follow Chicago's lead in retrofitting their juvenile courts with detention homes. In *Juvenile Courts at Work*, a report for the United States Children's Bureau, Katharine Lenroot and Emma Lundberg reported on ten cities in the early 1920s. Only six (Buffalo, Denver, Los Angeles, San Francisco, Seattle, and St. Louis) maintained "a special detention home for children."[41] Boston, the District of Columbia, New Orleans, and Minneapolis did not have such facilities. Lenroot and Lundberg were also dismayed to discover that in eight of the ten cities that they investigated, "detention of children in police stations or in jails was reported—in some as a rare occurrence and in others as a comparatively common practice."[42] Although the use of detention homes had become at least a fairly standard practice in urban juvenile courts by the early 1920s, across the nation in many instances children continued to be held in police stations and jails.[43]

Although detention homes were the most visible addition to juvenile courts in the early twentieth century, the development of professional probation staffs was equally important. In Chicago, members of the JCC, for instance, believed that public funding would help to make long-term careers in juvenile justice more attractive to gifted individuals. They also realized that a professionally staffed and managed probation department was required to keep tabs on the behavior of the increasing number of children in the juvenile justice system.

Influential members of the JCC like Julia Lathrop cautioned that it would be risky to pay probation officers from public funds for fear these jobs might become objects of patronage. This tension between demanding public support for the juvenile court but also desiring to retain control over its administration led to the creation of a hybrid system of juvenile justice, in which state power and private administration were often mixed together in a surprising fashion. The best example of this mixing of public responsibility with private administration was evident in the transformation of the probation department into a publicly supported branch of the court. The history of the development of the probation department came to serve as a blueprint from which the progressives worked to retrofit the juvenile court.

Probation officers were the "right arm of the court" because they investigated homes; interviewed neighbors, teachers and employers; made recommendations to the judge about what should be done with children; represented them during hearings; and supervised those on probation.[44] Scholars have described this entry by probation officers into the social lives of families as the beginning of a "therapeutic state," in which public officials work to "normalize" the social behavior of "deviants."[45] The child who got into trouble with the law, according to this interpretation, not only brought the state into his or her life but also opened up the family home to state intervention and extended supervision. Thus, the entire family, not just the child, became the subject for extended case work, which could involve demands to change jobs, find a new residence, become a better housekeeper, prepare different meals, give up alcohol, and abstain from sex.[46] A refusal to follow these commands could result in a probation officer calling on the power of the court to break up the disobedient family.

Yet, as Julia Lathrop sadly noted, in Chicago heavy caseloads that averaged between 50 to 150 children per officer made it unrealistic to expect a probation officer "to exercise much more than the somewhat humorously designated 'official parenthood' over most members of such a brood."[47] In fact, due to heavy caseloads, some officers in Chicago and other large cities even met groups of children at settlement houses or libraries instead of visiting them in their homes.

In addition, juvenile courts in their use of probation explicitly drew the color line. Officers of one race as a general rule did not visit the homes of children of another race. From its beginning, the Chicago Juvenile Court, for example, had assigned black children to the court's one black probation officer, Elizabeth McDonald, who volunteered her services to the court.[48] Along similar lines, the New Orleans Juvenile Court placed all black children on "probation to volunteer officers of their own race, and their cases were rarely investigated."[49] Thus the state did not always show an interest in investigating all homes.

In Chicago, the juvenile court's handling of the cases of black children became more complicated over time. The city's black population substantially increased in the early twentieth century from less than 2 percent of the city's total population in 1900 to nearly 7 percent in 1930. As the city's South Side "Black Belt" was being forged, most private child welfare institutions stopped accepting "colored" children. For instance, the Chicago Nursery and Half-Orphan Asylum (later Chapin Hall), which was founded in 1860, accepted "colored" children until 1914 but then excluded them. As the historian Kenneth Cmiel reported, "white hostility had risen after the race riots of the First World War. And migration from the South during 1917 and 1918 changed the racial composition of the city, hugely increasing the number of black children needing assistance. It was in this climate that Chapin Hall stopped serving African-Americans."[50] By the late 1910s, private institutions, whether Catholic or Protestant, were accepting children on the basis not only of their religion but also their "whiteness." By explicitly drawing the color line, private institutions limited the options that the juvenile court had in processing the cases of black children on the borderline of dependency and delinquency.

Beginning in the 1910s, the significance of race had become more apparent within the juvenile justice system as black children became disproportionately represented. The number of black boys in the system was "a little over twice the proportion of the Negroes to total population, and for Negro girls about three and one-half times." The rate of increase in juvenile delinquency was, however, much slower than the overall population growth for African Americans in the city. "Although the proportion for both Negro boys and girls increased from 7.9 percent in 1913 to 9.9 percent in 1919," as a leading study on race relations noted, "the Negro population for the same period increased over 100 percent."[51] In addition, it appeared that race did not make much difference in the types of offenses committed by children. Mary Bartelme, who handled girls' cases for the court, testified to the commission investigating race relations in the city: "I get all offenses committed by girls under eighteen years of age. I want to say that the offenses of white and colored are very much the same as far as those offenses come before me." With regards to boys' cases, the chief probation officer concurred. "From my experience," he said, "I would say that there is no significant difference between acts for which colored delinquent boys are brought to court, and the acts for which white delinquent boys are brought to court, with this exception: that larceny, as an offense, seems to have a considerable lead over other offenses."[52]

In 1927, the percentage of cases of African-American children in the juvenile court exceeded 20 percent for the first time. During that year, 495 out of the 2,197 cases that the Chicago Juvenile Court heard involved black children.[53] And the court itself reported that it had to handle the cases of black children differently from those of "white" children. In the court's annual report, the chief probation officer, Harry Hill, explained:

> The difficulty of providing adequate care for the dependent and neglected colored children constitutes one of the greatest problems with which the court has to deal. The situation is complicated by a lack of resources in the community comparable with those available for white children in the same circumstances. Practically no institutions are to be found in the community to which this group of colored children may be admitted.[54]

Due to this lack of facilities in Chicago's impoverished Black Belt and the refusal of private institutions to accept "colored" children, the juvenile court committed black boys to the state-run St. Charles School for Boys sooner than it would have in the cases of Jewish, Italian, or Polish children.[55] In effect, the court processed the cases of dependent black boys as if they were serious juvenile offenders. This handling of these cases contrasted with the processing of the cases of delinquent "foreign" children who had committed minor offenses. In many of these cases, due to overcrowding in juvenile reformatories, the court had committed these white juvenile offenders to institutions for dependent children.

Committing dependent black children to a delinquent institution had several consequences. First, St. Charles delayed the parole of black children if they did not have suitable homes into which to be returned.[56] As a result of early commitments and delayed releases, dependent black boys spent considerable amounts of time incarcerated in an institution for juvenile offenders. By the late 1920s, in fact, black boys comprised roughly a quarter of the inmates at St. Charles. Second, studies of recidivism from this period showed that "the chances of becoming a recidivist become greater as institutional commitments increase."[57] Thus, not only was the juvenile court treating dependent black boys as if they were juvenile delinquents, it may have also been helping them to become recidivists!

The juvenile court had even more limited options in the cases of black girls. As Hill noted, the situation was "desperate," since "the State Training School for Girls at Geneva is the only institution to which they are admitted . . . [and] they accept but a small number of those who should be sent there." He added: "delinquent colored girls have frequently been held for periods as long as six months in the Juvenile Detention Home after commitment before they could be admitted to the school at Geneva."[58] Due to a lack of space, the court had to return many dependent and neglected "colored" children to "unfit homes where, under unfavorable circumstances, the court is forced to carry out treatment when only a small degree of success may be expected."[59] Therefore, delinquent black girls spent long periods in the detention home, and neglected and dependent girls received few social services.

Thus, as the number of cases of black children appearing before the juvenile court grew over the course of the early twentieth century, the court's staff complained about the limited options in processing their cases. Whereas religion had been the most important consideration in the processing of the cases of children from "foreign" families at the turn of the century, as European immigrants were slowly becoming white Americans and more "colored" people migrated to American cities in the North and Midwest, the significance of race became more visible and tangible as the color line became more entrenched after World War I.

Although in the early twentieth century the limited number of probation officers certainly diluted the ability of the juvenile court to police the home, the authority to investigate homes did exist, and the progressives wanted to expand the probation department to take full advantage of this power. In 1905, Lathrop proposed two solutions to the problem of inadequate probation. First, she called for Cook County to fund the officers. Second, to ensure that these positions did not become subject to patronage, she declared that the Civil Service Commission should administer a merit examination to all applicants. From the highest scores, the commission could then compile a list of the most qualified candidates, from which the juvenile court judge would pick his officers. This approach to staffing promised to professionalize the court by hiring only those persons trained in the latest theories of social work.

The JCC drafted a bill to amend the Juvenile Court Act to allow for such a system. In February 1905, Chester Church, a Republican representative from Chicago, introduced the JCC's bill, which was unanimously passed by both houses of the General Assembly and signed into law by Governor Charles S. Deneen, a Republican who had made his reputation as the state's attorney for Cook County. According to the new law, the circuit court judges would inform the County Board of County Commissioners how many officers, including a chief probation officer, the juvenile court required for the coming year. The commissioners would then determine whether the number was appropriate and what their salaries should be.[60]

Julian Mack, who succeeded Tuthill as the presiding judge of the juvenile court in 1904, was responsible for implementing this new law. Mack had graduated from Harvard Law School and taught law at Northwestern University and the University of Chicago. He also later wrote the definitive law review article on the juvenile court that laid out its theory and practice.[61] In addition, he taught courses on juvenile justice at the Chicago Institute of Social Science, an extension of the University of Chicago. These courses were intended to develop a core of professionally trained probation officers to staff the court.

A citizens' committee developed the merit examination for probation officers, which tested spelling, arithmetic, and the applicant's understanding of the job, as well as his or her knowledge of the Juvenile Court Act. In addition, a series of sample cases forced the applicants to apply their knowledge to practical situations. Judge Mack, who was Jewish, ruled that all current probation officers would have to take the test, a decision that threatened to upset the delicate balance between Catholic and Protestant officers. Fortunately, all the officers scored highly enough on the examination for Mack to maintain the politically sensitive religious balance of the department.

Staffing the probation department, including determining who should direct it, also exposed ideological tensions among the founders about the court's mission. Although the founders all agreed that the court's primary purpose was to divert children from the harmful criminal justice system (what the criminologist Franklin Zimring has labeled "the diversionary rationale") they disagreed over the degree to which the juvenile court should intervene in the lives of children and their families.[62] Mack championed an interventionist approach, which envisioned that the juvenile court should be an agency that fostered social citizenship by providing needed services and supervision to children and their families.[63]

This tension between competing visions of juvenile justice was revealed when Henry Thurston, a professor of sociology at the Chicago Normal School, scored the highest mark on a separate examination given for the position of chief probation officer. As a result, Judge Mack named Thurston to replace John McManaman, an Irish-Catholic lawyer who had been critical of the interventionist direction in which Mack was taking the court. McManaman had raised concerns that "public officials [were] peeping into the home and attempting to establish a standard of living—a standard of conduct and morals—and then measuring all people by that standard."[64] McManaman's replacement by Thurston, who had no legal training but had been working for the JCC, only confirmed growing suspicions among Catholic supporters of juvenile justice.

Although Timothy Hurley, the court's first chief probation officer, was critical of Mack, he sought only to discipline the juvenile court, not to destroy it. In 1905, for example, at the annual meeting of the National Conference of Charities and Corrections in Portland, Oregon, Hurley had called for publicly appointed lawyers to represent children in juvenile courts and for the hearings to be more formal. Judge Mack did try to appease the Catholic reformers. For instance, he appointed John McManaman to serve as an attorney for children brought before the juvenile court. Perhaps as a result of such conciliatory acts, the growing mistrust in the Catholic reform community did not prevent reformers like Hurley from supporting additional amendments to the Juvenile Court Law passed in 1905 and 1907 that expanded its jurisdiction.

These amendments transformed *all* minors into potential wards of the court.[65] Now children found to be dependent, neglected, or delinquent would remain its wards until they reached the age of twenty-one or were discharged. This longer period of disciplinary control gave the court's probation officers an extended opportunity to work with children, including those who had been paroled from institutions.

Judge Mack and Chief Probation Officer Thurston were especially concerned about the behavior of children on parole and probation. Their concern grew out of the statistics kept by the court. Thurston discovered, for example, that close to 40 percent of the delinquent boys appearing before the juvenile court from 1904 to 1906 were recidivists.[66] Thurston believed that these children posed a threat to the legitimacy of the entire juvenile justice system because they openly flaunted its authority, which diminished its power to persuade other young people to respect the law. Thurston pointed out that every case of recidivism "tends to multiply itself many times among the associates of such delinquents." To prevent this from occurring, he urged that "boys and girls who persistently make no effort to improve under probation should quickly be put under such restraint that educational influences can get a chance at them."[67]

The "persistent repeater," according to Thurston, threatened to erode public support for the juvenile court. He cautioned that "all right-minded people are willing to have boys and girls have chances to do the right thing, but after they persistently throw chances away the same people have a right to insist that the young people be really controlled, even if it takes a criminal court process to do it."[68] Thurston was well aware that the juvenile court at this juncture could not afford to lose public support. The court was still an experiment and was not yet a permanent fixture of local governance.

The potential for the public to turn against the court for failing to solve "the boy problem" had been a constant worry because the juvenile court from its inception handled extremely difficult cases, including those involving children accused of serious and violent offenses. In fact, nearly 40 percent of the children who appeared before the court during its first few months of operations in 1899 had already had encounters with the law. Many of these children had spent time in a training or industrial school and, in some instances, the State Reformatory at Pontiac.[69] Moreover, the 1905 revision of Illinois's juvenile law granted the juvenile court original and exclusive jurisdiction over all cases of "any male child under seventeen years or any female child under the age of eighteen years."[70] This revised law, which raised the court's jurisdictional upper age limit from sixteen years, included no offense-related exceptions to the general principle that the juvenile court should hear all children's cases. Thus, the juvenile court had jurisdiction over the cases of serious and violent offenders, including ones accused of homicide.[71]

In the early twentieth century, however, the city's juvenile court judges did not assert their original and exclusive jurisdiction in every case. Initially, they had concerns about the constitutionality of the state's juvenile law, including the possibility that the Illinois Supreme Court might determine that the law's procedural informalities did not provide adequate due process protections to children and their families. They also did not want to give the Illinois Supreme Court an opportunity to declare that the criminal court, not the juvenile court, had original jurisdiction over persons committing a crime who were above the state's age of criminal responsibility, which remained at ten.[72] Instead, they entered into a "gentleman's agreement" with the state's attorney that allowed the juvenile court to hear most of the cases of serious and violent offenders but gave the state's attorney the opportunity to prosecute some cases in the criminal justice system. Under this informal system of concurrent jurisdiction, the state's attorney could potentially prosecute any child over the state's age of criminal responsibility.[73]

The Chicago Juvenile Court opted not to exercise its jurisdictional claims in the cases of older children who committed serious crimes while on probation, even though the court could retain jurisdiction over juveniles in the system until they turned twenty-one. Thus, judges, by not fighting to keep the cases of all children in the juvenile justice system, were using a form of "passive transfer" in which, by taking no action, the court allowed for a child to be tried as an adult.[74]

The juvenile court did also transfer a few cases each year to the criminal court, though much less than 1 percent of its calendar.

As Judge Merritt Pinckney, the third presiding judge of the court, explained,

> a child, a boy especially sometimes becomes so thoroughly vicious and is so repeatedly an offender that it would not be fair to the other children in a delinquent institution who have not arrived at his age of depravity and delinquency to have to associate with him. On very rare and special occasions, therefore, children are held over on a *mittimus* to the criminal court.[75]

Almost all of these cases involved boys who were recidivists and at least sixteen years of age, and the few cases of first offenders were those of boys close to seventeen years of age, whose crimes "included daring holdups, carrying guns, thefts of considerable amounts and rape."[76]

Transferred cases, however, were the exceptions to the principle that the juvenile court should adjudicate *all* children's cases. More typical than the cases of children accused of serious and violent offenses were cases like those of Edward Stark, a boy whose childhood experiences with the law began before the creation of the juvenile court and then continued into the twentieth century.[77] In 1897, when Edward was ten years old, a priest became worried about the boy's home, a site well known to the local authorities. The neighbors considered Edward's parents to be "habitual drunkards," and John Phelan, a district police officer, had arrested "some of the worst thieves Chicago ever knew out of their house." The father, an English Protestant, and the mother, an Irish Catholic, were having marital difficulties and paid little attention to Edward. In an attempt to save the neglected boy, the priest filed a dependent petition against him.

At a hearing in the Cook County Court, a six-member jury found Edward Stark to be a dependent child, and the judge committed him to St. Mary's Training School for Boys in Decatur, Illinois. Cook County then paid a monthly subsidy to the privately incorporated school, which Archbishop Patrick Feehan had founded in 1882. At "Feehanville," as the school was popularly known, Edward was slated to receive a good education and proper religious instruction.

Edward, however, had different ideas about his upbringing and escaped. His freedom ended two years later when he was arrested in Chicago for stealing an expensive suit of clothes. On July 24, 1899, Edward, who was now thirteen years old, became the 108th child to appear before the juvenile court.

This snapshot from Edward Stark's life reveals that the connections between the boy's parents, priest, and police pre-dated the creation of the juvenile court. The court, once established, relied on these older social connections to conduct its business. John Phelan, for example, the police officer who had arrested "known thieves" in the Stark house in the mid-1890s, was now the probation officer for the Eleventh District. He no longer wore a uniform, carried a weapon, or wore a badge, and much to Edward's chagrin became his probation officer. Over the next few years, their lives would intersect on the many occasions when Edward would again get into trouble with the law.

Judge Tuthill committed Edward to Pontiac, where he spent eight months. While Edward was in the reformatory, his parents deserted him, and he was consequently paroled to live with a "reputable citizen" in his old neighborhood. It took the abandoned boy less than two months to end up in juvenile court again. This time he was arrested by a police officer for "keeping bad company." Edward had been in an alley at 3:30 a.m. with two other boys, when the officer approached them. The boys all ran, and only Edward was caught. This time Judge Tuthill committed him to the John Worthy School, where Edward would spend the next year of his life.

The cycle then began again. Edward was paroled to another foster family and four months later was again in court. This time he had been arrested for throwing stones at a man. Probation Officer Phelan in his report to Judge Tuthill noted that Edward "when arrested . . . gave the name of John Kain [and] also claimed that I did not known [sic] him." Familiarity made it nearly impossible for Edward, now a fifteen-year-old, to use an alias to hide his checkered past.

The continuities revealed by Edward's case suggest that the significance of the juvenile court in its early years was its ability to centralize the preexisting system of policing children. Previously, a juvenile, just like an adult, could be brought before any one of the city's eleven police courts, but now when Edward was arrested he entered a juvenile justice system that had a probation officer who knew him quite well. This made it more difficult for Edward to slip through the cracks, but it did not deter him from further mischief.

Edward did outgrow his delinquency. The turning point was his enrollment in the Junior Business Club. Over the next couple of years, the club found him employment in the Navy and then helped him to get a job as a stockroom attendant for the Chicago Edison Company. What later became of Edward is not known, but he did, at least, survive a difficult adolescence and could be considered a success story for the new court.

After becoming chief probation officer in 1905, Henry Thurston applauded the efforts of the court's probation officers in handling cases like Edward's, especially their "missionary zeal," but after studying the department's administration, he announced that "the state of things was intolerable."[78] The informal system, which had relied on personal knowledge and cooperation among a small staff, no longer seemed adequate to keep track of the more than four thousand children on probation. A more sophisticated system, Thurston concluded, was required to prevent children from drifting through the system "without a record being made, except in the diaries of individual officers." Otherwise, it would be nearly impossible to determine how children "fared while they dwelt under the protection of the court and what happened to them afterwards."[79]

Thurston wanted accurate records of each child's history in order to calculate the juvenile court's success rate. A standardized approach to record-keeping promised to yield the sociological data necessary to study the problem of juvenile delinquency more systematically, which would allow social scientists like himself to integrate the individual experiences of children like Edward Stark into a composite sketch of the delinquent child. This knowledge would, in turn, help to explain the causes of delinquency and ultimately produce a cure for waywardness.

Thurston's efforts to modernize the probation department were hampered by the Cook County Commissioners, who did not provide him with the number of officers he requested, pay them a competitive salary, or even reimburse them for work-related expenses such as carfare. The result was heavy caseloads, an average of 120 children per officer, which discouraged talented individuals from becoming probation officers.[80] It also suggests that there was some truth to the historian David Rothman's wry observation that "it is an odd but perhaps accurate conclusion to note that the dependent and deviant may owe what freedom they have more to the fiscal conservatism of elected officials than to the benevolent motives of reformers."[81]

Chicago's overworked probation officers were not the exception to the national rule. Lenroot and Lundberg, for example, reported that "it is agreed that from 50 to 75 cases are all that one probation officer can handle effectively, but in only four of the [ten] courts studied was this standard generally observed. . . . In three courts it was more than 100."[82] Probation had certainly become a distinguishing feature of juvenile justice by the mid-1920s, but the majority of probation officers were generally underpaid and extremely overworked.

In addition to the problems associated with probation officers handling far too many cases, judges, such as Julian Mack, were also overwhelmed by their unwieldy calendars. In his first three years on the bench, Judge Mack had heard over fourteen thousand cases and was convening semiweekly sessions, which often lasted late into the night. This heavy caseload was the product of raising the court's jurisdiction to include older children and a growing acceptance of the court. As Breckinridge and Abbott reported, "a common belief seems to have been spreading through the community that any child, more especially any boy, whose conduct demanded supervision or discipline would be benefited by coming under the care of the court and the influence of the judge." They added: "The error of this view was, of course, apparent to the judge, who urged in every way and at every opportunity the adoption of preventive measures, and the importance of exhausting other methods of treatment before bringing the child to court, and the use of the court only as a last resort."[83] To gain control over his calendar, Mack needed to design a policy to prevent the cases that did not require his attention from coming to court. This change would not only free up his calendar for more serious cases but also would spare many children the unnecessary trauma and potential stigma of appearing before a judge.

The problem was that under the Juvenile Court Act the judge was required to hear *all* cases in which a petition had been filed. Mack had to find a method to limit petitioning, which was difficult, because any "reputable person" who was a resident of Cook County could file a petition against any child within the county. The fact that family members, principals, neighbors, child welfare workers, and probation officers all filed petitions only complicated matters.

Mack devised an ingenious remedy: the complaint system. He requested that concerned individuals should make an informal complaint to the court's probation department instead of filing a formal petition against a child. This procedural change allowed the probation staff to investigate cases to determine whether they merited judicial attention. After an investigation, an officer could dismiss the complaint if it appeared groundless, attempt to resolve any minor problems independently, file a petition against the child if necessary, or charge the parents or guardians with contributing to the dependency or delinquency of a minor under a freshly minted state law.[84] This policy gave the probation officers the discretion to determine which children should be brought to court. It also allowed these officers to use the threat of future legal action as a means to encourage cooperation with their commands.

The complaint system served as an effective technique for managing the court's caseload. In 1912, for example, the presiding judge, Merritt W. Pinckney, estimated that only a quarter of the complaints received by the court led to petitions being filed.[85] By the 1920s, the criminologists Clifford R. Shaw and Earl D. Myers discovered that police officers, assigned as probation officers for their precincts, were filing petitions in less than 10 percent of the cases that they handled.[86] Thus, only a small percentage of all the children who had contact with the juvenile justice system, including the police, had their cases adjudicated. The Chicago Juvenile Court had indeed become a court of last resort.

Other juvenile courts adopted variations on the complaint system in the early twentieth century. Lenroot and Lundberg discovered that "the proportion of delinquency cases adjusted without formal court action varied from 43 percent to 86 percent in the four courts which utilized this method to any considerable extent and for which statistics were available."[87] Thus, by the mid-1920s, the complaint system, like detention and probation, had become a distinguishing feature of progressive juvenile justice.

P rivate hearings, the final distinguishing feature of progressive juvenile justice analyzed in this chapter, involved removing the general public from juvenile court hearings. As already mentioned, the sponsors of the 1899 Illinois juvenile court legislation had wanted juvenile court hearings to be closed to spectators, but as a result of the campaign by the industrial school lobby the controversial provision had been removed from the legislation. The local papers did, in fact, cover the new court's early cases, such as Henry Campbell's, and published stories about the children, including their names, addresses, and alleged offenses. Spectators also came to the court to see the most sensational cases.

Although the progressive child savers learned how to use publicity to help legitimate the juvenile court, they still wanted to limit public access to juvenile court and give judges as much control of the courtroom as possible. It is significant, for example, that in 1910 when the *Annals of the Academy of Political and Social Science* published an issue devoted to "the administration of justice in the United States," it included an article, "Private Hearings—Their Advantages and Disadvantages," that addressed this question. Judge Harvey H. Baker, the presiding judge of Boston's juvenile court, wrote the article. In the introduction, he noted that "the limitations on publicity now being introduced in juvenile courts vary in strictness all the away from an under-standing with the newspapers that the offenders' name shall not be published, to what may be called for convenience a private hearing."[88] That these limitations on publicity were being written into state laws ten years after the invention of the juvenile court was telling, but even more revealing was that Baker deemed it necessary to explain what a private hearing was and why it was a potentially good thing.

Judge Baker used a series of analogies, comparing the role of the juvenile court judge to that of a parent, teacher, and physician, to support his argument in favor of private hearings, whose main feature was "the reduction of the number of persons present to minimum." Ideally, the judge, he believed, should talk with the child alone. The major advantage of the private hearing was that it allowed the "judge the closest approach to the conditions under which the physician works." The danger of this analogy, Baker pointed out, was that a judge, unlike a doctor, had the power to deprive children of their liberty and parents of their natural authority, and a private hearing represented a "radical departure from the hard-won and long-established principle of full publicity in court proceedings." Potentially, as Baker acknowledged, a system of private hearings could shield not only the privacy of children and their families but also shelter the "carelessness, eccentricities or prejudices of an unfit judge."[89]

Judge Baker concluded on a cautionary note. He recommended that "until the private hearing has been fully tested by experience, communities where the citizens are doubtful can proceed with caution, taking preliminary steps by suppressing newspaper reports of the name of the children and excluding all minors from the hearing except the offender and juvenile witnesses one at a time."[90] Thus, even in 1910 one of the nation's leading proponents of private hearings did not think that they had been in existence long enough to be considered "fully tested by experience." Private hearings had not yet become a defining feature of progressive juvenile justice.

Beginning in the 1910s, a number of juvenile courts, however, hired women referees to conduct private hearings for girls who were accused of juvenile delinquency. A referee acted like a judge, but did not have the legal authority to sign court orders. Accordingly, a judge had to review and sign off on her decisions. These women referees helped to legitimate the use of private hearings.

Although the number of cases of girl delinquency was much smaller than boys' cases (for every case of girl delinquency there were more than three cases of boy delinquency), the rate of girl delinquency increased during the early twentieth century.[91] In Chicago, Abbott and Breckinridge discovered that this increasing rate of girl delinquency was due to "the growing knowledge of conditions responsible for delinquency among [girls] and to increasing skill on the part of the officers of the court in seeking out girls who had fallen under the influence of these conditions."[92] This conclusion suggested that the building of the juvenile court and the defining of "juvenile delinquency" were interrelated, and that how the court defined the "delinquent child" helped to determine which children appeared before it. Unlike boys, who were primarily charged with property crimes (i.e., theft), girls were almost exclusively charged with either "immorality" or "incorrigibility," code words for sexual activity or what Steven Schlossman and Stephanie Wallach have called "the crime of precocious sexuality."[93]

Parents played an integral role in this process of using juvenile courts to police the sexuality of their adolescent daughters. Single mothers, as the historians Mary Odem and Steven Schlossman have discovered, especially relied on these courts to help them discipline their sexually active daughters who demanded more control over their own lives and bodies.[94] Fearful that sexually active girls would become "lost women," judges incarcerated girls at substantially higher rates than boys, who were considered better candidates for probation. Thus, girls were brought to juvenile court for different reasons from boys and had their cases processed in a different manner.

Cases of "precocious sexuality" placed male judges, not to mention the girls themselves, in uncomfortable positions because a confession by the delinquent in court was considered to be a critical step in the rehabilitation process. This meant that an older man had to question an adolescent girl about her sex life in a crowded courtroom. In "The Square Deal with Children," published in *American Illustrated Magazine*, the journalist Henry Kitchell Webster described how Judge Mack handled the case of a girl about "fifteen, pretty, blond, innocent, immaculate in white duck, a little flat sailor hat set on her yellow hair." Judge Mack motioned for the girl to approach him, so that she could quietly explain why she was in court. "No one knows," Webster explained, "what questions he asks, no one hears the long story she tells him, but it may be seen that before it is half through she is crying." When she finished, the judge called the mother before the bench and told her that he was going to take her daughter away. "We want," Mack explained, "to make a good woman of her. If she's to grow up to that she will have to get a good many things out of her mind that she has there now, and she won't do that as long as she has her old companions about her." The distraught mother cried, "I'll kill myself if you take her away from me!" After some reflection, Mack decided to negotiate with the mother: "If you will move away, move to an entirely new place, where her old companions won't find her, and where she will find new ones, you can have her. Unless you do, or until you do, she will have to go to Geneva [the State Home for Female Offenders]."[95]

The awkwardness of these cases in which a male judge quizzed an adolescent girl about her sexual history raised questions about the appropriate roles for men, women, and the public in the exercise of the state's power of *parens patriae*. Based on their observations of Chicago's model court, Breckinridge and Abbott concluded that the success of juvenile justice depended on both men and women playing integral roles in its future administration. They wrote: "Any real substitute for the care of the natural parents will contain the elements of both the paternal and maternal character, and will involve, *when the machinery of the court is fully developed*, the representation of the maternal and the paternal in the final decision."[96] They said that women had to be judges because "even when the [male] judge is a genius at understanding the child, or devotedly kind and genuinely sympathetic, there is often the need not merely of advice from a woman, but of deciding power exercised by a woman."[97] A woman's advice and power, they argued, were especially critical in the cases of delinquent girls.

This claim for special expertise by women over delinquent girls was part of the process in the nineteenth and twentieth centuries of women carving out professional roles. In 1913, the Chicago Juvenile Court hired Mary Bartleme to serve as the woman referee to adjudicate girls' cases. Since 1897 Bartleme had worked as a public guardian for dependent girls in Cook County; now she heard girls' cases in a quiet chamber away from the bustle of the courtroom. In the 1920s, she also became the first woman to serve as presiding judge for the Chicago Juvenile Court.

The successful use of private hearings in girls' cases, by referees like Bartleme, helped to popularize the notion that all juvenile cases should be adjudicated in closed courtrooms or a judge's private chambers. By the 1920s, when many of the most influential studies of juvenile justice were first published, private hearings had become fairly standard. Lenroot and Lundberg's *Juvenile Courts at Work* (1925) and Herbert Lou's *Juvenile Courts in the United States* (1927), for example, declared that "the exclusion of the public from hearings of children's cases is generally recognized as a fundamental feature of juvenile-court procedure."[98] Later in the twentieth century, scholars relied on these important studies from the 1920s, many of which were reprinted in the 1970s, to make generalizations about "the progressive juvenile court," including the assumption that private hearings had always been one of the distinguishing features of juvenile justice. Left out of these historical accounts was the controversial and long process of limiting public access to the juvenile court, echoes of which could still be heard in Herbert Lou's 1927 description of private hearings. He noted, for instance, that "it is to the advantage of the court to permit acquaintance with its work that will win the understanding and cooperation of the community and free the court from the suspicious criticism of holding 'star chamber sessions.' Undue privacy may be as injurious to the work of the court as undue publicity. Privacy should not appear to be secrecy."[99]

Juvenile courts, including Chicago's model one, were not immaculate constructions; they were built over time. It took more than a generation to pour form and substance into the idea of a juvenile court. The length of this construction process, which—due to American federalism—varied from state to state, reveals that the history of juvenile justice has not been a simple story of a decline or fall from high foundational principles. Instead, it is much more instructive to view the juvenile court as a work in progress whose "defining features" were a series of additions that only later became standard practices. This corrective lens helps us to see not only the continuing influence of private associations and institutions in Progressive Era state-building but also how social concerns about religion, class, race, and gender all shaped the development and administration of juvenile justice. The work-in-progress perspective also demonstrates that some practices developed in the 1910s, such as the administration of welfare programs (the subject of the next chapter), ceased to be considered appropriate functions for juvenile justice. Thus, an examination of the relationship of the juvenile court to the emerging welfare state is essential to a more precise understanding of the evolution of juvenile justice in the early twentieth century.

THREE

It is significant that it was in America that the first juvenile
court arose, for from America about the same time the
civilized world received its first warning that all was not
well with that ancient institution, the home.
—*Miriam Van Waters, Referee, Los Angeles Juvenile Court,*
  1925

Preserving the Family

On December 23, 1912, a Hungarian father brought his three young daughters (ages three, five, and seven) to the Chicago Juvenile Court to file dependent petitions on their behalf, alleging that their mother had deserted the family, stolen their savings, and disappeared. As a single father, he could have and probably did argue that it was unreasonable to expect him to work and to raise his young children simultaneously. On Christmas Eve, after a six-man jury found each girl to be a "dependent child," Judge Merritt Pinckney ordered them committed to the Lisle Industrial School and arranged for their father to pay $15 a month for their support. Thus, the single father had used the juvenile court to arrange for a private institution to raise his now motherless children, who, because they were the same sex, were at least allowed to grow up together in the same industrial school.[1]

The death of the girls' father in February 1914 and the reappearance in May of their mother, who petitioned the juvenile court for custody, raised new questions about the girls' dependency. At a time when the Chicago Juvenile Court was running one of the largest mothers' pension programs in the country and paying some mothers to raise their dependent children at home, in this case, the mother, who as an alien was not eligible for state relief, had to prove to the judge that she not only was a capable mother but also had enough resources to provide for her daughters. In her petition the mother described herself as a loyal but abused wife, "the almost unceasing victim of [her husband's] brutality and abuse," who had been forced away from her home and children on the very day that her husband had filed the initial dependent petitions. She had found a job at a restaurant on Halsted Street to support herself, but once her husband "had succeeded in getting the children placed in the said Industrial School he came to the place where [she] was then employed and induced her to return to their home." Shortly thereafter, the father was critically injured in an industrial accident. His wife secured employment at a West Side dispensary and supported the couple during the husband's long and eventually unsuccessful convalescence, which ended on February 17, 1914. Now, two months later, the mother appeared in Judge Pinckney's courtroom to declare that she "has always been a good mother to the said children" and could provide them with "a suitable place," and that "it is consistent with the public good and the good of said children; that they be restored to the custody of your petitioner."[2] Judge Pinckney concurred, but for the girls' safety placed them on probation with their mother until the end of the year. He permanently discharged them nearly two years after the date on which they had become wards of the court.[3]

The three sisters had entered the juvenile court at a formative moment in welfare history. Beginning in 1911 with Illinois's passage of the Funds to Parents Act—the first statewide mothers' pensions legislation—the Chicago Juvenile Court built a two-track system for dependency cases that used the gender of single parents to track their children. The first or "institutional" track followed a nineteenth-century model of family preservation that poor families had relied on since before the Civil War, in which parents had used institutions to provide short-term care for their children during hard times.[4] As the historian Kenneth Cmiel has noted, managers of late-nineteenth-century asylums understood this reasoning and, accordingly, "did not think of the children as unique individuals, separate from the accident of their parents. . . . Instead, they thought of the children as an integral part of a family unit, a unit the orphanage was struggling to maintain."[5] Thus, although children might be physically separated from their parents for periods of time, they were still considered to be part of a "natural" family and were expected to return to their own homes when conditions improved.

The juvenile court also established a "home-based" track for dependency that reflected a new model of family preservation. Progressive child savers denounced the nineteenth-century model of family preservation that relied on institutionalization because they claimed that institutions were too regimented and did not prepare children to live in the outside world.[6] As scholars of social welfare have long noted, the 1909 White House Conference on the Care of Dependent Children rejected institutionalization and instead endorsed the new model of family preservation in its famous resolution: "Home life is the highest and finest product of civilization. It is the great molding force of mind and of character. Children should not be deprived of it except for urgent and compelling reasons."[7] Accordingly, families, if at all possible, should remain physically together in their own homes.

The actual practice of family preservation in the early-twentieth-century Chicago Juvenile Court did not result from the ascendancy of the "home-based" model over the "institutional" one but rather from a mixture of old and new approaches.[8] Children placed in the "institutional" track, as the three sisters initially were, lived in training or industrial schools until they could be reunited with their families; children placed in the newer "home-based" track remained at home, partially supported by a state disbursement paid to their mothers. Moreover, gendered assumptions about single parenthood by parents and the court influenced how children were tracked. Motherless children generally ended up in the "institutional" track and fatherless ones in the "home-based" track. Once in either track, a child became a ward of the court, thus making a judge, not the parents, the final decision maker in questions about the child's welfare and in effect placed the entire family under the court's jurisdiction.

Progressive reformers were concerned about whether the family could survive in the modern world. The expansion of the wage economy and the spread of market processes, the rise of large-scale industrialization, rapid urbanization, and mass immigration were all radically transforming American life. The family, symbolized by the image of the home, appeared to be fracturing under these new pressures. As the referee of the Los Angeles Juvenile Court, Miriam Van Waters, observed, "parenthood itself began to weaken, so that not only were thousands of children brought before the court who in happier conditions would never have come, but the children themselves had no conception of what a wise, good father and mother ought to be."[9] Clearly, the state had to exercise its authority of *parens patriae* over these practically parentless children.

The question of why progressive child savers thought that the juvenile court was the *natural* choice to administer welfare programs merits consideration, before examining how this decision allowed for the construction of a two-track system for family preservation.[10] The legislative history of the Funds to Parents Act hardly explains why the juvenile court gained jurisdiction over mothers' pensions, for no public campaign led to the law's passage.[11] As the historian Joanne Goodwin has documented, since the turn of the century there had been discussions about mothers' pensions at national conferences of charity and social workers, social research into the subject by Chicago's leading social justice feminists, and calls by Chicago's juvenile court judges for family preservation programs. However, she notes that "the first state law that authorized voluntary public funding to families with dependent children slipped into existence without their consultation," and the actual origins of the Funds to Parents Act remain quite mysterious.[12] State Senator Carl Lundberg, a Republican from Chicago, introduced the bill, which was amended once, passed without opposition, and signed by the governor on June 5, 1911.[13] This bill, which had received little public attention before its passage, quickly became famous as word of its existence spread throughout Chicago and the nation.

The decision to entrust juvenile courts with the administration of mothers' pensions reflected both a nineteenth-century tradition of judges "governing the hearth" and a newer faith in the capacity of urban courts to police social problems.[14] In the United States over the course of the nineteenth century, as the legal historian Michael Grossberg has revealed, courts, not legislatures, had often played a leading role in establishing child welfare policies. With the creation of the nation's first juvenile court in Chicago in 1899, this trend of judicial intervention into domestic relations continued into the twentieth century.

Once a city opened a juvenile court, reformers began to think of it as the local child welfare center and as an institution that could be expanded to meet new needs. This tendency was especially pronounced in midwestern and western states, in which social services were less developed than in the East.[15] Moreover, progressive child savers conceived of all children as being different from adults and, accordingly, did not draw sharp distinctions between dependents and delinquents and believed that a unified children's court could serve both.[16] Thus, the juvenile court appeared to many progressives, who saw the roots of delinquency in dependency, to be the obvious site for administering mothers' pensions. In "Pensioning the Widow and the Fatherless," a 1913 article published in *Good Housekeeping*, Frederic C. Howe and Marie Jenney Howe made this argument matter-of-factly. They said that the juvenile court already had "charge of child life" and "could be enlarged to take over one more department, and more appropriately so than any other agency, since the children who suffer from lack of home care are those brought to the juvenile court. When delinquency is due to this cause it can be looked into and remedied by a Mothers' Pension."[17] As a result of such reasoning, legislatures entrusted juvenile courts with the administration of mothers' pensions in the majority of states that passed pension laws in the early 1910s.[18]

Some early critics questioned the expansion of the juvenile court into all areas of child welfare. In 1914, Thomas D. Eliot, a professor of sociology at Northwestern University, warned about the consequences of adding "extra-activities" to juvenile courts, which transformed them "into all things to all men" and taxed their limited resources.[19] More disturbingly, as Eliot pointed out, many of these new functions, such as mothers' pensions, were not "essentially judicial in character."[20] This pronouncement echoed the growing concerns of social workers and some juvenile court judges, who believed that juvenile courts were "ill adapted" to administer welfare programs. It also foreshadowed criticisms by legal scholars in the 1920s, who warned about the dangers of "socialized" courts, which disregarded the rule of law in the pursuit of "individualized" justice.[21]

Though the Funds to Parents Act epitomized the process of adding "extra-activities" to the juvenile court that Eliot had criticized, the law offered the possibility of preserving homes in a seemingly disorderly city. Chicago, the nation's fastest growing city, as the muckraking Lincoln Steffens observed, was "first in violence, deepest in dirt; loud, lawless, unlovely, ill-smelling, new; an overgrown gawk of a village, the teeming tough among cities. Criminally it was wide open, commercially it was brazen; and socially it was thoughtless and raw."[22] The Funds to Parents Act, which reflected faith in the capacity of the juvenile court to serve as a social welfare institution, promised to help restore social order by strengthening the home.

Sometimes judges get what they ask for. Merritt W. Pinckney, who became the third judge of the Chicago Juvenile Court in June 1908, had supported the idea of mothers' pensions because he believed that they would prevent the court from separating dependent children from their morally worthy but impoverished mothers. The Funds to Parents Act, which created the possibility for the juvenile court to build a "home-based" family preservation program, raised a host of administrative problems for the judge. It also thrust Pinckney into the national limelight, especially after the Russell Sage Foundation commissioned Carl C. Carstens, the director of the Massachusetts Society for the Prevention of Cruelty to Children, to investigate how the new program worked.[23] Social workers would be watching to see how the judge administered the welfare program.

Charity reformers since the Civil War had condemned outdoor relief, as the historian Amy Dru Stanley has argued, because it "constituted an 'unmitigated evil' that not only destroy[ed] the 'habit of industry' but also taught the poor to view dependence as a 'right' rather than a stigmatized status."[24] Although in the 1910s supporters of mothers' pensions tried to differentiate this new form of state aid from poor relief, they still shared many of the Gilded Age's assumptions about the potentially pauperizing effects of public aid to the poor. Thus, even though Pinckney supported the Funds to Parents Act, he feared creating new forms of adult dependency and knew that Carstens and other social workers would examine the family preservation program to see whether it would "inevitably create a new class of dependents."[25]

Part of the problem that Pinckney faced was that while the progressive child savers did not want to make adults into dependents, at the same time reformers did want to make children and adolescents into a dependent class. Through truancy, compulsory education, and child labor laws aimed to keep children off the streets, in school, and out of the labor market, progressives attempted to prolong youth dependency.[26] The founders of the juvenile court had in fact envisioned that the court, by removing juveniles from the adult criminal justice system, would be part of this larger project to prolong child dependency.

The juvenile court, however, had never done a good job of defining what exactly constituted "child dependency." This difficulty stemmed in part from the belief that "all children are dependent, but only a small number are dependent on the state."[27] If all children were dependent by definition, how could a judge determine which ones required state assistance? In addition, the multiple meanings of dependency, which, as the historian Sylvia Schafer has noted in her work on French child welfare, can also include "negative facts," not just a lack of material resources, complicated the issue.[28] In its annual reports, the Chicago court, for example, had listed the causes of dependency generally as "lack of care" without explaining what specific "care" was missing from the child's life. The reports also specified cases in which a child was dependent because of an "abnormal" family situation created by desertion, sickness, death, insanity, imprisonment, immorality, cruelty, or separation of the parents.[29] Over the years, dependency cases had accounted for about half of the annual calendar, but, given the court's ambiguous reporting system, it is unclear why some cases were classified as "lack of care" and others assigned more specific causes.

Before the passage of the law in 1911, the judge had limited options in a dependency case.[30] He could allow the child "to remain at its own home subject to friendly visitation of a probation officer," place the child under the guardianship of a "reputable citizen" who would find "a suitable home for the child," or commit the child to a private institution.[31] These options, however, did not include providing financial assistance to destitute families. Consequently, the judge could be forced to remove a dependent child from worthy parents who could not provide for their offspring.

In a December 1911 speech before Chicago's Hamilton Club, Pinckney explained that his "chief endeavor has been to keep the home intact—to preserve the family circle," but that before the passage of the Funds to Parents Act earlier that year, he had often made the painful decision to break up destitute families and send the children to private institutions.[32] These brutal moments in the courtroom, when he ordered the separation of a mother from her children, haunted him. "Words cannot express a child's fear or a mother's agony at such a time," he said. He asked the audience to think of the heartbroken mother: "Will she survive the test and continue to lead an honest upright life or will she drift along the lines of least resistance ending in the brothel or in the mad house? It was just such a problem as this some three years ago that first challenged my attention. Such cases have multiplied and made me realize the need of this new law."[33] The Funds to Parents Act now allowed the judge to keep such children at home with their mothers.

The law, however, was not exactly what he had envisioned and proved to be an administrative nightmare. It consisted of a single, loosely worded paragraph:

> If the parent or parents of such [a] dependent or
> neglected child are poor and unable to properly
> care for the said child, but are otherwise proper
> guardians and it is for the welfare of such child to
> remain at home, the court may enter an order finding
> such facts and fixing the amount of money necessary
> to enable the parent or parents to properly care for
> such child, and thereupon it shall be the duty of the
> County Board, through its County Agent or otherwise,
> to pay to such parent or parents, at such times as
> said order may designate the amount so specified for
> the care of such dependent or neglected child until
> the further order of the court.[34]

The lack of guidelines created the possibility for disparate interpretations by judges across the state, because no limits on aid were set, no standards for eligibility were specified, and no means for raising revenue for the program were provided. Although the law was considered to be the first statewide *mothers'* pension legislation, its inclusive language did not limit aid to mothers. If the original intent of the law was that funds would be given only to mothers, constitutional concerns about "class legislation" are one explanation for the gender-neutral wording of the act.[35] It is also possible that its author and the legislature did envision that financial assistance would be given to poor two-parent families to tide them over difficult times.

After the law went into effect on July 1, 1911, a flood of applications left the staff of the juvenile court reeling. They had expected that pension cases would emerge from the daily operations of the court; instead churches and newspapers spread the word and encouraged single mothers to apply.[36] Judge Pinckney, after realizing that his current staff was neither properly trained nor adequately equipped to handle all these new cases, created a separate mothers' pensions department (later known as the Aid-to-Mothers Division) to oversee the handling of the cases in the court's new "home-based" family preservation program. He also sought assistance from the Cook County Board of Commissioners "to meet these new conditions."[37]

The Funds to Parents Act, however, by vesting its administration in the juvenile court, had divided the jurisdiction over "outdoor," or noninstitutional, poor relief between the court and the county board. The county board's meager response to the judge's request for additional funding strained the already tense relationship between the two agencies. The county board had been solely responsible for public relief before the creation of the juvenile court. It still ran the county's poorhouse, located in Oak Forest, as well as a system of outdoor poor relief, which provided in-kind benefits to destitute families in the form of coal, food, clothing, and medical care. By allotting the court only $2,000 for the first fiscal year the law was in effect, July 1 through November 30, 1911, the county board rendered administration of the new law nearly impossible.[38] For the following year, it did grant $75,000, but this was still only 60 percent of the $125,000 Pinckney requested. The judge had to look elsewhere for help with the implementation of the new law.

The judge sought to make the Chicago court into a model of scientific administration. As Pinckney explained to social workers from across the nation, gathered in Cleveland in 1912 for the National Conference of Charities and Corrections, the Funds to Parents Act was "either the best law for our dependent poor ever enacted, or else it is the worst, depending upon its administration."[39] Effective administration, in his opinion, required incorporating the casework techniques developed by private charity organizations to infuse the new law with the spirit of scientific charity.[40] Like the leaders of the Charity Organization Society movement who crusaded against outdoor relief in the Gilded Age, Pinckney worried about the pauperizing effects of public aid on its recipients and the possibility that governmental intervention might loosen family ties.[41] He did not want to either break a mother's "spirit of self-dependence" or encourage "indifferent husbands" to abandon their families.[42]

Frustrated by the county board, Pinckney opted to work with the leaders of Chicago's private charities to formulate scientific guidelines for the new "home-based" program and to assist him in its administration. By bringing the city's philanthropic community into the process, the juvenile court merged public power with private resources, as it had many times since its creation. "It was but natural," Pinckney stated, "to turn for assistance to those great charitable, social and civic welfare societies and associations in Chicago which are most active in relief-giving and in advancing the cause of good citizenship and a purer body politic."[43] The leaders of the philanthropic community selected Julia Lathrop of Hull House, Mrs. L. L. Funk of the Children's Day Association, James F. Kennedy of the St. Vincent de Paul Society, Sherman Kingsley of the Elizabeth McCormick Memorial Fund, and Reverend C. J. Quille of the Catholic Charities to serve as an executive committee to work with the judge to determine eligibility requirements, fashion a workable system for investigating applicants, devise procedures for supervising the recipients, and select a staff of qualified social workers to run the program.[44]

The committee established a searching process of review for all applicants.[45] Observers of the review process, such as Carl C. Carstens, were appalled by its "brutality."[46] A staff probation officer conducted the initial investigation and presented his or her findings to the citizens' committee, which met on a semiweekly basis. Unfortunately, Peter Bartzen, the president of the county board, who was trying to wrest control of the juvenile court away from the city's progressives, had appointed a number of temporary probation officers who lacked charity work experience, and their findings were often inadequate, in the opinion of the committee members.[47] These officers had to make multiple inquiries and report on a case two or three times before the committee had enough information to make a decision. If a family appeared eligible at this point, its name and address were forwarded to the county agent, who had ten days to conduct a second investigation. This followup might include spreading rumors about the mother's immorality in the neighborhood to "arouse interest in his inquiry, and by means of which he hoped to get incriminating information."[48] The family would then have its day in court, along with the probation officer and a representative from the county agent's office.

This entire review process for a family attempting to enter the "home-based" track for family preservation could be time-consuming, costly, and demeaning. Judge Pinckney, nevertheless, declared this system to be "the ideal co-operation of society and the state in administering a worthy law."[49] He was pleased by the fact that this procedure produced a rejection rate of well over 60 percent during the period from July 1, 1911, to September 30, 1912, when only 522 out of the 1,450 families who applied received pensions.[50] This high rejection rate ostensibly demonstrated that the review process guaranteed that only morally worthy mothers with no other means of support would receive aid. Moral considerations such as "unfit parents or home," "no established home," "illegitimate child in the family," and "unmarried mothers" accounted for roughly one tenth of the rejected applications. Significantly, economic factors such as, "income sufficient," "family had money or interest in property," "husband alive and able to support" and "relatives able to support" led to more than one half of the rejections.[51] The classification of "causes" for rejection provided additional evidence that the "home-based" program was being administered in a scientific manner that would promote traditional values, ensure that families met their legal obligations to provide for their relations and, most important, protect the taxpayers' pockets.

The judge also began meeting with the citizens' committee to draft a new piece of legislation to replace the open-ended Funds to Parents Act and to formalize the safeguards that in practice had narrowed the entrance to the "home-based" track for family preservation.[52] The chief probation officer, Joel Hunter, later called these new requirements the "safeguards" for the administration of the law. They included the following working principles:

1. No funds will be granted to any family where there are relatives able to support and liable for support of that family.[53]
2. No funds will be granted to any family that has been in the county less than one year.
3. No funds will be granted to any deserted woman whose husband has been away less then two years.[54]

These principles reflected the strong belief that family members must first meet their legal responsibility to provide for their own poor relations before public aid would be granted. In addition, these principles also demonstrated concerns about the welfare program becoming either a magnet that pulled poor families into the county or one that pushed fathers away from their wives and children.

Fortunately, the discovery of a series of case files from the year 1912 provides an opportunity to examine the impact of the original Funds to Parents Act on poor children and their families before the law was later revised. These records—the only extant files from the 1910s—cover the holiday season from Thanksgiving until Christmas, a time when Chicago relief agencies shouldered heavy case loads due to the arrival of winter.[55] An examination of the case files suggests that gendered assumptions about single parenthood by parents and the court contributed to the dual tracking of dependent children, in which fatherless children often remained in their own homes, while motherless children often ended up in private institutions.

The first track comprised the families to whom the court did not award pensions. The children in this "institutional" track were generally committed to training or industrial schools, although some stayed at home on probation and a few were placed in foster care. The majority of these children sent to institutions were, however, ultimately reunited with their families. The second track contained the "home-based" cases. The court awarded pensions to these families, and all these children remained at home.

None of the children from any of the families who received cash assistance spent any time in an institution, but their own homes became sites for state supervision and intervention. This staying at home contrasted sharply with the experiences of the majority of children from the "nonpensioned" families who spent from a few months to a couple of years and, in some instances, nearly a decade in industrial schools. The scholarship on the hidden history of family violence and reassessments of orphanages has challenged the idealized image of the home as a safe place and the Dickensian depiction of institutions as brutal warehouses for children and makes it difficult to generalize about which situation was better for the majority of the children.[56] Still, if the policy objective behind the Funds to Parents Act was to keep children in their own homes, then the law appears to have met its objective in the cases in which it was applied.

Since it opened in 1899, the juvenile court had devoted about half its annual calendar to dependency cases and had sent many of these children to private institutions, such as the Chicago Half-Orphan Asylum, "whose chief work [was] to provide temporary care for the children of parents who are in temporary distress."[57] The court continued this practice after the passage of the Funds to Parents Act, even though Judge Pinckney and his chief probation officer, John Witter, had condemned the practice of institutionalizing dependent children from morally worthy families. The court's annual report for 1910, for instance, employed the maternalist rhetoric of the campaign for mothers' pensions legislation to criticize the separation of children from their mothers. As Witter explained, "purely a lack of funds for support should never be reason enough to separate mother and child; to rob a child of that for which no institution can render a proper substitute—a mother's love."[58] He added: "Were we to consider this from the standpoint of expense alone, private organizations have proved, in a limited way, that the ordinary parent can, by keeping the family together, provide for the child with less money than it costs the state to care for the child in an institution."[59] Despite this antiinstitutional rhetoric, the court continued to use institutions to preserve families, especially single male–headed ones.

The "nonpensioned" dependency cases from 1912 reflected the disparate needs of the fifty-one first-time wards of the court. They ranged in age from Maud, an eight-day-old baby born out of wedlock, to Jane, a fifteen-year-old whose parents were "unable" to support her.[60] The juvenile court relied on many different institutions to preserve their families when possible. In this regard, the court in its role as a parent to these dependent children, legally its wards, used private institutions to serve as temporary "second homes" to tide families over in tough times. Pinckney committed thirty-two of these children to institutions, including Jane, who spent three months at the Illinois Industrial School for Girls before being paroled by the court to live with her parents.[61] The expectation, as in Jane's case, was that these children would be reunited with their families, and in close to 70 percent of the cases this did happen.[62]

According to this nineteenth-century model of family preservation, parents were expected to contribute to their children's upkeep in institutions because this would ensure that they retained a sense of responsibility toward their offspring. The parents, such as the Hungarian father discussed at the beginning of the chapter, were required to pay a monthly amount, typically $5 per child, to the clerk of the court. The representative of an institution or foster home collected the money from the clerk. This system of indirect payment also allowed the juvenile court to serve as a mediating force between the concerned parties, whether a parent and manager of an institution, or occasionally even family members. If a parent fell behind in child support, the juvenile court had the authority to bring contempt charges against him. Due to many parents' failing to make their payments, the court appointed an assistant probation officer in 1917 to devote all his time to handling contempt cases. In his first year, his efforts increased the amount of payments collected from $8,500 to $19,950.[63]

Long separations could strain these efforts to keep family ties secure through the use of institutions and financial contributions.

It could take years, and in some cases up to a decade, before parents and children were finally reunited. The three daughters of the Hungarian parents discussed earlier, for example, spent a year and a half at the Lisle Industrial School. This separation from their mother might have been much longer if their father had not died or if their mother had not convinced Judge Pinckney that she was capable of raising them.

In many cases, due to the death or desertion of both parents, the court had no chance to reunite children with their natural parents. One sad case, for instance, involved an unnamed baby boy born on September 9, 1912, to a poor couple, the Rileys, who lived in a rooming house.[64] The parents advertised the baby in the newspaper and gave him to a wealthy Hyde Park couple, the Smiths, to raise. The "care of the baby," however, made Mrs. Smith "a nervous wreck," forcing the couple to return the newborn to his parents. When the Smiths visited the baby the next day to see how he was doing, they were shocked at the poor care he was receiving. According to Mrs. Smith, "[he] was nearly nude when she recovered [him], had but little milk in bottle and [he] was cold." Again, the Smiths decided to take the baby, but Mrs. Smith's nerves were still not up to the task. This time they were unable to locate the baby's parents and decided to bring the child to the juvenile court.

During the hearing the Smiths produced a remarkable extralegal document, which had been drawn up by the baby's father. It read:

> This is to certify that we this day in our good sense
> and sober minds give our child to [the Smiths] for adoption
> for the reason that the said [Smiths] are in better financial
> circumstances and can therefore provide for and supply
> it's [sic] wants and give said child a more desirable home
> than we ourselves can at present. The said [Smiths] have
> shown all affections towards said child which leads us to
> believe that it will be properly and lovingly cared for, and
> that the promises made by the said [Smiths] will be
> faithfully fulfilled. We the undersigned can in no way

claim said child and cannot compel the said [Smiths] to give it back unless the said party become financially embarrassed and cannot give the said child its proper care.

The father added that he and his wife required sixty day's notice in case of any unforeseen misfortunes "to prepare for and receive our child."[65] An angry Judge Pinckney demanded that the parents, who had given away their baby, be found and brought to court. They never reappeared, and the unnamed baby was sent to St. Vincent's Infant Asylum, where after six months he became legally eligible for adoption.[66]

Close to one quarter of the children from "nonpensioned" families, such as Baby Maud, were "illegitimate" and legally had no father.[67] The sketchy nature of the records for these children makes it difficult to determine what happened to many of them. A few were placed on probation with reputable citizens to locate foster homes for them, several appeared to have stayed with their mothers, and at least two were adopted.[68] These "fatherless" children tended not to be institutionalized, which suggests that the court found homes, not institutions, for dependent children in cases where family preservation was not the goal.

The court did, however, institutionalize children from single male–headed families, whose cases did not fit the ideological framework for mothers' pensions. Supporters of mothers' pensions had focused on the role of "a mother's love" in raising good citizens and not the role of men as fathers. According to the maternalist rhetoric of the mothers' pensions campaigns of the 1910s, if a father died, the children lost both their parents because the mother would be forced to assume the dual roles of bread-winner and homemaker.[69] This meant that the mother would have to go to work and leave her children improperly cared for or unsupervised. Accordingly, a pension that paid her to care for her children at home could solve this social problem. The supporters of mothers' pensions, on the other hand, did not publicize the plight of children from single male–headed families. This silence about single fathers may have derived from assumptions about the inability of men to serve as primary caretakers for young children and the belief that men could either hire somebody else to look after their children or remarry.[70]

The juvenile court did not award any pensions to single fathers, although nothing in the Funds to Parents Act precluded this possibility. Instead the "institutional" track for preserving these father-only families was utilized.[71] As cases like the three sisters suggest, fathers probably requested that the court use private institutions to care for their children. In six out of the eight father-only families the children were institutionalized, and (with a single exception) these "motherless" children were later reunited with family members, generally with their fathers.[72] In these cases, the father, if financially able, contributed from $5 to $10 per month for each child's stay in an institution.[73]

Although these father-only families were generally reunited, the road to reunion could be long and rocky. The court had to threaten one father with contempt for nonpayment, and in another case a girl spent ten years in the juvenile justice system, first as a dependent and then as a delinquent child.[74] Yet even these children, who entered the juvenile court at the respective ages of five and six, were reunited with their fathers, though a decade later and when they were old enough to work legally. Thus, in the "institutional" track single fathers paid the state to act as a mother and raise their dependent children.

By contrast, in the new "home-based" track, the state acted as a father and paid a mother to raise her children. During the holiday season of 1912, the court ordered cash payments to eleven families who had a total of twenty-nine children, ranging in age from two-month-old Hilda to thirteen-year-old Mary.[75] These children, who were now considered "dependent," became wards of the court. They were approximately the same age as their fellow wards in the "institutional" track.[76]

Mothers and their children traveled to the county agent's office to pick up their monthly pensions. The monthly payments not only caused budgeting problems for women accustomed to working with weekly or biweekly wages, but the disbursement process also raised concerns among the city's charity workers. The citizens' committee, for example, criticized the process because it resembled the administration of outdoor relief. "The result," cautioned the committee, "is gossip among the women and consequent dissatisfaction. Such a public distribution is demoralizing and destructive of self-respect among these people. Moreover, children are being kept out of school to accompany mothers . . . on the day the funds are paid." The social work pioneers Edith Abbott and Sophonisba Breckinridge reached different conclusions. It appeared to them to be a social outing for some mothers, who seemed to "rather enjoy the excitement of the occasion and the opportunity for leisurely gossip." The judge ultimately ordered women to keep their children in school, and eventually payments were made on a biweekly basis, although the women still went to the county building to receive them.[77]

Once a mother accepted a pension, she had to structure her life according to the standards set by the juvenile court. Home visits by a probation officer brought the state into a family's life on an intimate basis and transferred the authority to make decisions for the family's welfare from the mother to the official. Studies from the late 1910s reveal that families were generally visited at least once a month and occasionally more often.[78] These encounters resembled the "friendly visits" of private charity workers and guaranteed a continued state presence in the social lives of the wards of the court. Moreover, many of the women were "enabled or persuaded to move to new quarters."[79] According to a December 1914 report, 116 out of the 313 families receiving pensions during the preceding three months had moved. Thus, not only did a probation officer visit the home, he or she often helped to decide where the home would be.

Though it is nearly impossible to tell how the women involved in these cases viewed these moves, the reasons for uprooting families offer some clues. In over 70 percent of the cases a family left because of "bad" housing conditions, which included poorly ventilated rooms, dark basements, rundown buildings, and overcrowded quarters. A change of residence in such instances was probably welcomed. The other fourth of the families had to move because of "bad moral surroundings" or high rents.[80] These cases are more ambiguous, and one can imagine situations where a mother's conceptions of proper morality or an appropriate rent clashed with the views of a probation officer.

The kitchen was another potential site for conflict between a mother and the state, as a court dietician worked with mothers to help them economize, especially with respect to family meals.[81] Women were encouraged to use sample menus, which left little room for ethnic tastes. For a mother and her six children, the following was suggested:

> Breakfast—Oatmeal with sugar and top milk; corn-meal muffins with home-made caramel syrup; coffee for adult; cocoa for children.
>
> Lunch—Puree of split peas served over stewed carrots; home-made bread with butterine; tea for adult; cambric tea for children.
>
> Supper—Flank steak, braised, with brown gravy; baked potato; home-made bread and stewed figs; cocoa [for all].[82]

An individual's gender, age, and "size and degree of muscular activity" determined the quantity of food that he or she required.[83]

In addition to regulating the lives of women and children in the "home-based" track, the court used the ages of children, their race, and the status of their fathers to narrow the entrance to the new welfare program. The court, for example, considered any child above fourteen years to be ineligible for relief.[84] At that stage of his or her life, a child was expected to find work and help support the family. Thus, when Mary, the oldest girl in this track, turned fourteen the following April, the juvenile court entered an order permanently staying the $8 a month her mother had been receiving in child support. Her mother continued to receive pensions for Mary's four young siblings for several more years. These funds allowed the family to stay together, and none of the children was placed in an institution.

The court also limited the number of African-American families in the "home-based" track. Although roughly one third of all dependent children's families were pensioned during the fiscal year, African-American families were pensioned at the startlingly low rate of 3.1 percent. The assumption that African-American women had always worked and raised families and could continue to do so without adversely affecting their children may have accounted for this differential treatment.[85] The low rate of pensioning African-American families contrasted with rates of over 40 percent for Austrian, English, Irish, and Russian families.[86]

The court also excluded children whose fathers had deserted the family. Pinckney feared that mothers' pensions could have the unintended consequence of encouraging desertion, so he decided not to give relief to women deserted by their husbands.[87] The judge believed that aid in these cases would activate the "desertion microbe" of "indifferent men" and start "a migratory epidemic."[88] He admitted that "amending the law so that deserted wives will not be eligible for relief will necessarily work a hardship to a few worthy cases." Still, in his opinion, "the good of the few must, however, be sacrificed for the good of the many."[89] The consequences of this decision led to some children's separation from mothers who could not care for them. One brother and sister, for example, were committed to separate institutions and spent close to five years apart from each other and their mother.[90] In cases where the missing father was presumed to be dead, Pinckney made an exception to the desertion rule and provided pensions.[91]

Along somewhat similar lines, Pinckney granted one pension to a two-parent household, in which the father was presumably incapacitated. The family received $21 per month for almost a year, but only the mother appeared for the court dates. The probation order also specified that the cash payment was for the mother. Pensioning families with an injured or institutionalized father became a feature of the welfare program and suggests that the court considered these families "fatherless" because of the man's physical or mental inability to fulfill his role as a breadwinner.[92]

The judicial administration of mothers' pensions, during its first phrase under the loosely worded Funds to Parents Act, was clearly an effort to safeguard the entrance to the "home-based" track and to scrutinize those families allowed in. The judge and the citizens' committee were creating ad hoc procedures, but ones that reflected concerns about public assistance undermining traditional values and legal obligations among family members for mutual support. When Pinckney wrote more stringent eligibility guidelines into the law in 1913, he ensured that the juvenile court would continue to administer the "home-based" welfare program. This decision created a new division in the court, additional staffing, and a heavier overall caseload. The state had expanded the juvenile court, as critics like Eliot feared, by broadening its jurisdiction to address a social problem, whose structural source, the uneasy position of the working class in the new American economy, compounded by gender inequality, was beyond the ability of the court to resolve.

In 1912 Judge Pinckney traveled to Cleveland to defend his administration of the new welfare program before an audience of charity and social workers at the National Conference of Charities and Corrections. Pinckney announced that a period of ideal cooperation between society and the state in the administration of the Funds to Parents Act had laid the groundwork for a promising future in which the public would assume more responsibility for those in need.

The new era, however, began with a more restrictive and gender-specific *mothers'* pensions law. On July 1, 1913, the "Aid to Mothers Law," which Pinckney had drafted with the help of the citizens' committee and Joseph Meyer, the county agent, went into effect.[93] This revised law included: stringent new eligibility requirements (the mother now had to be a citizen of the United States and a resident of the county); caps on awards (aid was limited to $15 per month for the first child and $10 per month for additional children up to a $50 ceiling); and a new county tax of three-tenths of a mill to finance the program. This narrower scope left only widows and women with permanently incapacitated husbands eligible. Women who had been deserted, were divorced, had husbands in jail, or were unmarried were excluded from receiving aid.

The court, moreover, did not grandfather in prior recipients, and these newly excluded families had to turn to private charities. In Cook County, 172 families had their pensions stayed that July; nearly 80 percent of these cases involved mothers who were "aliens," and another 18 percent were deserted or divorced women. The court referred all these families to the county agent and the private charity societies. Remarkably, only seven families (4 percent) were forced to place their children in institutions.[94] This result provides some evidence that prior to the passage of the Funds to Parents Act, private charities had probably managed to keep many families together. It is unclear what would have happened, however, if the pensions of *all* the families receiving relief had been terminated. Evidence about changing patterns of philanthropy in this period, charted by the historian Kathleen McCarthy, suggests that private relief would not have met the needs of all these families.[95]

During the next two years, over thousand applications for aid were rejected because of the new citizenship requirement, but this period of more restrictive legislation was for the most part coming to an end. The criticism of the harsh treatment of "American" children, for example, led to the law being amended in 1915 to make "alien" mothers with American-born children under the age of fourteen eligible for pensions. The mothers, though, had to file for citizenship and meet the other criteria. In addition, two years later, the law was again amended to restrict pensions to women whose husbands were residents of Illinois at the time of their deaths or permanent incapacitation.[96] After World War I the trend was to make the law more inclusive, as "organized women became a more visible and vocal advocacy group for the expansion of the mothers' pensions law."[97] In the 1920s, amendments to the law made "deserted women" eligible, raised the upper age limit for children to sixteen, adjusted the tax rate, and at the end of the decade initiated state reimbursements to counties for half their costs.[98]

Pinckney's promise of a new era was only half fulfilled. During his tenure on the bench the Aid-to-Mothers Department became an important part of the court system and continued to expand after he retired in 1916. By 1920, the department handled a quarter of the juvenile court's caseload.[99] Although the department had become a vital part of the court system, financing continued to be a problem, and limited appropriations created a long waiting list for pensions in the late 1910s. The United Charities of Chicago often assisted, albeit grudgingly, families on the waiting list.[100] The charity's board argued that supporting these families was a public responsibility. The "home-based" track for family preservation, thus, did not become an entirely public program in the Progressive Era.

Moreover, like many progressive programs, mothers' pensions were never uniformly implemented. Many rural county court judges in Illinois never instituted mothers' pensions programs. On the other end of the spectrum, some continued to use the more inclusive Funds to Parents to Act to justify more generous giving. These extremes clouded the progressive vision for a centralized, modernized system of public relief in Illinois. Nationwide, fewer than half of the counties in the United States had operative mothers' pensions program before the enactment of the Social Security Act in 1935, and this problem continued into the 1940s.[101]

It is too simplistic to dismiss mothers' pensions as an experiment that failed because of the tenacity of localism. The mothers' pensions programs administered by juvenile courts did centralize the administration of home relief, albeit on the county level. The women lining up at the county building twice a month to pick up their checks were evidence of this centralization. They were all literally in the same place at the same time. These single female–headed families also remained physically together and embodied the new, progressive conception of family preservation. But as long as the court continued to categorize and treat other wards as belonging to the "institutional" track, there would be a dual approach to family preservation in early-twentieth-century Chicago.

As the two-track approach to family preservation continued in the 1920s, the experiences of the children diverged because those in the "institutional" track spent more time in institutions and less time at home. It appears that the progressive child savers' efforts to prolong child dependency had the unintended consequence of prolonging the time that some dependent children spent in institutions. As Howard Hopkirk, the executive director of the Child Welfare League of America, later noted,

> before 1900 elementary education in institutions generally led up to apprenticeship or to work on the farm or in domestic service. During the past thirty years various changes in the customs and attitudes affecting children generally in the United States and certain radical revisions of the policies of child-care agencies have tended to prolong the dependence of children under care of those agencies. There has been a growing tendency on the part of institutions to keep many of their intellectually more promising children under care until they have been graduated from high school and occasionally, in the case of students able to profit from college training, even to twenty or twenty-one years.[102]

Thus, the progressive efforts to keep children in school kept some dependent children in institutions for long periods of time.

A series of extant case files from September 1921 reveals the implications of the division of dependency into two tracks.[103] Sixty percent of the children from families not receiving pensions were institutionalized. All eighteen of these wards came from motherless families.[104] These motherless children remained in institutions longer, which stretched the nineteenth-century ideal of family pre-servation and challenged its underlying assumption that these families, while physically separated, remained together in spirit. Although roughly the same percentage of the institutionalized children were later reunited with their families as in 1912 (70 percent), a growing number of the children were staying in institutions until they turned eighteen and aged out of the system.[105] Overall, the average period of confinement lengthened to almost five-and-half years for girls and over eight years for boys, and these averages would have been higher without the deaths of a twelve-year-old boy and an eleven-year-old girl in training schools.

In 1921 an inadequate appropriation by the county precluded awarding pensions to any new families until the fall, but new legislation improved the situation.[106] The passage of amendments to the law raised revenue, removed family caps on aid, and raised pensions for a first child from $15 to $25 a month. The amendments also allowed for corresponding increases for additional children from $10 to $15 per month. In September, there were again funds to pension new families, and according to the extant case files, fifteen fatherless families with a total of thirty-five children were added to the rolls in September. These children, with one exception, spent no time in institutions.[107] As in 1912, there was also one two-parent family with children receiving a pension. The father was incapacitated but lived with his family.[108]

The case files also reveal a major change in the administration of the "home-based" family preservation program. Mothers in good health were now expected to work a few days a week outside of the home.[109] Eight of the fifteen mothers did so. As Joanne Goodwin has noted, this work requirement represented yet another chapter in the history of the devaluing of a mother's work in the home. Rhetorically, the progressives valued mothering, but in practice they demanded that a mother leave her own home to labor productively.[110]

The decision to place the administration of mothers' pensions in juvenile courts, which had seemed natural in the early 1910s, came under close scrutiny by the 1920s. In 1921 the chief of the United States Children's Bureau, Julia Lathrop, observed that "the present tendency of expert opinion is undoubtedly toward placing responsibility for actual administration of mothers' pensions in a separate body qualified to deal with the matter scientifically and not in the spirit of the old poor relief."[111] Such critiques were part of a growing concern among social justice feminists over the failure of mothers' pensions to modernize the administration of public relief and move beyond the traditional stigmatization of the poor. In the 1920s and 1930s many states removed the administration of mothers' pensions from juvenile courts and placed these programs in local or state welfare agencies.[112] The removal of mothers' pensions from the juvenile court helped to make welfare and juvenile justice appear to be separate systems with very different purposes, even though many of the same children passed through both systems in the twentieth century.

Critiques of the judicial administration of mothers' pensions also raised questions about the expansion of the juvenile court, which contributed to the reconsideration in the 1920s of the proper role of courts in American society. Conservatives concerned about the intervention of government into private life directed attention to the juvenile court. For example, in 1925, President Calvin Coolidge appeared before the international convention of the Young Men's Christian Association to criticize this development. "There are too many indications that the functions of parenthood are breaking down," proclaimed the popular president, a second-term Republican who had successfully built his career campaigning for law and order, less government regulation, and more traditional values. "Too many people," he explained, "are neglecting the real well-being of their children, shifting the responsibility for their actions, and turning over supervision of their discipline and conduct to the juvenile courts." This spelled trouble because "it is stated on high authority that a very large proportion of the outcasts and criminals come from the ranks of those who lost the advantages of normal parental control in their youth. They are the refugees from broken homes who were denied the necessary benefits of parental love and direction. . . . What the youth of the country need," the president concluded, "is not more control through Government action but more home control through parental action."[113] The juvenile court had become a clear target for critics of the progressive efforts to make the state into a parent.

FOUR

This is not a question of politics. It is religion.
—*Mary McDowell, head of the University of Chicago*
  Settlement, 1911

Legitimating Juvenile Justice

By passing the Funds to Parents in July 1911, the Illinois General Assembly not only allowed the Chicago Juvenile Court to begin construction of the two-track system for handling the cases of dependent children but also further politicized the administration of juvenile justice. Substantial increases in the system's budget, including the hiring of more probation officers to run the new welfare program, encouraged machine politicians to view the juvenile court as a rich source from which to distribute jobs and pension funds to supporters; in addition, critics of the court attacked its handling of dependency cases in order to challenge the basic premises of progressive juvenile justice. They questioned whether the best interests of the child and the state were really the same and rejected the idea that the state should become a superparent whose decisions trumped those of natural parents. In response, the child savers fought vigorously to keep their court system out of patronage politics, while simultaneously defending its administrators against serious allegations of misconduct.

The election in November 1910 of Peter Bartzen to the presidency of the Cook County Board of Commissioners had spelled trouble for the juvenile court. The *Chicago Examiner*, owned by the newspaper magnate William Randolph Hearst, had championed the candidacy of "Battling" Pete, a building contractor and fiery Democrat from Bowmanville on the city's far north side: A self-proclaimed man of the people, Bartzen had campaigned against the "hypocritical horde of reformers," among whose numbers he happily counted the women of Hull House.[1] Bartzen, who had gubernatorial aspirations, now presided over the fifteen-member board that controlled the county's finances, which for the fiscal year of 1911–12 would exceed $10 million.[2] The board managed the county's public services, roads and bridges, institutions, and civil service.[3] The powers of the president included a line item veto over appropriations, which required a four-fifths vote of the board to override. The president also appointed the superintendent of public service, who purchased supplies for the county; the county agent, who administered outdoor relief; the superintendent of the Oak Forest Institutions (the poorhouse and tuberculosis hospital); the warden of County Hospital; the county architect; the county attorney; the superintendent of the Juvenile Detention Home; and the three civil service commissioners, who administered competitive merit examinations for job-seekers and discharged inefficient county employees.[4]

In his inaugural address, President Bartzen promised to "jealously safeguard the interests of the unfortunate people, who, through their poverty, are compelled to become objects of public charity."[5] As a starting point, he ordered the civil service commissioners to launch investigations into the operations of the county's hospital, insane asylum, poorhouse, and juvenile detention home. There was precedent for such an undertaking. Two years earlier, a tragic accident at the Asylum for Feeble-Minded Children in Lincoln, Illinois, that had left a sixteen-year-old maimed had triggered a politically motivated investigation by the legislature into the state's hospitals and correctional institutions.[6] Members of the General Assembly had hoped to discredit Governor Deneen with their findings. Bartzen followed a similar strategy by ordering investigations into institutions still run by his predecessor's appointees. It appeared to be a shrewd political move. The discovery of any scandalous conditions would bolster

Bartzen's claim that he was the defender of the oppressed as well as open up patronage positions for him to fill. Bartzen had positioned himself as the true defender of the dependent, and his calls for investigations into county institutions set the stage for the defining moments in the struggle to legitimate progressive juvenile justice. Child savers across the nation carefully monitored this political battle.[7]

William H. Dunn, a manufacturer and former bailiff of the Cook County Circuit Court, emerged as the most persistent actor in this drama. His allegations that the juvenile court worked with private organizations to remove children from their families in order to sell them as a source of cheap labor cost the child savers many sleepless nights. Henry Thurston, the former chief probation officer of the juvenile court and now president of the Illinois Children's Home and Aid Society, was so concerned that he hired a stenographer to follow Dunn around the state and transcribe his speeches. Thurston also ordered an internal review of his society's placement of children in private homes.

A dispute with the Chicago court had upset Dunn. He had come to the court to seek the release of his business partner's children, who became wards of the court when their mother had died mysteriously and their father had been held as a suspect.[8] When the court denied Dunn's request, he began to monitor its operations and determined that the court declared children dependent so that it could rip them from their families. At a gathering of women's organizations in July 1910, he accused Thurston of running the state's child-slavery ring. Mrs. Elizabeth Prescott, the president of a local chapter of the Ladies of the Grand Army of the Republic, seconded Dunn's allegations by declaring "the state of Illinois is the worst slave state in the union, for it allows traffic in both white and colored children."[9] After Bartzen assumed office, Dunn announced to the Chicago press that he was going to file a complaint with the Civil Service Commission against the juvenile court. "I will see that the commission," he declared, "get[s] a complete picture of the chamber of horrors. . . . I will show them how families are torn asunder over the protests of weeping mothers and pleading fathers."[10] "The State of Illinois," he concluded, "is the father of the traffic in children. Our juvenile law is rotten to the core."[11]

Dunn lambasted the practice of letting private organizations export children. In 1905 the Illinois General Assembly had established a Department of Visitation of Children and Homes to monitor the treatment of children placed in family homes, but after five years the state agent reported: "It has been found impossible to visit the 882 children placed outside of the State, because of the inadequacy of funds, though it has been found, is some instances, that this class of children need the protection afforded by the State more than many others."[12] This meant that private home-finding societies were entrusted with the protection of the children whom they exported. Dunn charged that these national home-finding societies that had branches in several states were "charity trusts" whose real motive was monetary gain, not promoting child welfare. Their search for children threatened poor families because it was at their doors that the insidious child slavers came knocking. Dunn declared to audiences around the state that the juvenile court had been established to terrorize the poor. Why else, he asked, would it have been placed in the ghetto? He even claimed that probation officers, by threatening to remove children from poor families, were assisting slumlords in collecting their tenants' rent.[13] "The poor people of Chicago," he explained, "are afraid to ask the county agent for aid because they fear that their children will be seized by the Juvenile Court's officers."[14] Technically, he was right. According to the state's broad definition of dependency, a child on public support could be declared dependent by the juvenile court. Thus, a request for poor relief could theoretically lead to the removal of a child from an impoverished family.

The annual reports of the juvenile court provided Dunn with additional evidence that the court snatched children from their destitute parents. The 1904 report, for example, listed "poverty of the mother" as the cause of dependency in nineteen cases and "the poverty of the father" as the reason in three others. Even more ominously, in 1908 Chief Probation Officer Thurston had used the ambiguous classification of "lack of care" to describe the cause of dependency in over 60 percent of the reported cases.[15] Dunn seized on this vague classification to argue that children were being routinely taken away from their poor mothers. As Dunn told a gathering of the Daughters of the American Revolution, "Out of 600 [children] taken into the Juvenile Court, 400 were for 'lack of care,'—that terrible crime, 'lack of care'—and the mothers of these children have lost them."[16]

Dunn compared himself to early abolitionists, such as the Illinois printer Elijah Lovejoy, whose death at the hands of a mob in 1837 had shocked the nation and converted many northerners to the cause. Like these radicals, Dunn recounted vivid stories of families being torn apart. To help him spread the word, his sister Harriette Dunn privately published a pamphlet entitled *Infamous Juvenile Law: Crimes against Children under the Cloak of Charity* (1912), which was reminiscent of an antislavery tract.[17] The pamphlet, which she sold at her brother's speeches, reprinted lengthy excerpts from *People v. Turner*, a famous 1870 decision by the Illinois Supreme Court that had struck down key provisions of the state's reform school laws.[18] The pamphlet also included commentary by lawyers who declared that the current Juvenile Court Act was unconstitutional. The cover depicted a terrified mother desperately holding onto her young daughter, who was about to be snatched out of their apartment by an enormous hand crashing through the doorway. The hand was labeled "Juvenile Court Law." Among the stories inside was a newspaper account of a boy who reported being "raised by a speculator, with lots of others." The boy stated, "I grew up—long years and years—with no father, no mother, no sister, not a living soul that cared for me: Nothing but whippings, scoldings, and starving." If the parallels to slavery were not clear enough for the reader, the caption "CHILDREN OF CHANCE—MERE CHATTELS" settled the issue.[19]

Although most of Dunn's specific charges were outlandish, his underlying claim that the child savers had increased the power of the state to police children and their families was right on target. Through compulsory attendance laws, bans on child labor, and health measures such as vaccination laws, states were now making more decisions about children's lives. The establishment of juvenile courts was only one of the more obvious symbols of the state becoming a parent. In his testimony before the House Committee on Labor and Industrial Affairs of the Illinois General Assembly, Dunn railed against a bill to regulate school-aged children engaged in street trades as "another bill to abridge the rights of the child. The same people are back of it. There was a time when the board of education exercised control over the child only when it was in a public school."[20] Now, however, truant officers patrolled the city, giving the board control over all children "every hour the school is open, no matter where the child is."[21]

Timothy Hurley, who had played such an important role in establishing the juvenile court, also condemned its aggressive policing of poor families. Dunn himself pointed out that Hurley's *Juvenile Record*, the first national journal to chart developments in juvenile justice, had already announced: "A movement is setting in against the Juvenile Court."[22] Catholics, in particular, had begun to sour on the new institution, along with other progressive experiments in paternalism. In a telling editorial in the *Juvenile Record*, Hurley chastised child savers across the nation for allowing the "philanthropic side" of the juvenile court to eclipse its "legal side." This development endangered the "rights of the parents, the child and its relatives." This meant that the court's workers were now proceeding "on the theory that they are 'holier' than their fellow brethren and being encouraged by a lucrative salary, have at all times been anxious to exploit the great work that they are accomplishing."[23] This arrogance and disregard for personal liberties, Hurley argued, threatened to erode public support for juvenile justice.

Although Dunn and Hurley voiced somewhat similar concerns about the expansion of state power over children and their families, their prescriptions for juvenile justice were quite different. Dunn sought to abolish the juvenile court; Hurley, on the other hand, wanted to reform the wayward institution. He still believed that the court could do much good. It was, however, Dunn's sensational cries of child slavery, amplified by exposes in Hearst's *Chicago Examiner* that alleged child abuse in the juvenile justice system, that placed the court and its supporters on the defensive in the early 1910s. Yet Dunn refused to file a sworn statement of his charges with the Civil Service Commission, even though he had already provided the press with details about specific cases, including a fourteen-year-old ward of the court whose guardian had allegedly impregnated her.[24] Why he decided not to submit a sworn statement at this time is unclear, although he did continue to speak out against the court and later filed for injunctions to halt its work.

In July, President Bartzen appointed Henry Neil to help the Civil Service Commission "make an examination into the conditions surrounding the dependency of children and their disposition through the Juvenile Court."[25] Neil had helped to secure the passage of the Funds to Parents Act, claimed its authorship, and took every opportunity to publicize this innovative cash assistance program as the solution to the interrelated problems of juvenile dependency and delinquency. His argument was straightforward. Poverty bred delinquency. The truancy of a child, for example, often resulted from parents' inability to provide "Jimmy or Sallie clothing that would permit them to make a decent appearance in school. Sensitiveness on the part of the child naturally led to his or her playing truant and possibly making the acquaintance of questionable persons."[26] At this point, according to Neil, a delinquent was born. Providing "a nominal pension to enable the parents to clothe and feed their children," he stressed, "would go a long way toward remedying this condition."[27]

This narrative about the making of a delinquent career sounded remarkably similar to the environmentalist arguments put forth by respectable child savers like Judge Mack or Jane Addams. Yet the same group harshly criticized the choice of Neil. They considered him at best unqualified for the job and at worst a charlatan. This concern had to do partly with his lack of professional qualifications and training. Neil's characterization of the court also worried them; by trumpeting mothers' pensions as a panacea, he implied that the court *did* separate children from poor but morally worthy parents. In fact, Neil announced that the Civil Service Commission, which had just begun its inquiry, would recommend that the court stop removing children from their homes, except in cases where "it is found that the parents are wholly unfit to care for them."[28] Statements like this suggested that the court was reckless in its handling of dependency cases and lent legitimacy to Dunn's allegations.

In another move that worried the child savers, Bartzen appointed Ballard Dunn, the city editor of the Democratic *Chicago Daily Journal*, who was no relation of William H. Dunn, to be the new president of the Civil Service Commission. Ballard Dunn added "conspiracy" to the charges against the court. He declared: "A large number of persons connected with the various departments of the Juvenile Court are apparently doing all in their power to thwart our efforts to obtain the necessary evidence [of crimes against children].... This defensive attitude is only added proof to us that these people are implicated in [the] things we are investigating."[29]

To make matters more confusing, William H. Dunn reappeared on the scene. Apparently, he had been waiting for the right moment to make the dramatic announcement that he was filing for an injunction against President Bartzen, the county clerk, and county treasurer. If granted, the injunction would prohibit these county officers, who were Democrats, from allocating funds to the court, including paying the salaries of it staff.[30] Thus, the juvenile court and its predominantly Republican supporters were under political attack by Bartzen and the Democrats, and the Democrats who ran the County Board faced Dunn's lawsuit.

In this tense environment, Henry Thurston attempted to shift the debate away from the sensational allegations of child slavery to a frank discussion of child dependency. In a letter to the editor of the *Chicago Record-Herald*, he clarified what dependency meant, both in law and in practice. "The law distinguishes between dependent children with responsible parents on the one side and dependent children with either no parents or parents whom the court judicially finds unfit."[31] The law intended that the former families should be kept together and that only the latter kinds should be broken up for the sake of the children.

Moreover, there were specific criteria for declaring parents to be unfit: "depravity, open and notorious immorality, habitual drunkenness for the space of one year prior to the filing of the petition, extreme and repeated cruelty to the child, abandonment of the child or desertion of the child for more than six months."[32] Only if one of these conditions were met could the juvenile court, without the consent of the parents, order a child to be put up for adoption. Thus, Thurston stressed that there was "absolutely no difference of opinion between 'professional philanthropists' and the 'plain people' about the duty of society to keep parents who are merely poor with their own children." What had to be taken into account in the coming discussion of dependency, he argued, was that there were "natural parents who are persistent enemies and traitors to their own children."[33] These people clearly could not be entrusted with the care of the young, even though they had brought them into the world.

The heated rhetoric about the juvenile court cooled down, at least temporarily, during the first week of August, when President Bartzen announced that he would appoint a citizens' committee, or "quiz board," whose charge would be to make a systematic investigation into the juvenile justice system.[34] He named Professor Willard E. Hotchkiss, the dean of Northwestern's School of Commerce, to head the group, which would become known as "the Hotchkiss commission." Its other members were Mrs. J. E. Quan, the director of the Illinois Training School; Mrs. Hannah G. Soloman, a charity worker; Reverend J. C. Quille, the head of the Working Boy's Home; and Reverend August F. Schlecte, a Lutheran minister and missionary who worked with children. Perhaps to placate his enemies, Bartzen left Henry Neil off the committee.

The child savers were pleased with the composition of the committee and were now ready for the real investigation of the juvenile court to begin.[35] It took only a single meeting of the Hotchkiss commission to shatter the truce between Bartzen's forces and the child savers. At its first meeting, Ballard Dunn and the attorney for the Civil Service Commission proceeded to grill the first witness, Chief Probation Officer John Witter, for nearly two hours.[36] An enraged Chairman Hotchkiss could not understand why "the civil service commission should have anything to do with *our* hearings, to say nothing of directing the whole inquiry."[37] Ballard Dunn explained that the Civil Service Commission had begun its investigation "of those departments of the Juvenile Court service which come under the civil service" and would continue to do so because the law required no less.[38] He also expected that the Hotchkiss commission would "act in harmony with us, but of course if they wish to refuse, that is the affair of the committee."[39]

By late August it became apparent to all involved that the Civil Service Commission and the Hotchkiss commission would conduct simultaneous investigations of the juvenile court. As the two investigations proceeded throughout 1911 and into the election year of 1912, they assumed very different forms.[40] The Civil Service Commission hearings turned into a show trial of Witter, whereas the Hotchkiss commission became a privately funded investigation that searched for structural problems in the administration of juvenile justice.

The probation department became the focus of both investigations, and for good reason. From the inception of the court, probation officers had been hailed as the key to its success or failure.[41] These men and women did most of the court's work. They investigated the complaints filed with the court, visited homes, policed neighborhoods, and were expected to be community role models.[42] If there were problems with the court system, whether individual malfeasance or structural faults, it seemed reasonable to search for them in the work of this vital department. The overlapping investigations placed the probation officers in an awkward bind, especially when they were subpoenaed to appear before both bodies on the same day at the same time in different parts of the city! The *Chicago Record-Herald* observed: "The question now becomes pertinent to probation officers as to which is the real committee and which would it be safer to offend."[43]

Investigating the work of the probation officers raised the thorny question of whether the county board or the presiding judge of the juvenile court had jurisdiction over the department. The child savers alleged that President Bartzen was attempting to use the crisis over the juvenile court as an opportunity to make the department's forty-three positions into political appointments for the Democratic machine.[44] They had feared for years that if the position of probation officer became just another patronage job, then the whole experiment in juvenile justice would fail. The stakes of the investigation for the child savers became a battle to keep partisan politics out of probation.

It would be a mistake to accept the child savers' interpretation of the crisis at face value because they too had a political agenda. Their progressive vision for modernizing the city included controversial ideas about how to govern it. The juvenile court epitomized a new vision for urban governance that called for experts, efficiency, centralization of power, and the application of social scientific research to solve basic social problems.[45] The juvenile court represented, in fact, one of the few progressive success stories in Illinois. In 1911, Chicago's progressives fought so hard to keep the court "out of politics" because it was the only major institution of local governance that they actually controlled, and they did not want to lose it.

The child savers also had genuine concerns that President Bartzen's administration was endangering the practitioners of juvenile justice as well as their clients. Judge Merritt Pinckney was furious that Bartzen had reneged on his promise to improve the sanitary conditions of the juvenile court building. As he told his packed courtroom on the opening day of the fall term:

> Personally I am nearly worn out by this state of affairs. The courtroom is so unsanitary and ventilation is so difficult that it is impossible for me to keep well—and what applies to me is also true for the other employes [sic] of the court and for the women and children who have to be present. The health and welfare of the children of the county are being jeopardized and work of the officers of the institution is made unnecessary difficult. In humanity's name something should be done.[46]

Pinckney, who suffered from kidney disease, announced that he could not continue to hear cases under these conditions and would move the juvenile court back to its original home in the county building. The state of the detention home, which was chronically overcrowded, also upset Pinckney. Even after a scarlet fever epidemic had led to a six-week quarantine, the county board had not acted on a proposal to build an isolation ward. As a result of overcrowding, exacerbated by periodic quarantines, boys and girls were once again being held in the city's police stations. "On several occasions in previous months," the judge announced, "as many as eight girls have been brought in at one time from the annex at Harrison street: These girls are always in filthy condition."[47] Pinckney's public statements about Bartzen's mismanagement of the county board intensified after the president surprised everyone by suspending Chief Probation Officer John Witter before the Civil Service Commission had concluded its investigation and Pinckney, the key witness in the case, had testified. As Bartzen told the press, "it looks as if Mr. Witter has been under the influence of Hull House. He ought not to be listening to a bunch of old women all the time."[48]

The suspension of Witter and his subsequent firing in January energized the city's child savers. They had convinced the Republican and Progressive parties to run Alexander A. McCormick as their joint candidate against Bartzen for the presidency of the County Board in the 1912 election, although due to a court ruling McCormick's name could only appear on the Republican ticket. McCormick, the editor of the *Chicago Evening Post*, the director of the Immigrant's Protective League, and a member of the citizens' committee of the juvenile court, was one of Bartzen's fiercest critics. In a scathing piece entitled "The Blight of Bartzen," his *Post* denounced the "hard-fisted, unintelligent boss contractor" for not sparing "the children's court" from his political chicanery.[49] This was shameful because "more arduous and disinterested labor than has, perhaps, been put into any other institution in the city" had gone into its creation and administration. "It represented the best of our idealism, the thoughtful endeavors of people like Miss Jane Addams, Miss Julia

Lathrop, Mrs. Joseph T. Bowen, Judge Mack and Mr. Henry W. Thurston."[50]

McCormick entered the political ring to keep their idealism alive. To counter public perceptions of him as a stereotypically effeminate reformer, he wrote about his love of boxing for the *Cherry Circle*, the Chicago Athletic Association's journal. The local press that supported his campaign then ran stories about McCormick's prowess at "the manly art," including reporting on his impressive six-round sparring match with the former world champion "Ruby Rob" Fitzsimmons. The same papers later celebrated when during a heated county board meeting "Battling" Pete Bartzen called McCormick an "unprintable name" but then backed down from his invitation for a fistfight.[51]

Many of the city's foreign language papers, as well as the *Chicago Daily Socialist*, endorsed McCormick. In the weeks leading up to the election, Hugh Mann wrote an almost daily column for the socialist paper defending the administrators of the juvenile court against the charges of Hearst's *Chicago Examiner*. His articles explained in careful detail how the juvenile court processed children's cases and argued that the progressive child savers, not the city's machine politicians, were the truer friends of the working class.[52]

Although women could not vote in Illinois at this time (the state did not pass a woman's suffrage law until 1913), they played an active role in the McCormick campaign. A week before the election, the presidents of the city's women's clubs met at the Fine Arts Club, so that they could "put Peter Bartzen on the black list and order their army of workers out for a merciless fight to bring about his defeat at the polls."[53] On the Sunday before the election, the head of the Juvenile Protective Association, Louise de Koven Bowen, told a crowd gathered at the Illinois Theatre that Bartzen had disgraced Chicago by damaging the reputation of its juvenile court.[54] "People came from all over the world . . . to study its methods," she said, but under the present administration "it has perceptibly deteriorated. Civil service has been cast to the winds. Efficient probation officers have been dismissed, and in their place political hangers on have been put, who know nothing about the court or about the treatment of children."[55] She called for "the men of Cook County, [to] wake up and acquaint yourselves with what your public servants are doing. This is a call for public service. We need men at the polls next Tuesday. You put Peter Bartzen in. You can put him out. What are you going to do about it? Who will respond?"[56]

The child savers wanted to whip Bartzen badly in order to send a clear message to politicians in Chicago and elsewhere that an attack against juvenile justice would be an act of political suicide. The election for county board president, however, turned out to be too close to call. Mechanical problems with many of the county's voting machines complicated matters, but ultimately McCormick was declared the winner by a few hundred votes.[57] In this year of the Democrat, which saw the party capture the White House for the first time in twenty years, McCormick was one of only a handful of Republican candidates in Cook County to win his race. The closeness of the election made it difficult, if not impossible, to determine precisely why (or even if) McCormick prevailed. Yet the child savers used his victory as evidence with which to fashion a myth about the sacredness of the juvenile court. By 1934, for example, in her thesis about the development of the court's probation department, the social worker Elisabeth Parker could note matter-of-factly: "since the case of Mr. Witter, politicians have been wary of attacking the Juvenile Court and the problems of child welfare for political reasons.... The rise of public indignation in 1912 showed that the Juvenile Court of Cook County and its Probation Department have a large popular support that must be reckoned with at all times."[58]

In the immediate aftermath of the McCormick victory, the child savers were not so optimistic. The final report of the Hotch-kiss commission, which was released in January 1913, said that there were serious structural problems with the juvenile justice system, most significantly a "break in the juvenile court's authority."[59] The problem was that once the court committed a dependent child to an accredited private institution, it lost jurisdiction over the child until he or she was released. This meant that probation officers had no authority to visit children committed to industrial schools and that children could become lost in the juvenile justice system, especially since institutions were not required to update the court about the status of their wards. Without the court's knowledge, an industrial school could release a child or place him or her in foster care. As a result, the court could not always tell concerned parents where their children were. In his testimony before the Civil Service Commission, Judge Pinckney explained that parents whose children had been institutionalized because of "misfortune of poverty or other mischance" should be able to ask him: " 'Where is my child?' and learn where their child is."[60] It would be tragic if after recovering from a temporary setback, parents could not recover their child because no information existed about his or her whereabouts.

Any attempt to fix this structural problem would be risky, for the Hotchkiss commission had discovered that "eminent lawyers and jurists whose loyalty to the Juvenile Court Law is unquestioned have expressed grave doubts of its constitutionality. Until the Law is passed upon by the State Supreme Court, the enforcement of any new legislation enlarging the powers of the Juvenile Court...is likely to meet with legal resistance."[61] Thus, more than a decade after the establishment of the world's first juvenile court, fundamental questions about its constitutionality remained unanswered.

The legal drama about the constitutionality of the juvenile court began during the height of the political crisis of 1911–12 and played out in four acts. William H. Dunn took center stage for the first and final acts. Although it is unclear how many followers Dunn enlisted in his crusade against the juvenile court, he did discover a legal weapon—the injunction—that made it possible for him almost singlehandedly to shut down the court by cutting off its funding. Dunn, who was trained as a lawyer, realized that he could render the juvenile court inoperative if he could persuade a judge to grant an injunction restraining the county treasurer from paying the salaries of the court's staff, including its probation officers. He first attempted this strategy in July 1911, when he petitioned for an injunction from the Superior Court of Cook County.[62] The petition had left the sword of Damocles hanging over the children's court, and offered any Superior Court judge willing to entertain it a litany of reasons to cut the thread.[63] The explanations for why the Juvenile Court Act violated the state constitution fell, with a couple of exceptions, into four broad categories: perpetuation of child slavery; denial of due process protection; unwarranted interference with the parent-child relationship; and invasion of privacy. These were serious charges, and as the *Chicago Record-Herald* cautioned, "a constitutional lawsuit is not something to take chances with or treat lightly. Judges need the aid of competent counsel in unravelling legal knots and applying old legal principles to new situations and new social currents and movements."[64] The newspaper called for private associations to help secure able lawyers to defend the juvenile court.

This rights-based critique of the Juvenile Court Act questioned the basic assumption of progressive juvenile justice: that the best interests of the child and the state were the same. The specific charges challenged the progressive efforts to make the state into a parent whose authority outweighed that of a child's natural parents. The first charge, for example, condemned the juvenile law for permitting "the seizing of a child and depriving said child of its liberty and the giving of said child to a stranger because said child or its parents be poor."[65] Another criticized the authority given to the probation officer to be both the petitioner and the officer of the court who executed its orders. This dual power created "unwarranted interference with and the insecurity and disruption of the relation of parent and child; [and] creates a system of intrigue and espionage leading to unlawful and unreasonable searching into private affairs."[66] The petition also presented a case for the sanctity of the home as a private space, not a social realm, which should be safe from state policing.

Although Dunn's lawsuit was dismissed in June 1912, the child savers appreciated the power of his critique and acknowledged that they had created some tricky legal knots that required careful unraveling. Moreover, five years later Dunn did succeed in cutting off the court's funding when a Superior Court judge issued an injunction based on a similar petition. The child savers were fortunate that this occurred in 1917 and not before the election of 1912. An injunction then would have shut down the court at a critical moment in their struggle to secure its legitimacy.

Shortly after Bartzen went down to defeat at the polls, in the second act of the legal drama the Illinois Supreme Court brought the Witter affair to a close. After his dismissal, the ex–chief probation officer had sued the Civil Service Commission, and his case made it all way to the state's highest court. Justice James H. Cartwright wrote the majority opinion for *Witter v. County Commissioners* (1912), which announced that neither the County Board nor the Civil Service Commission had the authority to suspend or fire Witter.[67] The decision granted the circuit court judges jurisdiction over the probation department.

A law review article by Julian Mack, the former judge of juvenile court, framed the issue for Justice Cartwright.[68] In that now famous article about the theory and practice of progressive juvenile justice, Mack explained that a revolution in thinking about the responsibility of the state for its children was sweeping across America, Europe, Australia, and other lands.[69] This revolution, Mack argued, was built on ancient foundations. For more than two centuries, courts of chancery in England and the United States had "exercised jurisdiction for the protection of the unfortunate child."[70] Mack pointed out that in 1846 the Illinois Supreme Court had acknowledged that this was "a power which must necessarily exist somewhere in every well-regulated society, and more especially in a republican government."[71] The juvenile court, Mack concluded, was simply the most advanced means for meeting this basic governmental responsibility.

This history lesson helped Justice Cartwright to think about where probation officers fit into the American governmental system of checks and balances. By imagining the juvenile court to be an updated version of a chancery court, Cartwright could view the responsibilities of the probation officer as analogous to those of a guardian ad litem, the individual appointed by a judge to represent a minor in a legal proceeding.[72] Thus, probation officers were like "attorneys, masters in chancery, receivers, commissioners, referees, and other similar officers," who, according to the court, were "mere assistants to the court in the performance of judicial functions."[73] As assistants to judges, they belonged to the judicial branch of government, and this branch could not "be separate from the other departments of the government" if they were selected by a commission.[74] Accordingly, the doctrine of separation of powers prohibited the County Board and the Civil Service Commission from overseeing the probation department.

Witter effectively ended the struggle for control over the probation department.[75] After the decision, the circuit court judges voted Judge Pinckney the sole power to appoint, remove, and supervise the juvenile court's probation officers. Instead of making these decisions alone, however, Pinckney appointed a committee of leading citizens to develop and administer competitive examinations for those applying to be probation officers. Although John Witter had been vindicated, he did not reapply for his former position and instead chose to work for the Chicago Boys' Club.[76] This important legal victory provided the child savers with more material with which to cement the legitimacy of the children's court. In her influential casebook *The Child and the State* (1938), Grace Abbott included Justice Cartwright's opinion as a foundational document in the history of the juvenile court movement.[77] This landmark decision also had far-reaching consequences. In 1954, one of the nation's experts on probation, Frank Flynn, explained that "the Witter decision has often been referred to as a bad decision in a good cause. While at the time in Cook County it may have served to correct a bad situation, it perpetuated the selection of probation personnel by the courts— an administratively unwieldy device which today hampers the development of adequate probation services in many parts of the nation."[78] Thus, a political victory secured through the courts during the crisis of 1911–12 that had helped to legitimate the juvenile court also stunted its development.

In its *Witter* decision, the Illinois Supreme Court did not rule on the constitutionality of the Juvenile Court Act. And, as the Hotchkiss commission cautioned, without such a favorable ruling it would be difficult for lawmakers to amend the juvenile court law to seal the jurisdictional gap in the administration of juvenile justice. The question of whether the juvenile court had the power to remove minors from their parents if the court considered them to be "traitors to their children" was also in doubt. In his testimony before the Civil Service Commission, Judge Pinckney declared that it was absolutely necessary to separate such parents from their offspring. Once a child was removed from abusive parents and placed in a family home, he cautioned, the parents had to be kept away. Can you imagine "a drunken father stumbling over your doorstep, or a prostitute mother entering at your door" to inquire about their child placed in your home? the judge asked.[79] Such a spectacle, he declared, would make it impossible to find decent homes for dependent children.

Pinckney argued that the juvenile court must be allowed to act as a gatekeeper in such cases. He explained: "When a father knocks at the door of the juvenile court and says, 'Where is my child?' the court can ask: 'Mr. Smith, how have you lived?' and 'Mrs. Smith, are you in the red light district?' 'Mr. Smith, are you a drunkard? If you are, the state of Illinois demands for the welfare of the child . . . that you see that child no more.' "[80] The judge admitted that deciding who was a proper parent was extremely difficult, and his attempt to resolve a custody dispute produced the much-awaited constitutional test of the Illinois Juvenile Court Act, the third act in the unfolding drama.

Ironically, this custody case did not involve members of the so-called dangerous classes that Pinckney often criticized in such harsh terms. Instead, the participants were members of a well-to-do Eastern family. On December 15, 1911, Charles R. Lindsay Jr. filed a petition with the Chicago Juvenile Court stating that his twelve-year-old nephew, Billy Lindsay, heir to the family fortune, lacked "proper parental care."[81] Billy's father had died in 1902 and left his son "an income amounting to $1200 to $1500 per year" paid by the Girard Trust Company of Philadelphia to his mother to cover the boy's "care, maintenance and education."[82] According to the uncle, the boy's mother, Elizabeth Lindsay, "was an improper guardian wholly unable to care for, protect, train and educate said child."[83] The legal description of Elizabeth's inadequacies was boilerplate, but the case became front-page news.

Elizabeth Lindsey and her son were followers of Dr. Otoman Zar-Adusht Hanish, a German émigré who was the leader of Mazdaznan, an obscure religious society that had temples in Chicago, Los Angeles, Lowell, Massachusetts, New York City, and Montreal. In 1910 Lindsay had met Hanish in New York and became a believer, and later sent Billy to travel across the country with her new spiritual leader. The boy's relatives grew concerned that Hanish was the leader of an immoral cult of sun worshippers and feared that he would corrupt Billy. After a coast-to-coast search for the boy, his uncle discovered Billy at the society's temple on Lake Park Avenue in south Chicago.

In the dependent petition, Charles Lindsay named both the boy's mother and Hanish as having custody and control over Billy.[84] Fearing that Billy's "immediate health and welfare [were] being jeopardized by his present care and custody," his uncle filed an affidavit claiming that a warrant was required to apprehend the boy.[85] Judge Pinckney granted the warrant, and the authorities took the boy to the juvenile detention home. Elizabeth Lindsay, however, convinced Judge Pinckney to parole Billy to her. The judge appointed a local attorney to represent the mother and son and scheduled a hearing for January 4, 1912. A week before the appointed day in court, the mother and son disappeared. Their embarrassed attorney had to appear at the hearing to confess that he could not locate them. Judge Pinckney announced to the crowded courtroom: "I want to say . . . to the representatives of the press and to the public that I cannot help but believe from the information that has been brought to me that . . . in some way the members of the Mazdaznan are responsible for the circumstance that has been brought to light here to-day."[86] He appointed another attorney to represent the absent boy and proceeded to hear additional testimony about the boy's upbringing and disappearance.[87]

Spectators flocked to the juvenile court to watch the case, including Dr. Hanish's testimony. He read a prepared statement, swearing that "he never had control or custody of said child or power to produce him in court, and had no knowledge of the place where the child was or in whose custody or control he might be." William McEven, the petitioner's attorney, proceeded to grill him. According to the *Daily News*, Hanish's declaration that "he believes himself to be of royal lineage and spiritually and genealogically entitled to the designation of 'prince,' lent added zest to the sensations which the hearing developed."[88] McEven attempted not only to prove that Billy had been neglected but that Mazdaznan was immoral. He argued that the boy was "under the influence of a man whose acknowledged writings and publications are of such a character that if they were made public his followers and believers would be excluded from all decent and respectable society. His teachings violate all principles of nature, health and morals."[89] As evidence, McEven read into the record a chapter on marital relations from Hanish's *Inner Studies*, a book of conduct for his followers: The book, the attorney argued, belonged to Elizabeth Lindsay. Its contents prompted a number of women to leave the courtroom, and many of "those who remained held handkerchiefs to their faces and gazed at the floor."[90] Apparently, even its author blushed at the recital of his own words.[91] A photographer also triggered a melee when he took a picture of a true believer against her will. "The woman, who is not a small person," noted a reporter for the *Daily News*, "hurled herself at the photographer and only for the interference of several of the men followers of Hanish would have demolished his camera."[92] This very public hearing was not how the founders of the juvenile court had imagined it would operate.

Pinckney concluded the hearing by issuing a judicial decree. It declared that Billy was "a neglected and dependent child, having no guardian of his person other than his mother," who because of her "religious fanaticism" was unfit to raise him.[93] Moreover, she had kept the boy out of school and allowed him to travel around the country with Hanish, who was "not a proper person to have control of said child."[94] The decree appointed the boy's uncles to become his new guardians and "authorized them to take him into their care and custody wherever he may be found, and to present to the proper court of Philadelphia a showing regarding the conditions surrounding said child."[95] The judge also found Mrs. Lindsay in contempt of court for "taking her child and leaving the [court's] jurisdiction."[96]

Although Elizabeth Lindsay appealed to the Illinois Supreme Court for a writ of error to overturn Judge Pinckney's decree, the high court determined that she could not apply for this writ until she purged herself of the contempt charge.[97] By fleeing with her son, Elizabeth had placed herself in a bind. She could not challenge the juvenile court's decree unless she brought Billy back, yet if she did the decree would go into effect and she would lose custody of him at least temporarily and perhaps permanently. On the other hand, the high court declared that Hanish, by appearing in the legal proceedings, was entitled to question the juvenile court's decree since it declared that he was an unfit guardian for a child. Thus, Hanish, who was not related to Billy and had sworn that he had never had custody or control over the boy, was entitled to sue for a writ of error.[98] Billy, who had not been cited for contempt, could also sue for the writ, although as a minor he required a lawyer to bring the suit on his behalf.

The Illinois Supreme Court decided it would review the Lindsay case again the following term because both Billy and Hanish had "a right to the writ of error."[99] In February 1913, the court announced its second *Lindsay v. Lindsay* decision in as many years.[100] In a unanimous opinion, Justice William M. Farmer declared that the writ raised three separate questions: "Did the Juvenile Court Act violate either the Federal or State Constitution? Were Elizabeth and Billy Lindsay as visitors passing through Illinois subject to the jurisdiction of the State's Juvenile Court Act? Was Billy a dependent, neglected, or delinquent child and was his mother an unfit person to have custody of him?"[101] For the child savers, the first question was the most pressing, since an affirmative answer by the court would strike down the state's juvenile law. The child savers took some comfort in an important decision by the Pennsylvania Supreme Court, *Commonwealth v. Fisher* (1905), in which the justices had upheld the constitutionality of that state's juvenile court law.[102] Yet Illinois's child savers had learned to expect the worst from their state's highest tribunal, which had earned a reputation for striking down progressive regulatory laws.

The plaintiffs leveled four principal charges against the juvenile court law: "It creates a new court"; "denies the constitutional right of trial by jury"; "reduces the child to a state of involuntary servitude in cases other than as a punishment for crime"; and "deprives children and the parents of children of liberty, property and the right to the pursuit of happiness without due process of law."[103] The justices easily dismissed the first charge by saying that the juvenile court was part of the circuit court and that the power of *parens patriae* had been exercised by courts of chancery for hundreds of years. They cited *Witter* to prove that this jurisdictional power now resided with the juvenile court.[104] To defend the use of six-member juries in the juvenile court, the justices drew a distinction between common law proceedings and statutory ones. In the former, the right to trial by jury existed because juries had always heard such cases. In statutory proceedings this was not so because juries had not been required. Thus, the right to a jury trial did not exist in those areas of law that had been previously jury-less affairs.

In response to the claim that the juvenile court stripped children and parents of their respective rights to due process, the justices quoted large chunks of their decisions in *Petition of Ferrier* and *County of McLean v. Humphreys* to reveal the necessity for paternalistic legislation on behalf of dependent people. These twin 1882 decisions had supported the power of the state to protect dependent girls. "We have quoted extensively from those two cases," they explained, "because the principles involved in them are similar to those involved in this case, and we think they answer the objections here made to the Juvenile Court act."[105] The court used these decisions that predated the juvenile court to uphold the proposition that it served to protect and not punish children. They also praised the law because its intent was "unquestionably in advance of previous legislation dealing with children as criminals."[106] Thus, they rejected the claim that the law violated due process.

After determining that the law was a legitimate exercise of state power, the justices turned to the particulars of the Lindsay case. They noted that Billy was "a modest, unassuming boy... without any bad habits and no apparent evil tendencies, devoted to his mother and obedient to her wishes."[107] He was clearly not a juvenile delinquent. Was he, however, a dependent or neglected child? The justices acknowledged that his mother had sent the boy to accompany Hanish for a seven-week tour. Hanish and Billy, they added, had "sometimes occupied the same room and also slept together."[108] Yet because "the boy took no part in the services at the temple and was not employed by Hanish," their friendship appeared acceptable despite attempts by the boy's relatives to imply a sexual relationship.

Mrs. Lindsay's social standing deeply impressed the justices. They observed: "She appears to be a woman of culture and refinement and of more than ordinary intelligence."[109] She also seemed "attached to [Billy] and very solicitous in regard to his health and welfare."[110] They concluded: "She may have been misguided in her religious views and mistaken as to the best method of educating and training her boy, but we search the record in vain for evidence that he lacked food, clothing or shelter or was being reared in immoral or indecent surroundings."[111] The only evidence to suggest otherwise was the book of conduct read into the record, but there was no proof that "Mrs. Lindsay or the boy had ever seen or read the book."[112] Although the justices strongly disapproved of *Inner Studies*, they said that without evidence that "its principles were being taught to the boy or that he had access to it, we would not be justified in concluding that association with its author would show such a lack of parental care as to make the boy dependent, within the meaning of the statute."[113]

The justices declared that the juvenile court law was intended "to extend a protecting hand to unfortunate boys and girls who, by reason of their own conduct, evil tendencies or improper environment, have proven that the best interests of society, the welfare of the State and their own good demand that the guardianship of the State be substituted for that of natural parents."[114] Although they argued that the statute should be "given a broad and liberal construction," it was important not to extend it "to cases where there is merely a difference of opinion as to the best course to pursue in rearing a child."[115] There had to be "evidence of neglect, abandonment, incapacity or cruelty on the part of the parent or that the child is being exposed to immorality or vice" before the state should intervene.[116] Otherwise, "the right of parents to the society of their offspring is inherent and courts should not violate that right upon slight pretext nor unless it is clearly for the best interests of the child to do so."[117] Consequently, the Illinois Supreme Court overturned Judge Pinckney's decree, and Mrs. Lindsay retained custody of Billy.

The Illinois Juvenile Court Act had finally received judicial blessing, albeit through an strange case. Even though the juvenile court primarily handled cases of juvenile delinquency, the justices had relied extensively on cases involving dependent children that predated the juvenile court to uphold its constitutionality. Moreover, they used a custody dispute over the heir to a large estate to legitimate a system designed to police working-class families. Dependency, in the eyes of the justices, appeared to be firmly rooted in social class. Significantly, the justices did stress that parents have an inherent right to raise their offspring, a principle that the United States Supreme Court affirmed in a series of decisions in 1920s. This principle serves as the foundation for today's "parental rights doctrine," a firmly entrenched tenet of American constitutional law that holds that "the family relationship is so fundamental that government intervention must be circumscribed."[118] Thus, the *Lindsay* decision, which scored a major victory for the child savers, can also be read as a parental rights case that restricted the parental powers of the state.

Although the Illinois Supreme Court had finally declared the Juvenile Court Act to be constitutional, the Lindsay case did not close the curtain on the juvenile court's legal problems in the 1910s. On March 30, 1917, a week before the United States entered World War I, William H. Dunn petitioned once again for an injunction to prevent the County Board from paying the salaries of the juvenile court's 113 employees, who collectively earned close to $150,000 a year.[119] This time he found an obliging Superior Court judge to issue the injunction. As a result, the county treasurer refused to pay the staff's salaries, for two reasons. First, if he disregarded the judicial order he could be held in contempt of court. Second, and more important, if the Illinois Supreme Court upheld the injunction, the treasurer would be personally liable for all the funds he disbursed. The treasurer concluded on the advice of his lawyer not to risk his own financial future. Thus, Dunn's injunction left the court's employees potentially without pay for months to come. The final act in the legal drama had begun, and unless something was done quickly the juvenile court would have to shut down. This possibility alarmed the child savers, because the likelihood of the United States entering the war suggested that delinquency rates in American cities would soar during wartime, thus Chicago would require the services of its juvenile court.

The staff responded to the crisis by forming a committee and electing the popular Chief Probation Officer Joel Hunter to be chairman. With the help of the woman's referee Mary Bartelme, Hunter convinced the former judge Charles Cutting to serve as their legal counsel. Cutting warned that even if he successfully won the initial hearing over the injunction, Dunn could appeal the case to the Illinois Supreme Court and the salaries of the staff would probably not be paid until December.[120] Hunter then privately interviewed every employee to see whether he or she would continue to work in spite of the injunction. All agreed to continue. The majority of the employees even told Hunter that they could at least temporarily get by without their salaries. Twenty-five, however, were in desperate straits: Hunter calculated that these individuals were "in immediate need of $1,685.00."[121] He promised them that he would try to get a loan "for them from outside without interest."[122]

Hunter sought assistance from Julius Rosenwald, the president of Sears, Roebuck. The prominent philanthropist had given to the court before and had even offered to pay for all the legal expenses in the Witter case.[123] Hunter explained the situation to

Rosenwald's personal secretary, William Graves, and asked that Rosenwald loan them the needed funds.[124] From the perspective of the child savers who had fought to establish the world's first juvenile court, it must have appeared as if the entire experiment in juvenile justice were unraveling. Throughout its history, the juvenile court had relied on the city's philanthropists for support, but this request was different. Previously, philanthropists had been asked to help launch new programs. Now the court was asking them to pay for nearly all of its operating costs. Hunter explained that it would be unfair to ask "one person in the community" to be solely responsible for helping the court through the crisis, but added: "If there are a sufficient number of individuals who feel that the court is worthwhile these individuals should either pay the salaries of the employes [sic] of the court directly, or else should give their notes to the County Treasurer, guaranteeing the salaries to the Treasurer if the decision of the Supreme Court should uphold the injunction."[125] Thus Hunter recommended that a small number of private citizens should assume full responsibility for funding this important public institution.

Graves wrote to Rosenwald to inform him not only of the juvenile court's problems but also about a series of petitions that Dunn had filed to stop the county from paying subsidies to sectarian industrial schools. He charged that these payments were a blatant violation of the separation of church and state, and his petitions for injunctions threatened the Louise Training School for Boys and the Amanda Smith Orphan Home for Girls, both of which served the city's African-American population.[126] Rosenwald, who was on his way to the Tuskegee Institute in Alabama, asked to be kept abreast of the developing crisis. He also agreed to lend the committee the money that Hunter had requested.[127]

Meanwhile, the Chicago Bar Association established a committee to help guide the juvenile court through the injunction crisis. Although the Superior Court judge Martin Gridley had thrown out Dunn's injunction, as predicted, Dunn had appealed the decision. The bar association committee struck a deal with the county treasurer, who agreed to resume payment of the staff's salaries if the committee would secure him against personal liability for the money disbursed.[128] A surety bond for $200,000, it was mutually determined, would provide such protection. The committee then searched for Chicagoans who would guarantee to indemnify a bonding company for this lofty sum.[129] To make their case to potential contributors, such as Rosenwald and John G. Shedd, the president of Marshall Field, they explained: "If the work of the employes [*sic*] of the Court was ever needed by the community, it is needed now: Since the war began juvenile delinquency has increased 34% in England and in Berlin over 100%: The Juvenile Court of Cook County is in a position to prevent such a large increase here."[130] Twenty-five Chicagoans, including Judge Pinckney, pledged $5,000 apiece to ensure that the court's staff would be paid until November.[131] That month the state legislature also passed a law allowing the county treasurer to pay salaries in such situations to prevent future interruption in the provision of vital governmental services.[132] The law, however, would not go into effect until after the courts had resolved the current crisis. At least in the future the juvenile court would be less vulnerable to injunctions. This change in the law made it almost impossible for one man like William H. Dunn ever again to threaten the entire court system.

After the surety bond expired and the county treasurer stopped disbursing salaries, an employee of the juvenile court sued him. In December, the Superior Court granted a peremptory writ of *mandamus* (command), ordering the treasurer to resume payment of salaries until the Illinois Appellate Court heard the case. On June 14, 1918, the appellate affirmed the ruling of the lower court. In October, Dunn's last appeal was denied.[133] The Illinois Supreme Court also upheld the constitutionality of the state's industrial school system, rejecting Dunn's contention that county payments to religious schools violated the separation of church and state. The legal drama of the 1910s had finally ended.

Without the support of philanthropists and the legal community, the Chicago Juvenile Court would not have survived these trying times. During the 1910s, the child savers forged coalitions, endorsed candidates, held political rallies, raised substantial amounts of money, and, most important, made the case to the city's many publics about the virtues of juvenile justice. This history serves as a reminder of how the institutions of civil society, including the political process, shaped child protection in the Progressive Era. Studying how the child savers legitimated the juvenile court offers lessons (and perhaps a ray of hope) for contemporary supporters of juvenile justice who wish to see policy experts reclaim some of the authority that they lost to populist movements at the century's end. This history also suggests that nongovernmental actors must continue to monitor closely the exercise of state power on behalf of children and their families. Moreover, these actors continue to have a responsibility to help frame public debates about the future of juvenile justice.

FIVE

*From knowledge of the springs of conduct in the offender we
may hope a thousand times more reasonably for a wise
adjustment of his case than from the application of artificial
legal rules and punishments.*
—William Healy, director of the Juvenile Psychopathic
  Institute, 1915

Medicalizing Delinquency

Although the earliest political battles waged over the juvenile
court focused on its handling of dependency cases, progressive child savers were also concerned that high recidivism rates in
delinquency cases, if unchecked, threatened to undermine the system's legitimacy. To prevent this from happening, Judge Merritt
Pinckney assembled a research committee to investigate the
problem of recidivism, which recommended that the juvenile
court install a clinic to study these persistent offenders. The subsequent opening in 1909 of the Juvenile Psychopathic Institute, the
world's first such institute dedicated to studying the causes of
delinquency, not only transformed the administration of juvenile
justice in Chicago but also helped to mold popular understandings of child development and rearing. The child savers'
response to the problem of recidivism thus paved the way for
intensive scrutiny of the emotional needs of the nation's children
and youth, the vast majority of whom never entered a juvenile
court.

The history of the medicalization of juvenile delinquency
(i.e., treating youthful offending as a mental condition that should
be adjusted through individualized treatment plans) owes a special debt to Ethel Sturges Dummer, who was born into an affluent
Chicago family in 1866. Her civic-minded father was the president

of the Northwestern National Bank, and in 1888 she married the bank's vice-president, William Francis Dummer.[1] After reading a series of articles about child labor in the *Outlook*, she decided in 1906 to volunteer at the juvenile court. Shocked to discover the contrast between her own childhood, "in which life was largely pleasure and joy," and the children of juvenile court whose lives were filled with "squalor, poverty and evil," she told her husband that "any one of the cases reported today would break the heart, but when thirty are heard, it hits the brain."[2]

Dummer believed that most of these children were the victims of unhealthy environments, but she was struck by several notable exceptions. Most memorable were "a deaf mute boy maturing physically, but lacking education, who was corrupting various groups as he went from one neighborhood to another, and a few girls showing distinctly amoral behavior."[3] Yet she could not bring herself to condemn these children as evil and instead sought to understand them. They might, she reasoned, be helped if a scientist could discover the causes of their delinquency, much like Louis Pasteur had successfully isolated the germs that destroyed plant, animal, and human life. Once Dummer realized that these disturbed children needed to be studied by a doctor, not sentenced by a judge, she achieved "a strangely keener consciousness, a new mental process." Now all that was needed was a scientist who could research this "unsolved problem of the atypical child."[4]

She was disappointed to learn that there were no specialists studying the psychological causes of juvenile delinquency. Moreover, the antagonistic relationship that had developed over the course of the nineteenth century between law and psychiatry also raised doubts about whether juvenile court judges would be willing to work with "alienists." Dummer later recalled "the torrent of legal phraseology poured out upon me by Judge Mack, even after the establishment of the clinic, when I suggested that a wise physician, rather than a man trained in the law, would be of value in a juvenile court."[5] There was at least precedent for physical examinations of the children brought to the juvenile court. In 1905, Mack had authorized the Board of Education to study select wards of the court to see whether physiological problems produced delinquency.[6] Also the same year, the Children's Hospital Society had begun sending a nurse to every session of the court to examine children, and after the opening of the detention home in 1907 the society had established a clinic in the building. Thereafter, all children admitted to the home underwent a general examination, which included tests for contagious diseases.[7] Concerns about venereal diseases, especially among the older girls, prompted the purchase of a microscope for the home's dispensary so that the results of children's tests could be known as soon as possible. If a child tested positive, he or she was immediately sent to the Cook County Hospital for treatment.[8]

Dr. James A. Britton, the physician for the detention home, made daily rounds. In addition to his concern about the high rate of venereal disease among the girls, he was also appalled by the poor condition of the children's teeth. One day, for example, he discovered that only four out of the fifty-eight detained children had ever used a toothbrush or seen a dentist. Collectively the children had 203 decayed teeth, an average of more than three per child. These findings prompted the superintendent of the Home, Bena Henderson, to note: "There is little question as to the bad effects of carious teeth on general health and nutrition; there ought not to be very much doubt as to the effect of an aching tooth on mentality and conduct."[9] Although Henderson believed that there was a relationship between physical ailments and delinquent behavior, she was not prepared to assume that "a child's truancy or delinquency is entirely due to hypertrophied tonsils, adenoids, defective hearing or vision." She did, however, recommend that "a psychopathic clinic" should to be established to study questions about causation.[10]

But what did the term "psychopathic" mean? In the early twentieth century, as the historian Elizabeth Lunbeck has demonstrated, psychiatrists began to use it in a new way.[11] At the turn of the century, *psychopathic* or *psychopathy* was often used to describe "soul suffering"—a literal translation of the Greek *psyche* (soul) and *pathos* (suffering)—which referred to someone who was abnormal and, most likely, institutionalized.[12] By the 1910s, psychiatrists in Germany and the United States were using the word to describe a wide range of personality disorders, from mere eccentricities to extremely violent tendencies. The increasing elasticity of the term, according to Lunbeck, provided psychiatrists with "a rubric that comfortably encompassed incarcerated criminals and dissipated high-livers, promiscuous girls and lazy men, deficiencies so various, so numerous, and, in the end, so elusive that some wondered whether it referred to anything at all."[13] The broad definition also served as one of the conceptual tools with which psychiatrists were able to engineer their great escape from the state asylums, in which they had traditionally plied their trade. This escape was part of the process by which the profession acquired the power to claim expertise over the realm of domestic relations.[14] By claiming to have solutions to the so-called crisis of the family, psychiatrists brought "everyday problems" under their purview and then established psychopathic clinics or institutes to treat these patients, who could potentially be anyone, not just society's outcasts.

By diagnosing such personal matters as sexual relations in scientific terms psychiatrists were able to ease the nation's transition from a Victorian world populated with distinctly moral and immoral characters into modernity, with its clashing and often contradictory personalities.[15] Ethel Sturges Dummer's desire to move "beyond good and evil" in order to acquire "a new mental process" is a perfect example of this use of scientific knowledge. It helped her come to grips with the messy problems of modernity in order to discuss things that as a child she had been taught were unspeakable. As a result of her wealth and social standing, she was in a position to accelerate this transformation in American culture. She preferred to be "old-fashioned," including using her husband's name, because this practice shielded many of the reforms that she supported from being criticized as either radical or immoral.[16] During the early twentieth century, she served as a harbinger of modernity by acting like a self-professed "switchboard, connecting people and ideas."[17] She literally spread the news about innovative research by mailing thousands of articles, pamphlets, and books to social and behavioral scientists across the country.

In 1908 Dummer invited a distinguished collection of child savers to her Lincoln Park Boulevard home to discuss equipping the juvenile court with a psychopathic institute. Her guests included Julia Lathrop, Louise de Koven Bowen, George Mead, a professor of philosophy at the University of Chicago, and Frank Church, a physician and member of the Children's Hospital Society. They elected Lathrop as their chairwoman to lead the search for a man of science to run this institute, which Dummer promised to fund for five years.[18] The committee sent out confidential letters asking for recommendations for possible candidates for the position of medical director. They sought the advice of leading scientists and educators, including the psychiatrist Adolf Meyer, the psychologist William James, and Charles W. Eliot, the president of Harvard University. Citing studies of delinquency by the Chicago School of Civics and Philanthropy and the findings of the medical clinic run by the Children's Hospital Society at the juvenile detention home, the letter stressed the "special urgency" of the situation. The director, it explained, would be responsible for designing and conducting a scientific investigation into the causes of juvenile delinquency, as well as "suggesting and applying remedies in individual cases whenever practicable as a concurrent part of the inquiry." The ideal candidate would also have to be a "physician with special experience in mental and nervous diseases in children and with an understanding of the methods of modern psychology."[19]

The committee's recognition of the special nature of child development reflected the success of the child study movement, begun in the 1880s by the psychologist G. Stanley Hall, who was now the president of Clark University. Hall, who had been nicknamed the "Darwin of the mind," had argued in his influential textbook *Adolescence: Its Psychology and Its Relations to Physiology, Anthropology, Sociology, Sex, Crime, Religion, and Education* (1904) that every individual recapitulated the stages of human civilization.[20] This theory had lent scientific legitimacy to the idea that children were qualitatively different from adults, and also focused attention on adolescence (the period in one's life from the onset of puberty to one's early twenties) as a particularly difficult developmental stage. In 1909 Hall helped to further secure his place in American history by bringing Sigmund Freud to Clark University to deliver a series of lectures on psychoanalysis.[21] It turned out to be Freud's only visit to the United States, although his ideas about how unconscious forces shaped human behavior had an almost unprecedented impact on twentieth-century American culture.

After reviewing a number of candidates, the search committee eventually offered the position to William Healy. The choice of Healy was appropriate partly because of his own underprivileged childhood. When he was nine years old, in 1878, his family had immigrated to the United States from England. Due to their poverty, Healy had to leave school before his fourteenth birthday to work as an office boy in the Fifth National Bank on LaSalle Street in Chicago's Loop. Although Healy helped to support his family, he also grew frustrated with the moralizing of his fundamentalist father and began to attend meetings of the Ethical Culture Society. Its leader, Reverend William Salter, was the brother-in-law of William James. Salter was so impressed by Healy that he persuaded James to support Healy's application in 1892 to Harvard University as a special student. At Cambridge, the twenty-three-year-old freshman studied with James, who became both his friend and lifelong inspiration. After finishing his course work, Healy entered Harvard Medical School, but because of financial difficulties completed his degree at Rush Medical College in Chicago. He spent his first year as a physician in the Woman's Division of the Wisconsin State Hospital at Mendota before returning to Chicago to establish a private practice and to teach gynecology at Northwestern Medical School. Healy then became interested in neurology, a field of inquiry that developed in the United States in response to the carnage of the Civil War. He taught courses in this field at the Chicago Polyclinic before embarking on a European trip to conduct postgraduate research; he returned in 1907 to establish a private practice as a neurologist.[22]

Healy's medical credentials, broad interests, and connections in the Chicago legal community impressed the committee. His wife's father, Horace K. Tenney, was the senior partner of the firm of Tenney, Coffeen, Harding & Sherman and served on the advisory council of the proposed clinic.[23] The search committee understood that it would be essential for the medical director to work well with lawyers, especially Judge Pinckney, whose cooperation was essential for the success of the endeavor.

Before there were formal plans for establishing a psychopathic institute in Chicago, Julia Lathrop, whose interest in mental illness dated back to her days as a state commissioner in the 1890s, had written to Healy to ask him about the state of research into the mentally defective child. In his response, Healy pointed out that this area was still "virgin soil," although the possibility for such investigations was "large in scope." He explained: "That we possess at present only inklings of the causation of mental defect is probably due simply to a lack of thorough study with the many tools modern science has put into our hands." This ignorance led to a lack of help for these children "except in the most spasmodic and unintelligent way" until it was far too late to help them. It was time, he believed, that this sorry state of affairs be corrected and that "a thoroughly experienced and unbiased man" needed to master the existing literature, visit the world's leading institutions, and then examine at least one thousand cases, including "500 cases of really delinquents [sic] from the Juvenile Court." These examinations, requiring from one to two hours per child, should "involve all possible facts about heredity, environment, antenatal and postnatal history, etc." The same person, he stressed, would have to examine all the children in order to develop a "classical work on the subject," otherwise the results would become just "another bit of slip-shod social work." He estimated that "it is a task for four or five years, I should judge, to get anything like complete or commanding results out of this problem." Yet, if done correctly, this research would produce a book that would be as "classical as that of Lombroso" but "may be much more scientifically founded and a thousand times more practically beneficial."[24] Cesare Lombroso was an Italian physician and criminal anthropologist whose most influential work, *L'Uomo Delinquente* (The Criminal Man [1876]), posited that criminals were a distinct type who were throwbacks to an earlier era in human history. Their atavistic features, such as asymmetrical faces or skulls, ostensibly revealed their backwardness.[25]

Healy's fervently believed that analyzing case histories would move the study of delinquency beyond Lombroso's crude anthropology. He also knew that the probation officers of the juvenile court already filled out "History of the Case" forms on all the children who entered the system and explained to Lathrop that this valuable data could be put to good use in the construction of case histories.[26] The challenge was to classify these social facts in order to isolate the predominant causes of delinquent behavior among recidivists. By offering Healy the medical directorship of the institute in 1909, the search committee provided him with the opportunity to test all the leading theories of the day, including the idea that criminal traits were genetic, and to produce the classical study of juvenile delinquency that he had outlined for Lathrop.

At age forty, Healy gave up his lucrative private practice to accept the position and, with funding from Dummer, embarked on a trip across the United States to see what other researchers were doing and to collect ideas about how to proceed with his own work. He discovered that nobody was compiling "well-rounded studies of the[ir] cases" and that only a few people, such as Henry H. Goddard, the director of the Vineland Training School for Feebleminded Girls and Boys in New Jersey, even administered mental tests to children.[27] These scientists told him that he would have to "blaze a trail."[28] Writing to Dummer from New York City, Healy announced: "With all the advice and practical suggestions I have received, my fingers finely itch to get at work on our problem."[29]

The Juvenile Psychopathic Institute, which was officially incorporated with Lathrop as its president and Dummer as its treasurer on April 19, 1909, was ready for Healy's return.[30] The institute occupied three rooms on the ground floor of the detention home, and, as an article in the *Chicago Record-Herald* proclaimed, it would "study the souls of children."[31] Jane Addams, a member of its executive committee, told the press: "We intend to examine into the child's mental condition, investigate his environment and the record of his family, thus seeking the causes which brought about his criminal actions." She added: "There is no doubt that a great deal of youthful criminality is caused by nervous diseases, subnormality and mental aberration, brought about through heredity or home environment."[32] This focus on heredity and environment was a reminder that progressive child savers such as Addams and Healy believed that nature as well as nurture played critical roles in propagating delinquency.[33] Healy was later embarrassed by some of the initial tests that he and his staff conducted on children, including measuring their heads to see if they had any of the telltale stigmata of "born criminals" that Lombroso had popularized.[34] He also later joked about his friendships with committed eugenicists, such as the chief judge of the Chicago Municipal Court, Harry Olson, who served on the institute's advisory council and established a notorious psychopathic laboratory for his own court system.[35]

Healy appreciated that his work had the potential to challenge the authority of juvenile court judges. He was thus accordingly grateful that Judge Pinckney welcomed him as a friend to the court and even asked him to attend daily sessions to help solve perplexing cases.[36] Healy quickly discovered that without thoroughly examining a child he could offer little, if any, constructive advice, and realized that he had to devise techniques for classifying children, especially their range of mental abilities, so that he could make informed recommendations. During the institute's early years, Healy and his staff devised a series of schedules, which listed all the data that should be collected for a case.[37] They included information about a child's heredity, physical, mental and moral development, as well as anthropometrical, neurological, psychiatric, and psychological evaluations.[38]

Measuring a child's "mental age" appeared to be a particularly promising point of departure. In France, a few years earlier, the government had commissioned Alfred Binet, the director of the psychology laboratory at the Sorbonne, to devise tests that could reveal which children needed special attention in the class-room.[39] Healy, who initially used some of Binet's tests, soon learned that they could not be effectively administered to the court's "cosmopolitan population."[40] The high percentage of immigrants made it necessary "to eliminate the language factor as much as possible" from testing.[41] Healy worked with James Angell, a professor of psychology at the University of Chicago, and Grace Fernald, the institute's first psychologist, to devise a series of task-oriented exams that did not require knowledge of English. They faced, however, the inherent problem in devising an "intelligence" test: Is it really possible to measure "mental ability" apart "from the individual's experience"?[42] The first test that the group created involved putting eleven pieces of a puzzle into their proper places. When completed, the puzzle showed a puppy with a mouse in its mouth walking next to its watchful mother. Healy noted: "If a boy observes, 'Oh, gee! that dog's caught a mouse,' or 'There's a baby horse standing by its mother,' one gets some impression of the subject's mentality. But if the attempt to put an animal's head in upside down is persistently made, that likewise bespeaks certain mental characteristics."[43] This test was also supposed to get the child interested in the examination process and allow the examiner to watch how he or she solved the puzzle. Through careful observation, Healy point-ed out, general conclusions about the child's mental ability as well as muscular coordination could be drawn without verbal communication.

Healy preferred to diagnose children with whom he could converse because this allowed him to administer a wider range of tests, including ones designed to gauge an "individual's con-sciousness upon ethical lines."[44] He asked children, for example, to pass judgment on somebody else's actions. One question asked: "In a Russian city last year there lived a man who could get no work. He had for a neighbor a sick widow with two little children, who were starving. The poor man took some bread that did not belong to him from a baker's shop, because he could get it in no other way and gave it to the widow and her children. Did he do right or wrong?"[45] Most of the children condemned the actions of the man in no uncertain terms, which bothered Healy because these children were "themselves chronic little thieves."[46] Frustrated by the sanctimonious answers that this question elicited, Healy decided to scrap it altogether. Instead, he asked a child how he or she would react to hostile Indians threatening to burn a settlement to the ground because of an alleged crime committed by a white man against the tribe's chief.[47]

He also relied on the child relating his or her "own story," which, like the moral tests, helped Healy to see into the workings of the child's mind. He used these autobiographical accounts to expose subconscious reasons for the child's repeated delinquencies.[48] These stories, in effect, opened up a window into the child's "mental insides."[49] Healy described this research as "characterology" and strove to understand a child's "mental life" because he believed that "conduct," including delinquent behavior, was produced in this inner world.[50] He later became a proponent of psychoanalysis and a leader in the child guidance movement that took off in the 1920s and sought to treat the emotional needs of children in general, not just those who entered the juvenile justice system.[51]

In the 1910s, however, Healy's self-identification "as a student of character" revealed that he, much like his patron Ethel Sturges Dummer, was making the transition from a Victorian upbringing to the challenges of modernity. The awkward phrase "characterology" rested uneasily on the middle ground between nineteenth-century concerns with the moral nature of human beings and the twentieth-century obsession with "personality."[52] In fact, as the historian Warren Susman observed, "at least five major studies of Jesus appeared" in the first decade of the new century, and their authors, rather than describing the Nazarene as "the achieving man of character and moral exemplar," portrayed him as a "miserably maladjusted fanatic."[53] In the modern world, even Christ apparently needed a psychiatrist or at least a reliable self-help manual.

Healy cautioned fellow researchers about the difficulties of peering into a child's mind. There was, he noted, the ever-present danger of the child willfully building "a wall in front of himself that is hard to break down" or to see over.[54] He also learned from early cases that it was extremely difficult to study incarcerated children. Not surprisingly, they displayed little interest in the prospects of an examination. On the other hand, "the individual before his case is adjudicated in any way, either in court or out of it, is, in the vast majority of instances, peculiarly keen to show the full extent of his ability."[55] In addition, Healy discovered that younger children were far better subjects than adolescents, for he could develop "the friendly relationships" with them that were "necessary for getting the scientific data."[56] This finding convinced Healy to focus his attentions on those who had not yet developed adolescent obstinacy.

The warnings sprinkled throughout Healy's writings about making children uncomfortable reveal that his subjects were not passive during their examinations but rather active participants in the process. The medical instruments that he used to measure them, including the stopwatch for timing their activities, fascinated them.[57] Yet too many instruments in the room, Healy cautioned, could make a child suspect that he or she was being "measured for identification," and this produced "an immediate revulsion of feeling" that ruined "the entire interview."[58] To avoid raising such suspicions, Healy cautioned, "there must not be the least flavor of police methods" in the examination process.[59] The difficulty, of course, was that the Juvenile Psychopathic Institute was located in the detention home and had become an official department of the juvenile court in 1914.

Healy sought to have his methods and findings taught in the nation's law schools. John Wigmore, the dean of the Northwestern School of Law, the nation's foremost authority on evidence and a member of the institute's advisory council, helped in this endeavor. He ensured that Healy's speeches and articles found a home in the innovative *Journal of Criminal Law and Criminology*, which Wigmore helped to found in 1910. The new journal was slated to address "the crying need for co-operative effort among lawyers and scientists," and its inaugural issue included Healy's essay "The Individual Study of the Young Criminal."[60] The essay emphasized the multiple causes of crimes (what criminologists now refer to as the crime-correlate approach) and also suggested that if there were multiple causes of delinquency then there must also be multiple cures. Healy went so far as to argue that no two delinquents were alike and for this reason intensive study of each individual case must be undertaken. The article described ten cases in detail and concluded with a remarkable list of "possible causative factors." The factors included:

> Bad companions; immoral mother; poverty; mental subnormality; cheap plays and nickel shows; bad heredity; very poor education; bandit ideas from books; morbid impulsion—kleptomania; mother away working—no one to look after the children; bad sexual habits; congested neighborhood; defective ante-natal conditions; neglectful father; innate laziness; epilepsy; difficult birth; degeneracy with stigmata; feeble-mindedness; recent immigration; densely ignorant family; desire for finery; careless, not ignorant, parents; hypersensitiveness; stepmother; mental peculiarities, perhaps the beginning of a psychosis; teasing by other children; alcoholism of parent; high mental capacity, out of all proportion to his environment; nervous irritability; poor general health; defective vision; defective hearing; and great love of excitement and adventure.[61]

Healy did not, however, suggest possible treatments for these cases.

The lack of proposed remedies in Healy's early writings should not obscure the real significance of his intentions. He lobbied to replace formal legal ideas about individual responsibility with a therapeutic approach to governance that applied the principles of juvenile justice to the society at large. In practice, this meant "appropriate physical, educational, or even disciplinary treatment under highly individualized surveillance" for those such as wild adolescents, senile old men, epileptics, and menstruating women who could not control themselves.[62] In this brave new world, Healy envisioned that the state would devise individualized control for those individuals lacking self-control, and judges would use specific knowledge about individuals in order to exercise their authority most efficaciously. Scientific testing promised to provide this vital information. As Healy declared, "to be able to say to the judge, or to any one with the power to take action, that the offender of 23 chronologically is mentally an individual of 10 years, puts the whole matter is an enticingly clear light."[63] It seemed obvious, in this case, that an adult with the mentality of a child should be treated like one. The concept of mental age, in effect, could help to transplant the disciplinary techniques employed in the juvenile justice system, such as probation and indeterminate sentences, into the adult system.

With Wigmore's help, Healy aimed to convince lawyers of the importance of rethinking criminal justice in terms of discipline instead of punishment. When Edwin Keedy, a professor of law at Northwestern, asked Healy about devising a course using some of his research, Healy happily passed the word along to Dummer. "This delighted me, for we are all agreed it is largely through ignorance on the part of the lawyers that so little advance has been made in the past along these lines."[64] Healy also informed her of the "arduous hours" that Wigmore spent helping Healy complete *The Individual Delinquent* (1915), an 830-page textbook of "diagnosis and prognosis for all concerned in understanding offenders." On Wigmore's suggestion, Healy chose the publisher Little, Brown, instead of the more prestigious Macmillan, because the former published "law books, and while our audience is already made among certain types of people, it would be best to have a concern well known to lawyers bring it out."[65] After the publication of *The Individual Delinquent*, which Healy dedicated "to Mrs. W. F. Dummer," he sent her a handwritten note expressing his satisfaction with the book's reception, especially its positive reviews in law journals. He was also astounded to hear that 1,131 copies had already been sold and pleased to learn that law professors, such as Wigmore, were using it in their courses.[66]

Criminologists credit *The Individual Delinquent* with directing their discipline away from hereditarian explanations of deviance and toward an appreciation for environmental factors and the necessity for individualized treatment plans. In addition, scholars studying serious and violent offenders at the end of the twentieth century reaffirmed many of Healy's discoveries about delinquency, including his assertions that there are multiple causes, "practically all confirmed criminals begin their careers in childhood or early youth," recidivists "have the greatest significance for society," and that it is important to begin "treatment early." According to the criminologist John Laub, the continuing validity of Healy's findings has revealed that "there is little evidence to suggest that the underlying causes of juvenile delinquency have changed over the last hundred years."[67] Laub argues that criminologists should not assume that every generation of youthful offenders is unique; instead they should use past studies of delinquency in order to examine current patterns of juvenile offending. Healy's Chicago research both changed the direction of criminological research in the early twentieth century and also continues to provide useful insights into juvenile delinquency.

Healy left Chicago soon after the publication of *The Individual Delinquent*. In 1916 he was offered the directorship of the Judge Baker Foundation, which was established in honor of Harvey Humphrey Baker, who in 1906 had become Boston's first juvenile court judge. Twice before his death in 1915, Baker had come to Chicago to study at Healy's institute and had called for more such clinics to be opened. Friends of Baker, including his successor, Frederick Cabot, thought that Healy, who had taught summer courses on his research at Harvard University, was the most qualified man to direct this new foundation.

Wigmore was outraged that Chicago might lose Healy and wanted philanthropically minded Chicagoans to match Boston's generous offer, which included a hefty annual salary of $12,000 for Healy and facilities twice the size of the Juvenile Psychopathic Institute. Wigmore explained:

> Chicago, through Dr. Healy's genius, has been "put on the map" (as the phrase goes) in this field of human progress,—just as the Mayo Brothers put Rochester, Minnesota, on the map for certain kinds of surgery. Does

Chicago care enough for this achievement to make the effort to hold it? Or must it be allowed to go East to Boston? It is a noble work in itself, helping to reduce crime and rascality in our midst. We need it just as much as Boston does. It belongs here.[68]

By this time, however, Healy had soured on Chicago. The political battles waged over the juvenile court, including the annual struggle to get adequate appropriations, hindered his work. During the height of the political turbulence of 1911–12, for instance, Healy had become alarmed that he might be forced to turn over to the Civil Service Commission the case histories that he and his staff were compiling. To protect the institute's records, William Francis Dummer allowed Healy to place them in his private vault, while the child savers waited for the political storm to pass. Crises like this frustrated Healy and influenced his decision to leave Chicago.

Boston also offered a more secure future and better options for implementing treatment plans. Healy had asked that the Bostonians raise enough money to guarantee that their new foundation could be run full-time for ten years, and his request had been met.[69] More significant, Healy believed that the child welfare system in Illinois, which was still structured around the Gilded Age subsidy system, was not conducive to his work because so many of the children he diagnosed were simply sent to institutions, where they did not receive the individualized care he prescribed. Until the early 1920s, as the historian Kenneth Cmiel has calculated, Illinois "had fewer children in foster homes than any other major industrial state."[70] Boston, on the other hand, had a long tradition of placing dependent and delinquent children in private homes, where they could be given more individualized treatment.

Healy felt justified in leaving the Juvenile Psychopathic Institute because he had found a capable replacement in Dr. Herman Adler, who was conducting research in Chicago for the American Association of Mental Hygiene.[71] Healy had first met Adler at the Boston Psychopathic Hospital, where he had worked with Healy's good friend from medical school, Elmer Ernest Southard. In 1917, the Illinois General Assembly created a state Department of Public Welfare that incorporated the Juvenile Psychopathic Institute, renamed the Institute for Juvenile Research (IJR), and Adler became the state criminologist for Illinois.[72] A branch laboratory of the department continued to operate in the detention home so that all of the delinquent children upon entering the home could be given a two- to three-minute psychological examination. The results of this test were then used to separate out the "mental defectives" from the "obviously normal children." The children who failed the test were then subjected to thorough psychiatric examinations and had their cases written up.

Healy's departure from Chicago replicated an emerging pattern. Leading child savers had established their reputations by helping to build the Chicago Juvenile Court and then left the city. Lucy Flower had gone to California to retire, Julia Lathrop had moved to Washington, D.C., to head the Federal Children's Bureau, Julian Mack became a U.S. Circuit Court Judge and a New Yorker, and now Healy left to direct the Judge Baker Foundation.

In the 1920s, however, many of these child savers reunited in order to assess the successes and failures of the juvenile court movement. Healy, for instance, wondered what had happened to the children he had examined in Chicago. In a long letter to Dummer in March 1920, he suggested that a followup study of these cases might make a nice tribute to Judge Pinckney. A few years earlier, Pinckney had told Healy that determining the results of their work together was "the one thing he wanted to have done before he died." It seemed only fitting to honor the final request of the man who had guided the nation's first juvenile court through its most difficult days. Moreover, as Healy pointed out, "isn't it interesting that here is this huge bit of machinery, as it exists in Chicago, with never any checking up of whether its out-put is really efficient or successful?" The possibility of evaluating Chicago's experiment in juvenile justice appealed to the empiricist in Healy. "It would be a glorious thing . . . to make the first attempt that has been made to get a good study of what can be accomplished by ordinary court and institutional methods. If these methods are inadequate they should be shown up as such, if not, they should be commended. In any case the truth should come out." Healy cautioned that the success of the Chicago court was probably limited because of its reliance on institutionalization. Dummer, who had been disappointed to see Healy leave Chicago, agreed to fund the followup study and sent him a check for $1,000 as the first installment to begin the project.[73]

The results revealed staggering recidivism rates. "It is simply appalling to see the number of boys who have gone on to criminal careers, simply because the common sense things have not been done for them," he explained to Dummer.[74] These results, which Healy shared with child welfare experts at conferences in the early 1920s, contributed to the growing pessimism about the effectiveness of the juvenile justice system to prevent juvenile delinquency and were reflected in professional discussions among social workers about "the passing of the juvenile court."[75]

This loss of faith occurred at a critical moment, because members of the progressive generation of child savers were trying to regain lost enthusiasm for the juvenile court movement by consolidating its gains through the creation of uniform standards and the preservation of its storied past. Yet, at this moment of consolidation, when older reformers were striving to make the distinguishing features of juvenile justice into standard practices, a new generation turned away from the juvenile court and focused its attention on ways to work with younger, more "normal" children who had only minor behavioral problems.[76]

This turning away from the delinquent child concerned Julia Lathrop, who was nearing the end of her long tenure as the chief of the United States Children's Bureau and was especially troubled by the finding presented by Evelina Belden in *Courts in the United States Hearing Children's Cases*.[77] Although forty-six out of the forty-eight states had passed juvenile court laws by 1920, Belden discovered that the law in action did not even come close to matching the law on the books. She noted, for example: "From at least one court in every State in the Union came reports of detaining children in jails."[78] In addition, less than half of the courts reporting had probation service, which was supposed to be the cornerstone of modern juvenile justice. Moreover, psychiatric services were available in only 7 percent of the courts."[79] Belden calculated that approximately 50,000 out of the 175,000 juvenile cases heard during 1918 were conducted by courts "not adapted to the handling of children's cases."[80] Reflecting on this state of affairs, she concluded: "Statistics can not adequately reveal the injury done these children through their association with adult offenders, their trial under the old criminal processes, and the absence of equipment for the study of their needs or for proper oversight and protection."[81] These troubling findings prompted Lathrop to take action.

In June 1921, the Children's Bureau along with the National Probation Association sponsored a three-day conference in Milwaukee to bring together child welfare experts to discuss "the fundamental problems of the juvenile court" exposed by Belden's report.[82] The sessions addressed questions of jurisdiction, the inherent tension between individual rights and socialized justice in chancery proceedings, the problem of extending juvenile justice into rural areas, and the best way to individualize treatment of cases. In attendance were many of the experts who had spent the formative years of their careers in the Chicago court system and were personal friends of Lathrop, including Henry Thurston and William Healy.

Lathrop, who was now in her early sixties and about to retire from the Children's Bureau, delivered the introductory address. She used the example of the Chicago court, "whose development I know personally," to highlight the "continuous cooperation between public and private agencies" that had characterized the history of juvenile justice.[83] She stressed that this cooperation, which had been so beneficial in the past, must continue into the future if the spirit of the juvenile court movement were to be kept alive. It was their mission, Lathrop declared, to reawaken public interest in the idea of the juvenile court. "If judges and laity could join in a committee to study practicable recommendations for juvenile-court standards," she asked, "would not much public interest be awakened in its work and a genuine advance be made in juvenile-court provision in those areas where it is now lacking?"[84] At the conclusion of the conference, she appointed a committee whose mission was "to carry on this work of standardization of juvenile court methods."[85] It took almost two years for this thirteen-member committee, chaired by Judge Charles Hoffman of Cincinnati, to produce its final report.

Healy served on the committee, while at the same time he was analyzing the preliminary results of his followup research on the Chicago cases. The findings convinced him that Chicago's reliance on institutionalization and failure to implement truly individualized treatment plans had contributed to its poor record.[86] He used this evidence to argue for more extensive psychological and psychiatric work with young children to prevent them from developing into juvenile delinquents. In addition, after the Milwaukee conference, Healy met with Barry Smith, the general director of the Commonwealth Fund, a foundation established in 1918 by Anna Harkness, the widow of a wealthy stockholder in John D. Rockefeller's Standard Oil Company, "to do something for the welfare of mankind."[87] The foundation had decided to put its resources into delinquency prevention and child health. Healy showed Smith his findings about Chicago, and their meeting foreshadowed the rejection of the juvenile court as the focus for child saving in the 1920s. Smith, for example, on the advice of doctors like Healy, decided that the Commonwealth Fund would concentrate its efforts on young children, not older ones already in the juvenile justice system. He said:

> The General Director is strongly of the opinion that the most effective program will not deal with delinquency beyond the stages of the Juvenile Court and Probation System. While undoubtedly there is a great need of more intelligent handling of crime and delinquency in our reformatories, jails, and prisons, the work with children in the earlier stages is far more hopeful, both as to the children served and as to general beneficial results to the country at large.[88]

As the historian Margo Horn has demonstrated, this focus on the young child anticipated a decision by the foundation to remove itself entirely from the field of juvenile delinquency.[89]

Thus, just at the moment when juvenile court standards were being completed, child welfare experts were turning their attention away from the delinquent child. In May 1923, the committee presented its final report to Grace Abbott, the new chief of the Children's Bureau. Abbott had been Lathrop's handpicked successor and, like her mentor, had begun her career in Jane Addams's Hull House.[90] In a foreword to the committee's recommendations, Abbott summarized the four principles underlying their report:

(1) That the court dealing with children should be clothed with broad jurisdiction, embracing all classes of cases in which a child is in need of the protection of the State, whether the legal action is in the name of the child or an adult who fails in his obligations toward the child;

(2) that the court should have a scientific understanding of each child;

(3) that treatment should be adapted to individual needs;

(4) that there should a presumption in favor of keeping the child in his own home and his own community, except when adequate investigation shows this not to be in the best interest of the child.[91]

The first principle reasserted Lucy Flower's initial vision for a children's court in Chicago, and the final one reflected the progressive belief in family preservation. The second and third principles revealed the influence of Dummer's and Healy's ideas. The addition of the Juvenile Psychopathic Institute to the Chicago Juvenile Court, which fourteen years earlier had been hailed as a revolutionary act, was now considered to be a necessary feature of juvenile justice—although, as the historian David Rothman has shown, this ideal did not become a reality for most juvenile courts in the first half of the twentieth century.[92]

The completion of *Juvenile-Court Standards* in 1923 established for the first time an official norm against which the actual operations of the nation's courts could be measured. The nation's experts agreed on what practices—chancery proceedings, broad and exclusive jurisdiction until at least age eighteen, private hearings, the complaint system, probation, confidential records, clinical examinations, and individualized treatment—should become standard. Yet Lathrop's predication that the standards would reawaken interest in the idea of the juvenile court did not materialize, despite a barrage of press releases, radio promotions, and the fact that the bureau printed and mailed ten thousand copies of the guidelines to courts across the country.[93] Although *Juvenile-Court Standards* failed to generate the public interest Lathrop had hoped for, the report did become the programmatic capstone for progressive juvenile justice and would be reprinted and distributed by the Children's Bureau without any changes until 1954.

The twenty-fifth anniversary of the Chicago Juvenile Court and the fifteenth anniversary of its clinic provided the progressive child savers with another opportunity to generate public interest in juvenile justice and to preserve the ideals of the movement. In the autumn of 1924, reformers in Chicago organized a Citizens' Anniversary Committee, which Jane Addams chaired, to plan a conference for the first week of the coming year.[94] The child savers were, however, somewhat apprehensive about celebrating the court and clinic at this time. The city was still recovering from the publicity surrounding the brilliant act of legal contortion performed by Clarence Darrow to save the lives of Nathan Leopold and Richard Loeb, known worldwide as the "boy-murderers" who had committed "the crime of the century."[95] Earlier that summer, Leopold (age nineteen) and Loeb (age eighteen), sons of Hyde Park millionaires and students at the University of Chicago, had randomly selected, kidnapped, and killed Bobby Franks (age fourteen), a neighborhood boy and a distant cousin of Loeb, on his way home from school. After being caught, Leopold and Loeb had eagerly confessed but showed no remorse. To avoid a trial by jury and the pitfalls of an insanity defense, Darrow had his clients plead guilty and take their chances with a sentencing hearing before a lone judge.

Darrow performed his magic by transforming Leopold and Loeb into maladjusted children whom the state had a responsibility to protect. In his legendary summation, Darrow reminded Judge John R. Caverly of the Cook County Criminal Court that

> the protection of childhood, is always one of the
> first concerns of the state.... I suppose civilization will
> survive if your Honor hangs them. But it will be a terrible
> blow that you shall deal. Your Honor will be turning
> back over the long, long road we have traveled. You
> would be dealing a staggering blow to all that has been
> done in the City of Chicago in the last twenty years for
> the protection of infancy and childhood and youth.[96]

Darrow's strategy relied on the testimony of medical experts, including William Healy, to explain his clients' antisocial behavior. The testimony of "these men of science" attracted national attention, and Robert McCormick, the publisher of the *Chicago Tribune*, even offered Sigmund Freud $25,000 to come to Chicago to psychoanalyze Leopold and Loeb.[97] Freud, however, declined this lucrative invitation.

In November, while the anniversary conference was being planned, the *Journal of Criminal Law and Criminology* published a symposium on the sentencing hearing.[98] John Wigmore, who had been Healy's leading booster in the 1910s, had become wary of socialized law and wrote a vituperative piece about the misuse of science. William I. Thomas, a leading sociologist and protege of Ethel Sturges Dummer, sent her an excerpt from Wigmore's article. It read: "As everyone knows, today is a period of reckless immorality and lawlessness on the part of younger people, at the age of 18–25. It is more or less due to the vicious philosophy of life, spread in our schools for the last twenty-five years by John Dewey and others—the philosophy which worships self-expression, and emphasizes the uncontrolled search for complete experience."[99] Wigmore called for the "special repression" of modern youth in general and, in the cases of antisocial individuals like Leopold and

Loeb, the death penalty, because "life imprisonment has not terrors to their minds" but "everybody has sufficient horror of [hanging]—except the crazy and the mere child."[100] At the end of the clipping, Thomas scribbled: "Pretty savage? Is he on the program?"[101]

Dummer, who was the cochair of the program committee for the anniversary conference, was not pleased. She questioned whether the World War I had somehow changed "all of the ideals to which we had evolved."[102] She pointed out to Thomas that the *Chicago Tribune* was now running so many articles about crime that it had become difficult for the finance committee to raise enough money for the upcoming conference. "We must plan cautiously," she explained, "lest our conference meet with antagonism and ridicule. People are considering the juvenile court somewhat sentimental and are taking boys of 16 and 17 to the police stations and the criminal courts."[103]

Healy had agreed to deliver a paper at the conference but expressed concern to Dummer because both he and Bronner believed that "there is so much that ought to be altered [in Chicago] that we doubt whether we would be in good odor if we said what we really think."[104] Dummer informed them that some of the other addresses would also "absolutely show up the inefficient work of Chicago" and assured them that they would have the freedom to say what they liked.[105] Thus, with some reluctance, Healy returned to Chicago to help commemorate the city's court and clinic.

The conference, which was hosted by the City Club of Chicago, located in the South Loop, opened with greetings from Mayor William Dever and Anton Cermak, the president of the Board of Cook County Commissioners, on Friday morning, January 2, 1925. The first session was devoted to the history of the juvenile court movement and included such pioneers as Julia Lathrop, Timothy Hurley, Louise de Koven Bowen, and Judge Benjamin Lindsey from Colorado. The highlight of Friday, however, was an anniversary banquet that evening at the nearby Congress Hotel, whose featured speakers were Judge Julian Mack, of the United States Circuit Court of Appeals, and Dr. Miriam Van Waters, the referee of the Los Angeles Juvenile Court.

Mack, who was approaching sixty years of age, was an obvious choice to deliver a keynote address because of his years on the bench in Chicago and his influential role in the juvenile court movement. Van Waters, a generation removed from the founding of the court and twenty years Mack's junior, was a rising star in the field of juvenile justice. She had earned her Ph.D. in anthropology from Clark University in 1913 and had worked for the Boston's Children's Aid Society for several years before moving to California. She became the superintendent of the Los Angeles Detention Home as well as the director of El Retiro, a halfway house for wayward girls.[106] Her work there attracted the attention of Ethel Sturges Dummer, who had grown concerned during World War I about sexually abused girls and prostitutes. She worried that these girls suffered from a condition similar to shellshock. Dummer made Van Waters into one of her proteges and introduced her to the Chicago network of reformers. In 1920, after Van Waters passed the California bar exam, she had been appointed referee of the Los Angeles court.

Significantly, both Mack and Van Waters cautioned against the growing obsession among professionals with the personality of the child.[107] Yet much of the conference was dedicated to the medicalization of delinquency. The published collection of the proceedings, *The Child, The Clinic and the Court* (1925), edited by Jane Addams, even placed all the medical papers and clinical ones in front of those describing the court and the history of the social movement. This reversal of fortune, which placed psychology and psychiatry before law, symbolized the fading importance of the juvenile court.

Mack's fiery speech recaptured the tenor of the original juvenile court movement and must have pleased Lathrop, who for years had stressed that the primary importance of the juvenile court was its ability to make unpleasant social truths visible. Mack argued that economic factors were still the primary cause of delinquency. Society's "fundamental duty" was "to see what the economic basis is that brings the children into court and correct [that] economic wrong," he announced. "Tear down your hovels and your slums give your working man the leisure by enforced limitation of hours of work to give thought to the raising of his family before you step in and say he is not competent to deal with his own children."[108]

Van Waters used her address to demonstrate that the administration of juvenile justice had become too bureaucratic and "routinized" life.[109] The state had become a rigid parent; as one little girl explained to Van Waters, "I don't like it to treat me like a mean mother."[110] Despite the growing pessimism among experts and the public about the juvenile court, Van Waters argued that it was "the only *force* that can be substituted legally for weakening parental control" and must continue to play a central role in the policing of the child.[111] Without these courts, child welfare would suffer. For society to move forward, Van Waters argued, local communities had to become more involved with their children. They also had to ensure that committed professionals, who could effectively communicate with children, worked in the juvenile justice system to "keep the juvenile court machinery from stamping out the juvenile court ideas."[112]

The conference concluded with a Sunday symposium, presided over by Dummer, that analyzed "the foundations of behavior from the standpoint of biology, psychology, psychiatry and sociology in the hope that through this scientific synthesis, new understandings may appear."[113] William Healy, not Julian Mack, had the final word. Although he agreed with Mack that the elimination of poverty was critically important, Healy pointed out that "delinquency has so many interrelated causative factors that it presents a problem not to be solved so simply." He added, however, that "a vast deal of delinquency can be effectively treated and prevented by a psychologically sound and scientific program."[114] Healy thus emphasized mind over social matters.

In an ironic twist, Healy's call for truly individualized treatment of children's emotional needs had a greater impact on the lives of American children outside of the juvenile justice system than within. As the historian Kathleen Jones has shown, "child guidance did not stay in the clinic during the 1920s and 1930s; nor did it remain a method simply for steadying the life course of juvenile delinquents and unruly dependents." During these years, "child guidance advice about emotional conflict, personality maladjustment, and the determining role of the family environment spread beyond the confines of social reform to become the discourse of private child rearing."[115] The idea that parents were responsible for taking care of their child's emotional needs, in fact, served as a major theme of Dr. Benjamin Spock's *Common Sense Book of Baby and Child Care* (1945), which became the Bible of the baby boomers' parents. As Jones observed, "Spock collapsed into one volume twenty-five years of child guidance popularization. Common sense and the medical professional had become one and the same; the emotional needs of children ranked on par with their physical needs; parents shaped the destiny of their offspring; and troublesome behavior was the norm."[116] Thus, the medicalization of delinquency, which began as a response to the persistent repeaters who appeared before the Chicago Juvenile Court during its first years of operation, ultimately contributed to millions of parents across the nation adopting a medical model as part of their everyday child-rearing practices.

[SIX]

*It appears that a fruitful program for the treatment and
prevention of delinquency and crime must necessarily
address itself to the community environment, the local social
world in which the delinquent and the criminal have their
genesis. The problem in realistic terms is one of achieving
a new organization of life in these local deteriorated
communities.*
—Ernest W. Burgess, Joseph D. Lohman, and Clifford
   R. Shaw, Chicago Area Project, 1934

Organizing the Community

Not only did the trail that William Healy blazed with his
pioneering research into the causes of juvenile delinquency
give birth to the child guidance movement but also his detailed life
histories of delinquents inspired sociologists to study the social
factors that contributed to juvenile offending. This sociological
research led to the discovery in the 1920s that certain areas of cities
had continuously high crime rates even though the ethnic and
racial composition of those areas had changed over time. On the
basis of these findings, Clifford Shaw, the director of the department of research sociology at the Institute for Juvenile Research,
launched the Chicago Area Project (CAP) in 1932. Shaw and his
associates sought to help local residents, including young people,
in these "natural areas" of high crime to establish their own delinquency prevention programs. During the Great Depression, the
efforts of this project, which stressed "the autonomy of the actual
residents of the neighborhood in planning and operating the
program," served as a model for later state and federal programs,
including key components of President Lyndon Johnson's Great
Society, and the more recent Communities That Care programs of
the 1990s.[1] At the same time that innovative community organizing programs flourished in Chicago, public concerns about
youth crime were on the rise. In this climate, the Illinois Supreme

Court stripped the juvenile court of its original jurisdiction in cases of children over ten years of age who were accused of committing criminal offenses. As a result, children could be prosecuted in either juvenile or criminal court. The 1930s thus witnessed both imaginative efforts to prevent juvenile delinquency at the local level as well as more punitive treatment of serious and violent juvenile offenders. Thus, a child growing up in a high-crime area in depression era Chicago might be able to participate in many community-run social programs but also faced the prospect of being tried as an adult if he or she committed a crime.

Community outreach programs had been a part of the juvenile court since its inception, beginning with the volunteer work of the Juvenile Court Committee, which had run the first detention home and paid the salaries of the court's first probation officers. In 1906 the committee invited Benjamin Lindsey, the popular judge of the Denver Juvenile Court, to deliver a luncheon lecture about his city's Juvenile Improvement Association. Lindsey praised the association's preventative work, which involved providing disadvantaged children with the opportunity to participate in structured recreational activities.[2] Judge Julian Mack and Chief Probation Officer Henry Thurston believed that a variation on this approach could be effective in Chicago and worked with the women of the JCC to establish a private organization based on the Denver model. By helping to develop an improvement association, the JCC reinvented itself at a critical moment in its history. With Cook County assuming responsibility for probation in 1905 and the detention home scheduled to open in 1907, the JCC appeared obsolete, and its leaders eagerly embarked on the new mission to prevent delinquency. In 1909, the committee changed its name to the Juvenile Protective Association (JPA) to reflect its reorientation and set up an office in Hull House.

The JPA's mission was to socialize neighborhoods, and its approach to delinquency prevention combined what the historian Paul Boyer has called "positive" and "negative" environmentalism.[3] The positive part of the program was similar to the work of the Denver association that focused on creating constructive alternatives to the temptations of urban commercial culture for children. The child savers believed that children should play together under responsible adult supervision in parks, playgrounds, and after-school programs. The JPA also used coercive or negative approaches to safeguard children. It sought to eradicate "neighborhood conditions which especially in the poorer districts lead to inevitable demoralization; to remove some of the temptations constantly put in their way, to stop 'can rushing' [children getting beer for workers for a tip] and cocaine selling, and to keep [children] out of the disreputable fruit stores and houses."[4] In addition, the JPA employed agents who did family casework, including investigating all the anonymous complaints filed with the juvenile court.

The JPA divided the city into districts, sent agents to map the uplifting as well as dangerous places in each district, and employed officers to patrol morally suspect sites like "disreputable cabarets and cafes." In addition, to expose the underlying conditions producing juvenile delinquency, the association conducted investigations of public dance halls, nickelodeons, and dime theaters, examined county jails, and assessed the pernicious effects of racial discrimination on African-American children.[5] The JPA put these findings to political use. In the 1910s it became an effective lobby for the expansion of a court-centered approach to social policing in Chicago. Under the leadership of Louise de Koven Bowen, the association successfully campaigned for the creation of a Boys' Court to hear the cases of "juvenile-adults" (i.e., boys who were above the upper age limit of the juvenile court, seventeen, but below the age of majority, twenty-one). They also succeeded in their efforts to establish a Morals Court to stamp out prostitution and a Court of Domestic Relations to discipline "home slackers" (i.e., fathers who did not support their families).[6]

By the mid-1920s, as faith in socialized law faded, some JPA staffers concluded that the association had also become old-fashioned and out of step with the Jazz Age. For example, Paul Cressey, a sociology graduate student at the University of Chicago who later wrote a notable book about taxi-dance halls (where men paid women a nickel or dime for a dance), spent the summer of

1925 working for the association.[7] He reported: "Speaking Sociologically, it may be said with truth that the chief function of the [JPA]—the appeal which it uses to get its funds—is to attempt to apply the mores of a small New England community to a great cosmopolitan city." He added: "Fundamentally, the [JPA] often finds itself fighting the very 'ecology' of the city. While very great efforts are being made by individual officers of the [JPA] to divorce themselves of any 'narrow' moral judgments—and this quite successfully I believe—it nevertheless finds itself in conflict constantly with relatively large groups of the city's population who do not even subscribe to the broad standards of the [JPA]." He stressed that "the metropolitan city is not a complex economic and ecological organization of people holding almost similar values. The mores of different groups differ profoundly and herein is the difficulty and also the 'raison d'etre' of the [JPA]. In some of its investigatory and coercive efforts it seems to be beating against a stone wall."[8] From his perspective, the JPA personnel, most of whom came "from the small towns of Illinois or Iowa," were unwelcome outsiders in the neighborhoods that they investigated, surveyed, and policed.

Cressey's use of the phrase "the ecology of the city" referred to the theory of urban growth that the Chicago School of Sociology, led by Robert Park and Ernest Burgess, popularized in the 1920s.[9] According to this theory, the expansion of a city disturbed its "metabolism," leaving some areas disorganized and without adequate social controls over their populations. In these transitional regions, where commercial and industrial development transformed residential life, social pathologies were rampant. As Park noted, "delinquency is, in fact, in some sense the measure of the failure of our community organizations to function."[10] Park and Burgess sent their graduate students into Chicago, which they considered to be a sociological laboratory, to investigate the "natural" processes of urban expansion, including their deleterious effects on city dwellers. "We need such studies," Park declared, "if for no other reason than to enable us to read the newspapers intelligently. The reason that the daily chronicle of the newspaper is so shocking, and at the same time so fascinating, to the average reader is because the average reader knows so little about the life of which the newspaper is the record."[11]

During the 1920s, through their studies of juvenile delinquency in urban areas, Clifford Shaw and Henry McKay became two of the most influential practitioners of this Chicago school mode of sociological investigation that blended qualitative data (e.g., life histories, interviews, and participant observation) with sophisticated quantitative analysis. Shaw hailed from Luray, Indiana, a small farming community, and after studying theology, which he thoroughly disliked, enlisted in the navy during World War I and completed his college education after its conclusion. In 1919 he moved into the "House of Happiness," a social settlement in an eastern European neighborhood in the inner city, and began his graduate studies at the University of Chicago. In the early 1920s, Shaw also worked part time as a juvenile parole officer for the Illinois State Training School for Boys at St. Charles, a reformatory for juvenile offenders, where he first encouraged boys to write autobiographies. He then served as a probation officer for the Chicago Juvenile Court from 1924 to 1926. He wrote:

> My activities in this position included the investigation
> of cases, preparation of petitions and other legal papers,
> home visits, presentation of cases in court, etc. This work
> was citywide and brought me into touch with the various
> agencies which offered services to children. My experience
> at the Cook County Court was valuable because it gave
> me contact with hundreds of delinquents and a familiarity
> with the details of court procedure.[12]

In 1926, on the recommendation of Ernest Burgess, Shaw was hired as the first director of the newly established department of research sociology at the Institute for Juvenile Research. Child savers, including Jane Addams, Ethel Sturges Dummer, and Herman Adler, had raised nearly $300,000 to establish the Behavior Research Fund that supported studies of children, including Shaw's investigations into the social causes of delinquency.[13] In 1927, McKay joined Shaw's staff as a clerical research assistant.

McKay, who, was from Orient, South Dakota, had also grown up on a farm and moved to Chicago to study urban sociology. McKay's quantitative skills complemented Shaw's ability to work directly with juvenile delinquents. Whereas Shaw befriended juvenile delinquents and encouraged them to write autobiographies, "McKay was the quiet statistician, a man who stayed removed at the Institute and plotted the maps, calculated the rates, ran the correlations and described the findings which located empirically and depicted cartographically the distribution of crime and delinquency in Chicago."[14] Shaw and McKay became the nation's leading experts on the social factors producing juvenile delinquency; in 1931, they coauthored the report on this subject for President Herbert Hoover's National Commission on Law Observance and Enforcement (popularly known as the Wickersham Commission and best known for its investigation of Prohibition). They asserted that "juvenile delinquency" was "traditional behavior in the disorganized areas of the city," that it was "group behavior," and that a continuing culture of juvenile offending in disorganized areas was "transmitted through personal and group contacts."[15] Accordingly, they argued that "a delinquent career is the product of a natural process of development" and "from this standpoint, a delinquent or criminal act is a part of a dynamic life process and should be considered as such in the analysis and treatment of cases."[16]

The life histories that Shaw compiled, including *The Jack-Roller: A Delinquent Boy's Own Story* (1930), *The Natural History of a Delinquent Career* (1931), and *Brothers in Crime* (1938), revealed how children in these disorganized areas became delinquents and suggested pathways to desistance.[17] As Ernest Burgess explained, Shaw used a delinquent's "own story" in order to enable himself to see the boy's life "as the boy conceived it rather than as an adult might imagine it."[18] In *The Jack-Roller*, Shaw famously used this method to create empathy for Stanley, a Polish-American boy from the rough "Back of the Yards" district. Shaw described this part of Chicago as "one of the grimiest and most unattractive neighborhoods in the city, being almost completely surrounded by packing plants, stock yards, railroads, factories, and waste lands."[19] Stanley spent much of his young life on these mean streets and in juvenile institutions before being committed shortly before his seventeenth birthday on the charge of "jack-rolling" to the Chicago House of Corrections, an adult facility, for one year. Stanley, who had begun running away from home when he was only six and half and started shoplifting at eight, had become a violent adolescent offender. Jack-rollers like Stanley worked in pairs or small groups in Chicago's rooming-house district on West Madison Street, where they preyed on intoxicated men and homosexuals. They assaulted and robbed their victims in deserted alleyways, abandoned buildings, and cheap hotels.

As Shaw explained in *The Jack-Roller*, when William Healy was the director of the Juvenile Psychopathic Institute he had thoroughly examined Stanley shortly before his eighth birthday. Healy had reported: "The home conditions in this case are very bad. Father heavy drinker. Boy poorly nourished and neglected. Dislikes step-mother. Says she beats him and sends him out to steal. Boy very unhappy at home. Wants to live in Detention Home. Should be placed in congenial foster home. Not likely to be any improvement if he remains in his own home." Unfortunately, as Shaw pointed out, "Healy's recommendation to place Stanley in a foster-home was not followed, and his career in delinquency continued."[20]

Stanley's own story, which Shaw verified and commented on, comprised the bulk of *The Jack-Roller*. Stanley's observations, reinforced by Shaw's commentary and a final discussion by Burgess, stressed that correctional institutions failed to rehabilitate children and instead only made them more antisocial by advancing their educations in crime as well as exposing them to sexual abuse by older inmates. The book also revealed how difficult it was for Stanley to change. He kept drifting back to his old haunts and criminal ways. Yet Stanley did ultimately settle down. After Shaw befriended him, found him lodgings in a middle-class neighborhood, encouraged him to go to night school, and eventually landed him a job he liked as a salesman, Stanley married and became a productive and law-abiding citizen. Stanley reported:

"Salesmanship is hard work, but I've learned to like it. It pays well and it puts a fellow on his mettle. You have to know how to meet different types of people in an easy and diplomatic way. I get a great kick out of putting over a deal on a customer, especially a stubborn customer." He added, "I have not gone over to the stock yards for almost two years. I want to forget the people over there. I am very glad that I escaped from that life, but feel sorry for the children who live there and have to go through the misery and hardship which were mine." Shaw concluded that Stanley "has developed interests and a philosophy of life which are in keeping with the standards of conventional society." These changes had grown out of his "participation in the life of conventional social groups."[21]

In his discussion of Stanley's successful treatment, Burgess highlighted that the young man's surroundings, rather than his personality, had changed. The significance of Shaw's work, according to Burgess, was that he "pays attention to the powerful factors of group and neighborhood influence." Whereas Healy had recommended that Stanley needed a new environment, Shaw helped him to establish one. At the turning point in Stanley's life, Burgess emphasized, "the decisive influence in this time of indecision was undoubtedly the continued contact with Mr. Shaw, the daily influence of his landlady, and the new associations he was forming at work and at night school."[22] Helping individuals like Stanley to escape from high-crime areas did not completely satisfy Shaw; he also wanted to help the residents of these areas organize their own communities.

McKay, "the quiet statistician," was also passionate about delinquency prevention but pursued his research in a more scholarly fashion. He was driven to provide a definitive empirical answer to the explosive "race" question: Were some nationalities and races criminally disposed? In Chicago, race relations had worsened after the bloody race riot of 1919. Nearly five days of rioting, in which youth gangs had played a major role, left 38 people dead and 537 persons injured and focused the nation's attention on "the problem of the relations between the white and the Negro races."[23] In the aftermath of the riot, the Union League

Club, an influential progressive organization, urged Governor Frank Lowden to establish a biracial commission to study the riot and race relations in the nation's second largest city. Robert Park, who had worked as Booker T. Washington's secretary for seven years and later served as the first president of the Chicago Urban League, helped to organize the research and writing of the report of the Chicago Commission on Race Relations, *The Negro in Chicago* (1922). On Park's recommendation, Charles Johnson, an African-American graduate student in the sociology department at the University of Chicago, served as associate executive secretary and directed the massive research project.

The report documented disturbing findings about white perceptions of "Negro criminality" and concluded: "There is, for example, no section of the country in which it is not generally believed by whites that Negroes are instinctively criminal in inclination."[24] The report added: "How, indeed, may the belief be avoided? Crime figures on Negroes are consistently unfavorable to any other conclusion." The commission's researchers, however, did not accept these statistics "without question" and instead investigated the operations of Chicago's justice systems. They found systematic racial basis.

> From the records and from the testimony of judges, in the juvenile, municipal, circuit, superior, and criminal courts, of police officials, the state's attorney, and various experts on crime, probation, and parole that Negroes are more commonly arrested, subjected to police identification, and convicted than white offenders; that on similar evidence they are generally held and convicted on more serious charges, and that they are given longer sentences.

Moreover, the report pointed out: "This bias, when reflected in the figures, serves to bolster by false figures the already existing belief that Negroes are more likely to be criminal than other racial groups."[25] The commission recommended that whites become more educated about Negroes.[26]

Beginning in 1920s, Shaw and McKay helped to discredit the idea that certain nationalities or races, including African

Americans, were inherently criminal. Through their ecological analysis of crime patterns in Chicago, Philadelphia, Richmond, Cleveland, Birmingham, Denver, and Seattle, they established the empirical basis for their landmark discovery that place, not race, produced high crime rates. As they explained in their report to the Wickersham Commission,

> when the Germans, Irish and other immigrant groups lived in the areas of high rates of delinquents they constituted a large proportion of the population of the juvenile court. As they moved out of these areas of high rates into areas of second and third immigrant settlements their children disappeared from the juvenile court at a rate far greater than the decrease in these nationalities in the total population of the city. They were supplanted in the juvenile court population by the Italians, Polish, Negroes, and other groups, all of whom moved into these areas of high rates of delinquents.[27]

They concluded that delinquency was due to the ecology of the city, not the nationality or race of its residents. And, as they later wrote in their influential textbook *Juvenile Delinquency and Urban Areas* (1942),

> it is difficult to sustain the contention that, by themselves, the factors of race, nativity, and nationality are vitally related to the problem of juvenile delinquency. It seems necessary to conclude, rather, that the significantly higher rates of delinquents found among the children of Negroes, the foreign born, and more recent immigrants are closely related to existing differences in their respective patterns of geographic distribution within the city.[28]

Shaw was especially gifted at communicating to disadvantaged youth how this important sociological finding about place related to them. For example, Anthony Sorrentino, who became the administrative director of the CAP after Shaw's death in 1957 and then the first executive director of the Illinois Commission on Delinquency Prevention in 1976, credited Shaw with inspiring self-confidence in him and his friends in the early 1930s.[29] These young men felt that they were being discriminated against in their quest to find decent jobs in Chicago's business district because they were Italian immigrants and lived in the infamous "Bloody" Twentieth Ward on the Near West Side (where the gangster Al Capone had his headquarters during Prohibition). In 1933, when Sorrentino was twenty years old, he and his friends heard Shaw speak at Hull House. Sorrentino recalled: "Essentially what he did was tell us that the problem of delinquency in this community was not a problem unique or prevalent only among Italian-Americans but the same area had high rates of delinquency when it was Norwegian, Northern European groups, and as ethnic and racial groups moved out of these areas the rates of delinquency decreased as they improved their socio-economic circumstances." He added: "So we were fascinated by Shaw's story but not only by these sociological ideas which he presented in a very charming way. He was a man of charisma. He was a kind and gentle person. We were especially impressed by how he viewed the delinquent as a human being."[30]

Shaw envisioned that CAP, through grants and training programs, could assist young men like Sorrentino to reorganize their own communities. Although there were some parallels between the content of the recreational and educational programs sponsored by CAP, settlement houses, religious organizations, and the JPA, Shaw and his associates pursued a fundamentally different method. They placed "great emphasis upon the training and utilization of neighborhood leaders" in contrast to depending primarily on "professionally trained leaders recruited from sources outside of the local neighborhood."[31] The project supported "indigenous" organizations like the West Side Community Committee, which Sorrentino and his friends helped to establish and incorporate in 1939. "The idea underlying our organization was a radical departure from traditional agency work," Sorrentino said. "In going to some of these local institutions we said, 'We, the young men of the community, would like to come in here and meet you and your staff to discuss the problems of our children and of the community. We would like to know what your institution is attempting to do in this regard; then we would like to suggest how we might cooperate with you in dealing with these problems.' "[32] Although the initial reactions to such visits were mixed, the committee eventually established good working relationships with most of these social agencies and became a clearinghouse for neighborhood residents seeking "aid and advice" about school placements, court appearances, employment opportunities, and social services.[33]

The West Side Community Committee worked especially closely with the public schools to help the principals and teachers get to know the neighborhood residents and the community conditions. The principal of Andrew Jackson Elementary School was shocked to recognize the "faces of men who had been rowdy, mischievous, and incorrigible boys—boys who had raided the school and done unmentionable things [including defecating on a teacher's desk]." The same boys were now responsible community leaders. The principal worked with them to improve the school facilities, and together they encouraged mothers in the neighborhood to start a Parent Teacher Association.[34] The committee also succeeded in having two of their members, who were former juvenile delinquents, appointed truant officers. These young men helped to bridge cultural differences between the teachers, the administrators, and the children and their families.

The West Side Community Committee also worked with the police and the juvenile court. "We were in and out of the police station regularly," Sorrentino recalled, "meeting with the juvenile police officer to talk over problems of children who were in trouble or to discuss community conditions related to these problems."[35] They also appeared with children during court dates, recruited adults to mentor them, found them jobs, and, most important, befriended and spent time with them. As a result of the committee's efforts, judges allowed more children to remain in the community under supervision. The committee thus worked as a diversionary program that helped to keep juvenile offenders out of correctional institutions. The committee members also worked with incarcerated young men. By working with a young man in jail or prison, the committee could "keep up a continuing relationship so that when he is released we can work with him, his family, the parole agency, and other persons who are interested in his welfare."[36] They believed that since the offender was "a product of the influence of his family and community," it was "the community's responsibility to welcome him back to the neighborhood upon his release from an institution and try to incorporate him into the conventional life of the community."[37] Although their efforts did not always succeed, Sorrentino explained: "As for our failures, this is our guiding rule: Never give up with the offender. One never knows when there will be a turning point. During periods of outward failure, subtle influences may be at work in ways we cannot understand at the time. Some former delinquents and adult ex-offenders who eventually became productive citizens have come to me and expressed their appreciation for how they felt we helped them."[38]

The growing concerns about crime, including youth violence, that prompted sociologists to study its social causes, and young men to organize their communities, also paved the way for more punitive treatment of juvenile offenders in Illinois. By 1930 most states had raised the maximum age of jurisdiction of their juvenile courts to eighteen, and Arkansas, California, Colorado, Iowa, and Wyoming raised theirs to twenty-one. At the same time state legislatures raised jurisdictional age limits they also began to exclude serious offenses, generally murder and other crimes punishable by death or life imprisonment, from the jurisdiction of their juvenile courts. Illinois did not follow this pattern. Rather than exclude specific offenses, it continued to rely on its informal system of concurrent jurisdiction, under which the state's attorney prosecuted some cases of children over the state's age of criminal responsibility, while the juvenile court heard almost all children's cases, including those involving serious and violent offenders. Beginning in the 1920s, the state's attorney disregarded this "gentleman's agreement" between his office and the juvenile court.[39] The breakdown of this agreement meant that the state prosecuted more juveniles as adults. It also set the stage for the Illinois Supreme Court to hear a series of cases—*People v. Fitzgerald* (322 Ill. 54 [1926]), *People v. Bruno*

(346 Ill. 449 [1931]), and *People v. Lattimore* (362 Ill. 206 [1935])—
that determined the extent of the juvenile court's jurisdiction.

These cases differed significantly from the ones the Illinois
Supreme Court had used to make the state into a parent. Those
earlier cases had involved prepubescent, dependent children. In
contrast, these three cases from the 1920s and 1930s involved
adolescents who had been convicted by criminal courts of committing violent crimes. Sixteen-year-old Richard Fitzgerald was
convicted of rape and sentenced to twenty years at the Illinois
State Reformatory at Pontiac; sixteen-year-old Tony Bruno was
convicted of armed robbery and sentenced to Pontiac for a term
of one year to life; and fifteen-year-old Susie Lattimore was
convicted of first-degree murder and sentenced to twenty-five
years at the Illinois State Reformatory for Women at Dwight.
Their cases not only raised technical questions about jurisdiction
but also ultimately led the justices to consider whether the Illinois
General Assembly had either the authority under the state's
constitution or the intention in 1899 to grant the juvenile court
original jurisdiction over all children's cases.

In *Fitzgerald*, the Illinois Supreme Court focused on sixteen-
year-old Richard's crime, not his age or legal status as a minor.
The court's opinion recounted how Richard and a friend had
abducted a twenty-one-year-old woman at gunpoint and then
raped her. In his appeal, Richard claimed that his confession had
been coerced and that the assistant state's attorney had prejudiced the jury against him. The prosecutor, in his closing re-
marks, had brought up another case in which a rapist was also
named Richard Fitzgerald and compared the defendant to Nathan
Leopold and Richard Loeb. Although the justices acknowledged
that there were "objectionable statements made by the assistant
state's attorney in his closing argument," they did not think that
these statements prejudiced the jury. In addition, they noted
that in this case there were "no extenuating circumstances, unless
it be [Fitzgerald's] age, which, no doubt, was taken into consideration by the jury in passing on the case."[40] Turning to the
critical question of which court system had jurisdiction over this
case, the court declared: "The criminal court and juvenile court

have concurrent jurisdiction over persons charged with a criminal offense who are below the age of seventeen years." There were only two exceptions to this rule. First, children under ten could not be tried in adult court because "the criminal code fixes the age below which there is a want of criminal capacity at ten years." Second, if the juvenile court had already declared a child delinquent, then "consent of the juvenile court *must* be obtained before the delinquent child can be prosecuted for a criminal offense in any other court."[41] Since the juvenile court had not declared Richard to be a delinquent child, the criminal court in this case did not need to seek its consent to try him.

Five years later, in 1931 the high court decided *Bruno*, a case that appeared to fall clearly under the *Fitzgerald* consent rule. Tony Bruno had filed for a writ of *coram nobis* ("in our presence")—a common law writ that asked a criminal court to vacate its own judgment in a case because the defendant had not presented a valid defense due to "duress or fraud or excusable mistake."[42] Traditionally, minors had applied for this writ in cases in which their guardians had not properly represented them. Without proper representation, courts had considered errors made by a minor to be excusable and grounds for vacating a conviction. Bruno's attorney argued that Tony had failed to raise two critical issues during his trial. First, he had not provided evidence to prove that he was in another part of the city at the time when the armed robbery was committed. His attorney argued that Tony "is immature in years" and "that on account of such immaturity he failed to appreciate and present this affirmative defense to the charges against him."[43] Second, in 1927 the juvenile court had declared Tony to be a delinquent child and committed him to the St. Charles School for Boys. The court had retained jurisdiction over Tony "for the purpose of making such further or other orders herein for the welfare of said child as may from time to time be found to be in accordance with equity and in accordance with the statute in such case made and provided."[44] Although the reformatory had released Tony, the juvenile court's decree was still in effect, and he remained under its jurisdiction at the time of his criminal trial in 1931. According to *Fitzgerald*, the juvenile court had to consent before one of its wards could be prosecuted in criminal court, but the juvenile court had not done so in this case.

The criminal court rejected Tony Bruno's application for the writ of *coram nobis*. Although the Illinois Supreme Court pointed out that Illinois had abolished this common law writ, the justices noted that its provisions had been incorporated into "section 89 of the Practice Act" and decided the case under the act's guidelines. The justices did not accept the argument that Tony's immaturity had impaired his judgment. Instead, they declared that Tony's own "negligence," not his immaturity, accounted for his failure to present to the criminal court either his alibi or status as a ward of the juvenile court. Since these errors were his own, Tony could not petition for relief. Thus, both the criminal and Illinois Supreme Court considered Tony's age to be irrelevant and, in effect, held the sixteen-year-old responsible for allowing a court without jurisdiction to sentence him to prison, possibly for the remainder of his life, for a crime that he may not have committed.

In the case of Susie Lattimore, the Illinois Supreme Court reevaluated the consent rule that it had sidestepped in *Bruno*. On February 23, 1935, Susie, a ward of the juvenile court, had fatally stabbed another girl during a fight in a tavern.[45] She was arrested and taken to juvenile court, and a psychologist from the Institute for Juvenile Research examined her. The psychologist determined that the African-American girl was a "high grade mental defective" with a mental age of only ten years and one month. Based on this finding, the institute recommended that the juvenile court have her committed to Dixon State Hospital for psychiatric treatment.[46] Instead, Frank Biecek, who had become the presiding judge of the juvenile court after Mary Bartelme's retirement in 1933, transferred Susie to the criminal court. After being indicted, Lattimore appeared on April 15 before Chief Justice Denis Sullivan of the Cook County Criminal Court, pled "not guilty," and waived her right to a jury trial.

Lattimore could not have ended up before a more hostile judge than Sullivan. At the time of her trial, Sullivan was leading a campaign to restrict the juvenile court's jurisdiction. He had drafted a series of proposed amendments to the Juvenile Court Act to limit the juvenile court to hearing only the cases of children charged with misdemeanors or incorrigibility. During the same week that Sullivan heard the testimony in Lattimore's case, the *Chicago Tribune* reported on his drafting of this proposed legislation. As Sullivan explained, "the outdated Juvenile Court Act permits highly dangerous gunmen and thieves, or even murderers to be accorded leniency intended only for bad boys and bad girls who have committed no serious crime and who are not habitual criminals. The act is clearly in conflict with the legal rights of the Criminal Court."[47] Given this statement, it is not surprising that Sullivan dismissed the public defender's motion to transfer Lattimore's case back to juvenile court. He found her guilty of first-degree murder and sentenced her to twenty-five years in prison. The public defender appealed to the Illinois Supreme Court.

In the meantime, children's advocates and organizations, including the JPA, worked to defeat Sullivan's proposed amendments. Although they successfully stopped this legislative attempt to rewrite the state's Juvenile Court Act, they could not prevent the Illinois Supreme Court from using *Lattimore* to reinterpret its meaning. In a suspicious move, the state's attorney had provided the court with an incomplete record of Lattimore's trial. This partial record allowed the justices to act as if the juvenile court had not consented to Susie's prosecution as an adult. As the Illinois Supreme Court said, "the sole question presented here for decision is whether the defendant, a ward of the juvenile court, who had been indicted for murder, can on such indictment be tried in the criminal court without the consent of the juvenile court."[48] The justices determined that the juvenile court may transfer cases to the criminal court but could not prevent the criminal court from prosecuting wards of the juvenile court. Constitutional interpretation and a misreading of history served as the basis of this finding. The justices explained that the Illinois Constitution of 1870 granted criminal courts their jurisdiction, including the authority to try children over the age of criminal responsibility.

The legislature thus could not invest an inferior court, such as the juvenile court that was only a statutory creation, with the power to block a constitutionally sanctioned court from hearing a case. Yet the justices did not end the opinion with the assertion that the legislature lacked the authority to grant the juvenile court exclusive jurisdiction over children's case. Instead, they stressed that it was inconceivable that the legislature had intended to give the juvenile court such power. Otherwise, the legislature would have made the juvenile court "into a haven of refuge where a delinquent child of the age recognized by the law as capable of committing a crime should be immune for punishment for violation of the criminal laws of the State."[49] This argument about legislative "intent" reflected concerns about youth violence in the 1930s, not the original intent or spirit of the founders of the juvenile court. These progressive reformers had believed that the juvenile court should have original, if not exclusive, jurisdiction over all children's cases. The high court's misreading of history helped the justices to legitimate a system of concurrent jurisdiction in Illinois, in which the state's attorney could prosecute any child over ten years of age. As the sociologist Benedict Alper pointed out, the Illinois Supreme Court had "completely reversed itself on the basic philosophy of the juvenile court act."[50]

Ominously, on the same day that the Illinois Supreme Court issued *Lattimore*, it also announced its decision in *People v. Malec* (362 Ill. 229 [1935]). Chester Malec, who was sixteen and a ward of the juvenile court, had been convicted in criminal court of larceny for stealing an automobile. He was initially committed to the Illinois State Penitentiary at Joliet, an adult facility, but then was transferred to the state reformatory at Pontiac, whose inmates ranged in age from sixteen to twenty-six. He filed for a writ of habeas corpus, contending that the criminal court had failed to receive the consent of the juvenile court and thus did not have the jurisdiction to try him. The justice reasserted their finding in *Lattimore* "that the legislature is without authority to abridge the jurisdiction of the criminal court of Cook County" and "that the legislature did not intend that the juvenile court should be able to bar the prosecution of a delinquent child old enough, in the eyes of the law, to commit a crime."[51] The court also used Chester Malec's case to overturn explicitly the *Fitzgerald* consent rule by declaring that "some of its language is not in harmony with our later decisions." The justices rejected Chester's petition for the writ of habeas corpus and used his larceny case to reinforce their judicially constructed system of concurrent jurisdiction. That system remained in place in Illinois until 1965.

It was in the troubling climate of the 1930s that advocates of juvenile justice turned to judicial waiver (i.e., a juvenile court judge transferring a child's case to criminal court) as a defense against the charge that the juvenile court was soft on crime. In the *Illinois Bar Journal*, for example, John Dickinson responded to *Lattimore* and *Malec* with a classic defense of judicial waiver. He argued that the juvenile justice system would not become a "veritable haven of refuge" for dangerous offenders because juvenile court judges were capable of exercising the necessary discretion to transfer appropriate cases to the criminal court.[52] "It would seem," he added, "that the benefits to be gained from having first offenders of low age dealt with apart from the criminal courts would outweigh the rarely possible exercise of poor judgment by a juvenile court judge in not turning over to the criminal courts an offender."[53] Apparently, the state's attorney agreed with Dickinson. His office prosecuted only the most serious crimes by adolescent offenders.[54]

Despite frustrations over decisions like *Lattimore* and *Malec*, children's advocates had at least made a strong case for the selective use of judicial waiver as the best way to protect both children and society. This frank acknowledgment of transfer, however, suggested that these advocates accepted the existence of a class of children who were not amenable to reform within the juvenile justice system. Thus, in a society increasingly concerned about youth violence, the threat to public safety served as the justification for transferring children out of juvenile court.

During the Great Depression, children's advocates had also accepted that the juvenile court by itself could not prevent crime. As Judge Charles Hoffman observed, "the juvenile court may not be able to stop the constant flow of delinquency and crime but it can in any event fulfill its primary mission which is that of standing like the walls of a fortress between a child and the cruel and medieval methods of the criminal courts incident to the trials of children."[55] He added: "Let us trust that civilization and culture will reach greater heights in the days to come, and that in spite of economic and social depression the time is not far distant when an enlightened people will not permit either a dependent or delinquent to be lost."[56] In Chicago, residents of some of the city's highest crime areas had already begun this new form of child saving.

Leaders of the community organizing movement, such as Clifford Shaw and Anthony Sorrentino, considered their efforts to be a continuation of the work begun by the progressive child savers. In defending CAP's use of local residents instead of trained professionals, Shaw explicitly linked his work to these pioneers in child welfare, noting that the greatest compliment he had ever received was from Jane Addams. She had said that if social settlements had succeeded in Americanizing immigrants, then Shaw's work was the next logical step in social welfare.[57] Sorrentino also described community organization as part of the evolution of juvenile justice. This process, he explained, began with the establishment of a juvenile court, continued with the opening of a psychopathic clinic, and then spread into local neighborhoods.[58]

The significance of CAP rests not only in its ideology of community mobilization but also in its historical timing and legacy. The radical organizer and theorist Saul Alinsky, for example, began his career by working for Shaw in the 1930s. His assignments included collecting life histories that he and Shaw planned to use to cowrite a book. In 1940, however, Alinsky left to establish his own community organization, the Industrial Areas Foundation. He later explained: "As a kid was telling me of an A & P store he robbed and another of a gas station he heisted, Hitler and Mussolini were robbing whole countries and killing whole peoples. I found it difficult to listen to small-time confessions."[59] Alinsky instead put his efforts into antifascist activities and labor organization. Although he was absolutely right to worry about the dangers of fascism, even during times of national and international crisis there still have to be responsible adults willing to commit their time and energy to help troubled young people, such as Stanley, find pathways to productive lives. The fact that Shaw and his associates launched and continued to operate innovative delinquency prevention programs during such disquieting times was remarkable. It is also inspiring.

The spirit of CAP also still guides the development and implementation of the most effective community-based prevention programs in this country and abroad, including the acclaimed Communities That Care program, which uses a risk-focused prevention strategy developed by David Hawkins and Richard Catalano.[60] During the 1990s the U.S. Office of Juvenile Justice and Delinquency Prevention (OJJDP) adopted this approach as part of its Comprehensive Strategy for Serious, Violent, and Chronic Juvenile Offenders. And as David P. Farrington and Rolf Loeber, who chaired the OJJDP study group that examined serious and violent juvenile (SVJ) offending, have concluded,

> several programs are effective in preventing SVJ offending, including home visiting/parent education programs, preschool intellectual enrichment programs, child skills training, parent management training, multisystemic therapy, and increased police patrolling of "hot spots" of crime. Cost-benefit analyses show that the monetary benefits of these programs outweigh their monetary costs. Programs offered to everyone living in high-crime areas, such as Communities That Care, are likely to be most effective.[61]

Although such programs strive to prevent delinquency and keep children out of court, it is worth remembering that these programs, much like mothers' pensions and child guidance before them, grew out of the juvenile court's experiential development.

Prevention, individualized treatment, rehabilitation, the
bywords of the juvenile justice system, are the best we have
to offer.
—*Judge Eugene A. Moore, January 13, 2000*

Conclusion

U sing his sentencing of Nathaniel Abraham to revisit the
history and theory of juvenile justice, Judge Moore drew on
the accumulated wisdom of child savers, such as John P. Altgeld,
Lucy Flower, Julia Lathrop, Jane Addams, Richard Tuthill, Ethel
Sturges Dummer, William Healy, Clifford Shaw, and Anthony
Sorrentino. By doing so, Judge Moore took a sensational case that
seemed to epitomize the unique problems of youth violence in
the 1990s and placed it squarely within the history and traditions
of American juvenile justice. Engaging the past helped Judge
Moore to escape from the constraints of the late-twentieth-
century crime complex that so limited sound considerations of
juvenile justice policy in the 1990s. Sounding like a Gilded Age
reformer, he criticized the impact of imprisonment: "To sentence
juveniles to adult prison is ignoring the possibility that we are
creating a more dangerous criminal by housing juveniles with
hardened adults."[1] Echoing the sentiments of a Progressive Era
child saver, he lamented a lost sense of "social responsibility" and
called for investigations into the "causes of juvenile crime" in
which "the question should be debated and analyzed by everyone
interested in helping children and reducing crime."[2] Finally, the
solution he offered was reminiscent of the Chicago Area Project.
Juvenile delinquency, he declared, "is a community problem with

community solutions. No court system, in isolation, can solve this problem. Only when the community comes together and recognizes the problems and factors which contribute to crime will we be able to tackle the problem."[3] Yet, as Judge Moore lamented, the Michigan legislature had opted not to focus on prevention and rehabilitation but rather passed punitive laws that treated "juveniles more like adults." As a result, he had to sentence Nathaniel under a "fundamentally flawed" law and urged "the legislature to lean toward improving the resources and programs within the juvenile justice system rather than diverting more youth into an already failed adult system."[4]

In reviewing his three options in the case at hand (i.e., sentence only as an adult; sentence as a juvenile; or use a blended sentence) Judge Moore began with the question "Should Nathaniel be sentenced today as an adult?" His answer was unequivocal. "If we say 'yes,' even for this heinous crime, we have given up on the juvenile justice system." He asked: "Can we be certain that between now and the time he turns 21 that we can't change his behavior? Must we say today that Nathaniel, at age 13, must be put into an adult prison system? No, the testimony and/or reports are clear that the adult prison system is not designed for youth. It is only a last resort, if the juvenile system has failed." He added: "Testimony and the psychological examination demonstrate that in the last two years, while awaiting trial, Nathaniel has made progress in the juvenile system. It is also clear that the adult system has very few treatment alternatives for a 13-year-old. In addition, Nathaniel may be subject to brutalization in prison that could destroy any hope of rehabilitation."[5] Thus, Judge Moore was not willing to discard either the juvenile court or abandon a child who had done "probably the worst thing any one can do and that is to kill another human being."[6]

Given the judge's concerns about predicting Nathaniel's future, imposing a blended sentence seemed like the logical choice. Why not delay the final decision about Nathaniel's fate for eight years? By then Nathaniel would be older, and the judge could evaluate his progress in a juvenile correctional center in order to determine whether he had been rehabilitated and no longer posed a threat to public safety. If not, the judge could impose the adult sentence and Nathaniel would be transferred to an adult prison. Yet, in a move that stunned court watchers, Judge Moore rejected this option, for "if we were to impose a delayed sentence, we take everyone off the hook."[7] Instead, he sentenced Nathaniel only as a juvenile, and ensured that he would be back in the community by his twenty-first birthday, even though he might not be rehabilitated and "may kill again."[8]

Judge Moore explained that his decision to keep Nathaniel solely in the juvenile justice system would force the community to make the rehabilitation of juvenile offenders a priority. "If we are committed to preventing future criminal behavior," he stated, "we will use our collective efforts and financial resources to rehabilitate him and all the other at-risk youth in our community." He further noted: "The safety net of a delayed sentence removes too much of the urgency. We can't continue to see incarceration as a long-term solution. The danger is that we won't take rehabilitation seriously if we know we can utilize prison in the future."[9] He emphasized that "the juvenile justice system has a *much higher rate of success* than the adult correctional system" and that in the long run it was better for society to keep most juveniles offenders in this system instead of committing them to adult prisons.[10]

Judge Moore directed his concluding words to Nathaniel Abraham. He said:

> We as a community have failed you, but you have also
> failed us and yourself. I will be keeping a very close eye
> on you and your progress. When you are able to fully
> understand what I am telling you, I urge you to take
> advantage of the help we are trying to give you. The only
> thing you can do to begin to repair the damage you have
> caused to the Greene family is succeed. Don't let
> Mr. Greene's death be in vain. Help us help you and in
> turn help many other children in this community. No
> one can do it for you. You must do it for yourself.[11]

Nathaniel Abraham, who had initially faced the prospect of life imprisonment without parole when his trial began, had been given a second chance, as the judge noted, to "grow as a person and develop the potential that all children possess."[12] It was unclear, however, how much of Judge Moore's decision Nathaniel could understand. The boy, who fidgeted and doodled during the judge's twenty-minute speech, turned to his attorney, Daniel Bagdade, after the judge had concluded, and asked, "What happened?" When Bagdade told him that he was going to a juvenile facility instead of an adult prison, the boy "just sort of looked down and shrugged his shoulders."[13]

Reactions to Judge Moore's decision were swift as well as mixed. Eliana Drakopoulos, a spokesperson for Amnesty International, which had used Nathaniel's picture as the cover of its report entitled "Betraying the Young: Human Rights Violations against Children in the US Justice System," declared: "This is a victory for human rights and, hopefully, a small step forward in the way the United States treats its children in the juvenile justice system." The Reverend Al Sharpton, who was present at the sentencing to show his support for Nathaniel, announced: "The judge said some strong and compassionate things. He convicted the system but he incarcerated Nathaniel. We do not believe Nathaniel is guilty of murder." Nicole Greene, sister of the victim, decried the verdict: "My brother did not deserve to be gunned down like a dog in the street. . . . A lot of people have forgotten who the real victim is—and it's Ronnie Greene Jr." Neither the defense attorneys nor the prosecutors were pleased with the judge's decision. Geoffrey Fieger continued to insist that Nathaniel was innocent and vowed to seek a new trial: "The fact of the matter is that Nathaniel isn't guilty of murder. He's a child playing with a gun."[14] The Oakland County assistant prosecutor, Lisa Halushka, who had asked for a blended sentence, said: "I'm disappointed. Disappointed and hopeful. I'm hopeful the judge is right and eight years can rehabilitate him."[15]

In the years since his sentencing, Nathaniel seems to be coming to terms with his killing of Ronnie Greene Jr. It has been a difficult process. In August 2002, Judge Moore told the sixteen-year-old Nathaniel that he was disappointed in him for focusing on being released instead of working to improve himself. As a result, he told Nathaniel that he would not be released early and would remain incarcerated until he turned twenty-one. Three months later, at another hearing before Judge Moore, Nathaniel appeared to be growing up. His counselors "reported significant progress in his schoolwork and therapy," and Nathaniel told the packed courtroom: "I took to heart the words you were saying— that you were disappointed in me. I was thinking within myself, I made my situation better. I'm doing what I need to do to better myself, to be more empathetic and more responsible." He added: "I haven't forgotten who the victim was, which was something I needed to address. Nobody else is a victim here except Ronnie Green." Although Greene's family did not attend the hearing, his sister said: "At some point you want to believe him. I hope that everyone who heard him is as hopeful as we are that he can make a change." And Judge Moore announced: "This is a much better day than the last one."[16] Whether Nathaniel Abraham will become a productive citizen remains to be seen, but at least the juvenile justice system has kept this hope alive.

In retrospect, what was so astonishing about Judge Moore's opinion was the perception that it was an astonishing decision. Viewed historically, this opinion fit perfectly into the long tradition of juvenile justice discourse that has seen debates periodically erupt over which young people belonged in this separate system. The contradictions between this interpretation and that of the sound-bite history of juvenile justice reveal the depth of misunderstanding concerning the court and its beginnings. According to this mythic history, an earlier world in which children committed heinous crimes and/or had their cases heard in juvenile court never existed. This misconception not only distorts the beginnings of juvenile justice but also exaggerates contrasts between then and now.

The first generation of child savers, who worked so hard to distinguish the juvenile court from the criminal court, began this process of myth-making. Through their reminiscences, they highlighted their own humanitarian motivations in establishing the juvenile court and presented a caricature of the institution. For example, as Jane Addams famously observed,

> there was almost a change in *mores* when the Juvenile Court was established. The child was brought before the judge with no one to prosecute him and with no one to defend him—the judge and all concerned were merely trying to find out what could be done on his behalf. The element of conflict was absolutely eliminated and with it, all notion of punishment as such with its curiously belated connotation.[17]

The idealized juvenile court that Addams and other leaders in the juvenile court movement spoke about so glowingly never actually existed, nor could have. For any court system that mixed children of widely ranging ages, circumstances, and offenses was bound to handle more than its share of hard cases. Controversy came with the territory, and it helped to spur innovations in juvenile justice.

Scholars of juvenile justice, such as Anthony Platt, Steven Schlossman, David Rothman, Mary Odem, Victoria Getis, and Anne Meis Knupfer, have all effectively critiqued the benevolent rhetoric of progressive child savers, including pointing out that they often worked from troubling assumptions about race, class, gender, and sexuality. Yet these scholars have not adequately reconstructed the actual workings of juvenile courts in the early twentieth century. The absence of a comprehensive institutional history of the juvenile court has had significant ramifications. Contemporary critics of juvenile justice, such as the law professor Barry Feld, have had little choice but to rely on these studies that have characterized the early juvenile court in static terms and downplayed its role in the development of social policy. On the basis of this reading of history, they argue that the juvenile court has been conceptually flawed from the beginning, cannot be fixed, and should be eliminated because it stifles innovative approaches to child welfare.[18]

This book, however, shatters the myth of immaculate construction that posits the juvenile court was born institutionally intact. As this history of America's first juvenile court reveals, juvenile justice evolved through trial and error. The most creative moments in this history have been when reformers sought to discover the root causes of juvenile dependency and delinquency. Such investigations led to the establishment of the juvenile court in the first place, its procedural innovations, and the development of family preservation programs, child guidance clinics, and indigenous community organizing programs. And, as this study has demonstrated, local politics shaped how these programs developed and operated. Thus, the juvenile court helped, not hindered, the establishment of innovative child welfare policies.

It has also been a failure of historians to dispel the lingering myth that the present is unprecedented, and that "kids today," whether in the 1930s, 1950s, 1970s, or 1990s, are a new breed of offenders.[19] As this book has shown, child savers in the early twentieth century struggled with many of the same issues that twenty-first-century policy-makers must address. Hard cases complicate the administration of juvenile justice and will no doubt continue to cloud its mission. The range of children entering the juvenile justice system guarantees nothing less. But still, we must remember that all these cases involve young people, and policy-makers should treat them as a part of an overarching youth policy that takes their developmental needs into account.[20]

The inherent tensions over addressing the needs and rights of children that were exposed in the creation of the juvenile court still exist. Concerns that juvenile justice has not met the needs of children and their families, adequately protected their constitutional rights to due process, or ensured public safety have all led to reforms of the juvenile court, even periodic demands to abolish it.[21] Contemporary critics of juvenile justice have exposed its many shortcomings, from overrepresentation of ethnic and racial minorities to inadequate educational opportunities and mental health services in correctional facilities. Their radical alternatives that seek to integrate children's cases into the adult system, however, all raise the deeply troubling prospect of discarding an institution worth preserving and severing our connection to its history. The juvenile court is in danger. Drawing on the accumulated wisdom of more than a century of juvenile justice can help us to escape from the tightening constraints of our crime complex. This wisdom includes diverting children from the criminal justice system, taking children's developmental differences into account, highlighting social responsibility for the young, searching for the root causes of offending, and mobilizing communities not only to prevent delinquency but also to reclaim offenders. Like Judge Moore, we too can use history to make more informed policy choices and to prevent the dangerous punitive excesses of the present from becoming further entrenched.

The Cook County Juvenile Court Case Files

Reconstructing the history of America's first juvenile court was a dirty job. Although the case files of the court had supposedly been destroyed in the late 1960s or early 1970s, I contacted Phil Costello at the newly opened Cook County Circuit Court Archives, located in the Richard J. Daley Center in Chicago. I mentioned that a Children's Bureau study from the early 1920s, Helen Jeter's invaluable book *The Chicago Juvenile Court*, had listed these records as public ones that were held by Cook County. Phil Costello and his staff discovered boxloads of case files in the county's warehouse. As Phil explained, the good news was that the case files dated back to the court's founding in 1899; the bad news was that they were impounded. Fortunately, the Honorable Sophia Hall, the presiding chief judge of the Cook County Juvenile Court, granted me permission to work with them. It was a mixed blessing. I spent many months sorting the documents, which were out of order and covered with nearly a century's worth of dust and grime. There turned out to be approximately twenty-seven hundred case files from 1899 to 1926, but it was not clear why these select records were preserved.

Every child who entered the juvenile court system was assigned a permanent case number, and all his or her subsequent legal papers were filed under this number in a folder. The amount of social historical data in the case files varied greatly. As a general rule, the delinquency cases before 1907 had "a history of the case" compiled by a probation officer, but the later cases did not. These more recent cases reveal, on the other hand, the rise of bureaucracy. They did not explain specifically why a "delinquent child" had been brought to court but instead were stamped in purple "Was and is delinquent." In dependency cases, which included applications for mothers' pensions, siblings were assigned consecutive numbers. Fortunately, there were runs of consecutive files, such as those analyzed in chapter 3, which allowed me to track over time what happened to different children who entered the juvenile court on the same day. To protect the confidentiality of the families involved, per Judge Hall's request, I have not used the real names of children from these case files.

Notes

PREFACE

1. There is a vast literature on the revolutionary nature of this era. See, e.g., Robert Kaczorowski, "Revolutionary Constitutionalism in the Era of the Civil War and Reconstruction," *New York University Law Review* 61 (November 1986): 863–940; Eric Foner, *Reconstruction: America's Unfinished Revolution, 1863–1877* (New York: Harper and Row, 1988); William J. Novak, *The People's Welfare: Law and Regulation in Nineteenth-Century America* (Chapel Hill: University of North Carolina Press, 1996), 235–248; Laura F. Edwards, *Gendered Strife and Confusion: The Political Culture of Reconstruction* (Urbana: University of Illinois Press, 1997); Amy Dru Stanley, From *Bondage to Contract: Wage Labor, Marriage, and the Market in the Age of Slave Emancipation* (New York: Cambridge University Press, 1998); Akhil Reed Amar, *The Bill of Rights: Creation and Reconstruction* (New Haven: Yale University Press, 1998), 137–294; and Bruce A. Ackerman, *We the People: Transformations* (Cambridge, Mass.: Harvard University Press, 1998).

2. Novak, *The People's Welfare*, 235–248.

3. Kathryn Kish Sklar, *Florence Kelley and and the Nation's Work: The Rise of Women's Political Culture, 1830–1900* (New Haven: Yale University Press, 1995), chap. 7. On the limited number of compulsory attendance and child labor laws in this period see Grace Abbott, *The Child and the State*, 2 vol. (Chicago: University of Chicago Press, 1938), 260.

4. Children also worked on farms in rural American, but early child labor laws generally applied only to mining and industrial workplaces. For a good overview of child labor in the late nineteenth century see Priscilla Ferguson Clement, *Growing Pains: Children in the Industrial Age, 1850–1890* (New York: Twayne, 1997), chap. 5.

5. *Thirteenth Annual Report* (1869), 42–43. In 1870 the United States Census recorded the occupations of child laborers for the first time. Clement, *Growing Pains,* 133.

6. "Petition for *Habeas Corpus,*" issued November 12, 1870, n.p., case no. 16472, Secretary of State Archives, Supreme Court Case Files, Springfield, Illinois.

INTRODUCTION

1. The following description of the Nathaniel Abraham case is drawn from David S. Tanenhaus and Steven A. Drizin, "Owing to the Extreme Youth of the Accused": The Changing Legal Response to Juvenile Homicide," *Journal of Criminal Law and Criminology* 92 (Spring & Summer 2002): 641–706.

2. Jim Dyer, "Children Accused of Killing Children; Young Life Lost, Younger One in Jeopardy," *Detroit News,* February 10, 1998, A1.

3. Judge Eugene A. Moore, "Sentencing Opinion: People of the State of Michigan v. Nathaniel Abraham," *Juvenile and Family Court Journal* 51 (spring 2000): 6.

4. Bryan Robinson, "Fieger Surprises Court, Emerging as Thirteen-Year-Old's Cocounsel in Murder Trial," available on-line at www.courtv.com/trials/abraham/101999_fieger_ctv.html.

5. Anthony Platt M. and Bernard L. Diamond, "The Origins of the 'Right and Wrong' Test of Criminal Responsibility and Its Subsequent Development in the United States: An Historical Survey," *California Law Review* 54 (1966): 1233–1234.

6. William Claiborne, "Thirteen-Year-Old Convicted in Shooting; Decision to Try Youth as an Adult Sparked Juvenile Justice Debate," *Washington Post,* November 17, 1999, A3.

7. Associated Press, "Boy, Thirteen, Convicted of Second Degree Murder," *Chicago Tribune,* November 17, 1999, 19.

8. Keith Bradsher, "Michigan Boy Who Killed at Eleven Is Convicted of Murder as Adult," *New York Times,* November 17, 1999, at A1.

9. "Betraying the Young: Human Rights Violations against Children in the US Justice System," *Amnesty International* (November 1998), 8–36, 60.

10. Keith Bradsher, "Fear of Crime Trumps the Fear of Lost Youth," *New York Times*, November 21, 1999, sec. 4, p. 3. Also see *The Changing Borders of Juvenile Justice: Transfer of Adolescents to the Criminal Court*, edited by Jeffrey Fagan and Franklin E. Zimring (Chicago: University of Chicago Press, 2000).

11. Fagan and Zimring, *Changing Borders of Juvenile Justice*, 40.

12. Victor L. Streib, "The Juvenile Death Penalty Today: Death Sentences and Executions for Juvenile Crimes, January 1, 1973–August 31, 2002" (manuscript in author's possession and available on-line at www.law.onu.edu/faculty/streib/juvdeath.htm).

13. David Garland, *The Culture of Crime: Social Order in Contemporary Society* (Chicago: University of Chicago Press, 2001), 163–164.

14. From 1994 to 1997, there was a 22 percent drop in the number of arrests of juveniles for homicide, rape, robbery, and aggravated assault. David P. Farrington and Rolf Loeber, "Serious and Violent Offenders," in *A Century of Juvenile Justice* edited by Margaret K. Rosenheim, Franklin E. Zimring, David S. Tanenhaus, and Bernardine Dohrn (Chicago: University of Chicago Press, 2002), 206. According the United States Supreme Court, the Constitution does not permit children to be put to death for crimes that they commit before age sixteen (*Thompson v. Oklahoma*, 487 U.S. 815 [1988]) but does allow the death penalty to be applied against children sixteen and older who commit capital offenses. Since 1994, Texas, Virginia, and Oklahoma have put people to death for crimes that they committed before their eighteenth birthdays. Streib, "The Juvenile Death Penalty Today."

15. Franklin E. Zimring, "The Common Thread: Diversion in the Jurisprudence of Juvenile Courts," in Rosenheim, Zimring, Tanenhaus, and Dohrn, *A Century of Juvenile Justice*, 142.

16. Barry C. Feld, *Bad Kids: Race and the Transformation of the Juvenile Court* (New York: Oxford University Press, 1999).

17. Moore, "Sentencing Opinion," 3–4 (italics in original).

18. See, e.g., Christopher P. Manfredi, *The Supreme Court and Juvenile Justice* (Lawrence: University of Kansas Press, 1998) and Feld, *Bad Kids*.

19. Feld, *Bad Kids*, 15.

20. See, e.g., Anthony M. Platt, *The Child Savers: The Invention of Delinquency*, 2nd ed. (Chicago: University of Chicago Press, 1977), James Gilbert, *A Cycle of Outrage: America's Reaction to the Juvenile Delinquent in the 1950s* (New York: Oxford University Press, 1986),

Victoria Getis, *The Juvenile Court and the Progressives* (Urbana: University of Illinois Press, 2000), and Anne Meis Knupfer, *Reform and Resistance: Gender, Delinquency, and America's First Juvenile Court* (New York: Routledge, 2001).

CHAPTER 1

1. Frederick H. Wines, "Address," *Fifteenth Biennial Report*, Board of State Commissioners of Public Charities (Springfield, Ill.: Phillips, 1899), 336.

2. The best accounts of Flower's and Lathrop's lives are Harriet S. Farwell, *Lucy Louisa Flower, 1837–1920: Her Contribution to Education and Child Welfare in Chicago* (Chicago: Privately Printed, 1924), and Jane Addams, *My Friend Julia Lathrop* (New York: Macmillan, 1935).

3. "An Act to Regulate the Treatment and Control of Dependent, Neglected and Delinquent Children," in *All the Laws of the State of Illinois* (Chicago: Chicago Legal News, 1899): 83–87.

4. Herbert H. Lou, *Juvenile Courts in the United States* (Chapel Hill: University of North Carolina Press, 1927): 23–25.

5. Graham Taylor, *Pioneering on Social Frontiers* (Chicago: University of Chicago Press, 1930), 450.

6. Farwell, *Lucy Louisa Flower*, 5.

7. Kathleen McCarthy, *Noblesse Oblige: Charity and Cultural Philanthropy in Chicago, 1849–1929* (Chicago: University of Chicago Press, 1982), 46. Also see Maureen A. Flanagan, *Seeing with Their Hearts: Chicago Women and the Vision of the Good City, 1871–1933* (Princeton, N.J.: Princeton University Press, 2002).

8. The most comprehensive account of transatlantic social politics in the late nineteenth and early twentieth centuries, although it does not discuss crime at great length, is Daniel T. Rodgers, *Atlantic Crossings: Social Politics in a Progressive Age* (Cambridge, Mass.: Harvard University Press, 1998).

9. On the ascendancy of wage labor and its cultural meanings in America, see Amy Dru Stanley, *From Bondage to Contract: Wage Labor, Marriage and the Market in the Age of Slave Emancipation* (New York: Cambridge University Press, 1998). On the transatlantic response to the expansion of market processes see Rodgers, *Atlantic Crossings*. On American progressivism generally, including the impact of industrialization on social thought, see Richard Hofstadter, *The Age of Reform: From Bryan to FDR* (New York: Knopf, 1955); Samuel P. Hays, *The Response to Industrialism, 1885–1914* (Chicago: University of

Chicago Press, 1957); and Robert H. Wiebe, *The Search for Order, 1877–1920* (New York: Hill and Wang, 1967).

10. For an excellent account of this phenomenon see David Garland, *Punishment and Welfare: A History of Penal Strategies* (Brookfield, Vt.: Gower, 1985), especially chap. 2; David Rothman, *Conscience and Convenience: The Asylum and Its Alternatives in Progressive America* (Boston: Little, Brown, 1980); and Michael Willrich, "The Two Percent Solution: Eugenic Jurisprudence and the Socialization of American Law, 1900–1930," *Law and History* 16 (fall 1998): 63–111. Willrich has emphasized that the search for "root" causes included biological as well as social explanations. Thus, many progressive reformers were comfortable implementing solutions that ranged from bettering the environment (e.g., the building of playgrounds for children) to eugenic practices such as the colonization or sterilization of mental defectives. As Willrich argues, reformers considered environmental and eugenic solutions to be complementary.

11. "Our Dark Places" was the title of a famous English exposé on the penal system published in the *Daily Chronicle* in January 1894; see Garland, *Punishment and Welfare*, 64.

12. Quoted in Martin Wiener, *Reconstructing the Criminal: Culture, Law and Policy in England, 1830–1914* (New York: Cambridge University Press, 1990), 24.

13. Ibid.

14. G. Stanley Hall, *Adolescence: Its Psychology and Its Relation to Physiology, Anthropology, Sociology, Sex, Crime, Religion and Education,* 2 vols. (New York: Appleton, 1904).

15. Janet E. Ainsworth, "Re-Imagining Childhood and Reconstructing the Legal Order: The Case for Abolishing the Juvenile Court," *North Carolina Law Review* 69 (1991): 1101; Elizabeth S. Scott, "The Legal Construction of Adolescence," *Hofstra Law Review* 29 (winter 2000): 547–598.

16. John P. Altgeld, *Live Questions Including Our Penal Machinery* (Chicago: Humboldt, 1890), 164.

17. Ibid., 181–182. According to Altgeld, the House of Corrections held: 1 eight-year-old, 5 nine-year-olds, 14 ten-year-olds, 25 eleven-year-olds, 47 twelve-year-olds, 68 thirteen-year-olds, and 103 fourteen-year-olds.

18. Ibid., 162.

19. Altgeld, *Live Questions*, 153.

20. Ibid., 189.

21. Ibid., 187.

22. Ibid., 2.

23. "Report of the Members of the Cook County Grand Jury," November 16, 1898, Chicago Historical Society, Chicago, 2.

24. Ibid.

25. They reprinted extracts from five earlier grand jury reports, dating back to November 1897. "Report of the Members of the Cook County Grand Jury," 3–5.

26. Ibid.

27. "Report of the Members of the Cook County Grand Jury," 2.

28. Quoted in Timothy D. Hurley, *Juveniles Courts and What They Have Accomplished*, 2nd ed. (Chicago: Visitation and Aid Society, 1904), 30.

29. Ibid.

30. "Will Not Make Criminals," article from unnamed newspaper, n.d. but c. 1892, in Lucy Flower and Coues Family Scrapbooks, vol. 3, Chicago Historical Society, Chicago.

31. "Seven-year-old in Jails," article from unnamed newspaper, n.d. but c. 1892, in Flower and Coues Family Scrapbooks, vol. 3.

32. Julian M. Lucas to Grace Groves Clement, December 8, 1922, Clement (Groves) Papers, Chicago Historical Society, Chicago.

33. A.D.G., "A Vital Question," *Chicago Inter-Ocean*, June 6, c. 1884, clipping in Clement Papers.

34. "Boys Made Criminal by Confinement at the Bridewell," *Chicago Herald*, c. 1893, in Flower and Coues Family Scrapbooks, vol. 3.

35. Ibid.

36. Ibid.

37. Ibid.

38. Joan Gittens, *Poor Relations: The Children of the State in Illinois, 1818–1990* (Urbana: University of Illinois Press, 1994), 103; Victoria Getis, *The Juvenile Court and the Progressives* (Urbana: University of Illinois Press, 2000), 32–33.

39. On the influential role of women's organizations in the creation and spread of juvenile justice in the United States see Elizabeth J. Clapp, *Mothers of All Children: Women Reformers and the Rise of Juvenile Courts in Progressive Era America* (University Park: Pennsylvania State University Press, 1998).

40. The bill is reprinted in Timothy D. Hurley, *Origin of the Illinois Juvenile Court Law: Juvenile Courts and What They Have Accomplished*,

3rd ed. (reprint, New York: AMS, 1977; Chicago: Visitation and Aid Society, 1907), 139–140.

41. Farwell, *Lucy Louisa Flower*, 29.

42. Ibid., 26–27. Also Mary M. Bartleme, "A Judge Speaks," *Illinois Voter* 12 (June 1932), in Graham Taylor Papers, Newberry Library, Chicago.

43. "Every Day Club," typescript of handwritten note, n.d., Lucy Flower and Coues Family Scrapbooks, 1858–1921, vol. 3.

44. Eric C. Schneider, *In the Web of Class: Delinquents and Reformers in Boston, 1810s–1930s* (New York: New York University Press, 1992), 58.

45. Grace Abbott, *The Child and the State*, vol. 2 (Chicago: University of Chicago Press, 1938), 330.

46. Lucy L. Flower to Louise de Koven Bowen, c. May 1917, Louise de Koven Bowen Scrapbooks, vol. 2, Chicago Historical Society, Chicago.

47. Ibid.

48. "Harvey B. Hurd," *Courts and Lawyers of Illinois*, vol. 1, edited by Frederick B. Crossley (Chicago: American Historical Society, 1916), 294–297.

49. By the end of the nineteenth century, California, Delaware, the District of Columbia, New York, Maryland, North Carolina, New Hampshire, Oregon, Pennsylvania, and Tennessee all made appropriations to some child welfare institutions within their borders. Homer Folks, *The Care of Destitute, Neglected, and Delinquent Children* (Albany: J. B. Lyon, 1900), 69–88.

50. Flower's letter to Bowen, Bowen Scrapbooks, vol 2.

51. Hurley, *Origin of the Illinois Juvenile Court Law*, 18.

52. "Address," *Fifteenth Biennial Report*, Board of State Commissioners of Public Charities (Springfield, Ill.: Phillips, 1899), 321.

53. Ibid.

54. Ibid., 288.

55. "Address," *Fifteenth Biennial Report*, Board of State Commissioners of Public Charities (Springfield, Ill.: Phillips, 1899), 324.

56. Paul Gerard Anderson used the term "industrial lobby." See Anderson, "The Good to Be Done" (Ph.D. diss., University of Chicago, 1988), 2:80.

57. Since the general assembly met biennially, the 1899 session would be the last one of the nineteenth century.

58. Hurley, *Origin of the Illinois Juvenile Court Law*, 22; Memorandum by Julia Lathrop, May 3, 1917, Bowen Scrapbooks,

vol. 2. According to Lathrop, the following representatives
were in attendance: Judge Hurd and Judge Orrin Carter (Chicago
Bar Association); Hasting H. Hart (Children's Home and Aid
Society); Lucy Flower and Ellen Henrotin (Chicago's Woman's
Club); Jane Addams (Settlements); Timothy Hurley (Catholic
Charities); Julian Mack (Jewish Charities). According to Hurley,
the following people were also present: the state representative
John C. Newcomer; the superintendent of public schools,
A. G. Lane; the county jailor, John L. Whitman, Carl Kelsey,
a probation officer who had worked in Boston and was now
working with youth in Chicago; and Frank G. Soule, an insurance
salesman, who at the time was the sitting foreman of the Cook
County Grand Jury.

59. Hurley, *Origin of the Illinois Juvenile Court Law,* 22.

60. The proposed bill is reprinted in ibid., 26–30.

61. Ibid., 28.

62. The mandatory language would be changed to permissive
language in the final version of the bill. Thus, justices of the police
and police magistrates could, but did not have to, transfer cases to
the juvenile court. A 1901 amendment to the juvenile court law did,
however, make such transfers mandatory.

63. *Petition of Ferrier,* 103 Ill. 367 (1882), and *County of McLean v. Laura
B. Humphreys,* 104 Ill. 379 (1882).

64. The following definitions were incorporated into the Bar
Association Bill: "For the purposes of this act the words dependent
child and neglected child shall mean any child who for any reason is
destitute or homeless or abandoned; or dependent upon the public for
support; or who habitually begs or receives alms; or who is found
living in any house of ill fame or with any vicious or disreputable
person; or whose home, by reason of neglect, cruelty or depravity on
the part of its parents, guardian or other person in whose care it may be,
is an unfit place for such a child; and any child under the age of
eight years, who is found peddling or selling any article or singing
or playing any musical instrument upon the street or giving any
public entertainment." Quoted in Hurley, *Origin of the Juvenile Court
Law,* 26–27

65. Ibid., 27.

66. Ibid., 28.

67. Ibid., 29.

68. Ibid.

69. Steven L. Schlossman, *Love and the American Delinquent: The Theory and Practice of "Progressive" Juvenile Justice, 1825–1920* (Chicago: University of Chicago Press, 1977), 61.

70. On the significance of individualized treatment see Rothman, *Conscience and Convenience,* chaps. 2 and 6.

71. Ibid., 39. In 1895, Illinois had established the State Home for Juvenile Female Offenders at Geneva.

72. "Child Slaves," *Chicago Daily Inter-Ocean,* February 28, 1899, pp. 1–2.

73. Ibid., 1.

74. On Brace and the Children's Aid Society see Charles Loring Brace, *The Dangerous Classes of New York, and Twenty Years of Work among Them* (New York: Wynkoop and Hallenbeck, 1872); Marilyn Irvin Holt, *The Orphan Trains: Placing Out in America* (Lincoln: University of Nebraska Press, 1992); LeRoy Ashby, *Endangered Children: Dependency, Neglect, and Abuse in American History* (New York: Twayne, 1997), chap. 3; and Stephen O'Connor, *Orphan Trains: The Story of Charles Loring Brace and the Children He Saved and Failed* (Boston: Houghton Mifflin, 2001). For good accounts of the nineteenth-century concerns about placing children out see *Foster-Home Care for Dependent Children,* United States Children's Bureau publication no. 136 (Washington, D.C.: Government Printing Office, 1926), and *State of Illinois Report of the Joint Committee on Home-Finding Societies* (Springfield, Ill.: Schnepp and Barnes, 1915).

75. "Child Slaves," 2.

76. Hurley, *Origin of the Illinois Juvenile Court Law,* 30–31.

77. "Child Slaves," 1.

78. Although Illinois passed its first compulsory attendance law in 1883, it would take twenty years before it would be rigorously enforced. See Edith Abbott and Sophonisba P. Breckinridge, *Truancy and Non-Attendance in the Chicago Schools: A Study of the Social Aspects of the Compulsory Education and Child Labor Legislation of Illinois* (reprint, New York: Arno Press, 1970; Chicago: University of Chicago Press, 1917), esp. chap. 5. As Abbott and Breckinridge recognized, before the compulsory education law could be successfully enforced, the state needed to restrict child labor laws, establish a juvenile court, and run parental schools to educate truants.

79. Hurley, *Origin of the Illinois Juvenile Court Law,* 28.

80. "Child Slaves," 1.

81. Lathrop Memorandum, Bowen Scrapbooks, vol. 2.

82. They accomplished this goal by amending sections 10 and 12 of the proposed bill. See Hurley, *Origin of the Illinois Juvenile Court Law*, 33–34.

83. Kenneth Cmiel, *A Home of Another Kind: One Chicago Orphanage and the Tangle of Child Welfare* (Chicago: University of Chicago Press, 1995), 15; Paul Lerman, "Twentieth-Century Developments in America's Institutional Systems for Youth in Trouble," in *A Century of Juvenile Justice* edited by Margaret K. Rosenheim, Franklin E. Zimring, David S. Tanenhaus, and Bernardine Dohrn (Chicago: University of Chicago Press, 2002), 80.

84. Hurley, *Origin of the Illinois Juvenile Court Law*, 39.

85. Ibid., 38.

86. "The Dependent Children's Bill," *Chicago Tribune*, March 10, 1899, p. 6.

87. "Juvenile Court Bill Amended," *Chicago Inter Ocean*, March 10, 1899, p. 4.

88. For an analysis of the bill's passage by the general assembly see Getis, *The Juvenile Court and the Progressives*, 42–44.

89. Lathrop, Memorandum, May 3, 1917, Bowen Scrapbooks, vol. 2.

CHAPTER 2

1. "Judge Richard S. Tuthill," *Courts and Lawyers of Illinois* edited by Frederic B. Crossley, vol. 2 (Chicago: American Historical Society, 1916), 453–454; "Case in Juvenile Court—Judge Tuthill Listens to the First Complaint Filed under the New Enactment," *Chicago Daily News*, July 3, 1899, p. 2; "New Court Begins Work," *Chicago Tribune*, July 4, 1899, p. 8.

2. T. D. Hurley, "Development of the Juvenile-Court Idea," in *Children's Courts in the United States: Their Origin, Development, and Results* (reprint, New York: AMS, 1973; Washington, D.C.: Government Printing Office, 1904), 8.

3. Ibid.

4. "New Court Begins Work," 8.

5. "Case in Juvenile Court," 2.

6. Ibid.

7. "New Court Begins Works," 8.

8. Ibid.

9. For an excellent analysis of contemporary understandings of the interconnectedness of the modern world see Thomas L. Haskell, *The Emergence of Professional Social Science: The American Social Science*

Association and the Nineteenth-Century Crisis of Authority (Urbana: University of Illinois Press, 1977).

10. Eric Foner, *The Story of American Freedom* (New York: Norton, 1998), 161.

11. Ibid., 153.

12. The fact that juvenile courts have always been statutory creations, which state legislatures can alter at will, has contributed to many differences among these courts. The most fundamental difference has been whether courts used chancery proceedings the Chicago model of informal hearings or continued to remain part of the criminal justice system, retaining most of the features of criminal procedure, as New York courts did until the 1930s. In addition, the emphasis on informal procedures in courts using chancery proceedings also accounted for individual courts adopting very different procedures. Still, by 1925 every state, except Maine and Wyoming, at least had a juvenile court law, and juvenile courts were operating in all the American cities with more than a hundred thousand people. Katharine Lenroot and Emma O. Lundberg, *Juvenile Courts at Work: A Study of the Organization and Methods of Ten Courts* (reprint, New York: AMS Press, 1975; Washington, D.C.: Government Printing Office, 1925), 1.

13. "Judge Richard S. Tuthill," 453–454.

14. "Judge Tuthill Trying to Simplify the Work of Juvenile Court," *Chicago Daily News*, June 27, 1899, p. 3. By not requiring the justices to transfer cases, the law avoided a potential constitutional pitfall. See Julia C. Lathrop, "The Development of the Probation System in a Large City," *Charities* (January 7, 1905): 345. A 1901 amendment to the juvenile court law made the transfer of cases mandatory. "Juvenile Court," in *Laws of Illinois* (Springfield, Ill.: Phillips, 1901), 142.

15. "Juvenile Law Is Good," *Chicago Tribune*, July 16, 1899, p. 15.

16. The social investigators Sophonisba Breckinridge and Edith Abbot discovered between July 1, 1907, and June 30, 1909, that 258 out of 908 boys (28.4 percent) brought to the juvenile court for "stealing" had stolen from the railroads. I have extrapolated from these figures to calculate the approximate number of railroad thefts in the period from 1899 to 1909. Breckinridge and Abbott offered a cultural interpretation for why these immigrant children stole from the railroads. They argued that these children's parents, many of whom had been peasants, considered the railroads to be like the communal lands in the old country. Thus, it was conceptually difficult for these former peasants "to understand why the sweeping from the empty freight

cars should be not appropriated to feed the chickens or pigeons at home; or why coal dropped from uncovered cars should not be carried home." Thus, many of these cases of "stealing" from the railroads may have represented clashing cultural conceptions of property rights. Sophonisba P. Breckinridge and Edith Abbott, *The Delinquent Child and the Home* (reprint, New York: Arno Press, 1970; New York: Charities Publication Committee, 1912): 32, 68.

17. Ibid., 32.

18. "Juvenile Law Is Good," 15.

19. *Chicago Open Board of Trade v. The Imperial Building Company,* 136 Ill. App. 606 (1907).

20. Ibid.

21. Henry W. Thurston, "Ten Years of the Juvenile Court of Chicago," *Survey* 23 (February 5, 1910): 661.

22. Ibid.

23. Ibid.

24. In *Jennie Gerhardt,* for example, Theodore Dreiser described the impoverishment of a family leading to a son being arrested for stealing coal from the railroad yards. Theodore Dreiser, *Jennie Gerhardt* (reprint, New York: Bantam, 1993; New York: Harper, 1911), chap. 6.

25. "Juvenile Law Is Good," 15.

26. Ibid.

27. "Chicago Bar Association Committee on Juvenile Courts Report," October 28, 1899, Chicago Historical Society, Chicago, 6.

28. On the significance of these institutions see Helen Lefkowitz Horowitz, *Culture and the City: Cultural Philanthropy in Chicago from the 1880s to 1917* (Chicago: University of Chicago Press, 1976).

29. Richard S. Tuthill, "The Juvenile Court Law in Cook County," in *Sixteenth Biennial Report of the Board of State Commissioners of Public Charities of the State of Illinois* (Springfield, Ill.: Phillips, 1901), 334.

30. Harriet S. Farwell, *Lucy Louisa Flower, 1837–1920: Her Contribution to Education and Child Welfare in Chicago* (Chicago: Privately Printed, 1924), 39.

31. Emily Dean, "Dedication of Oakdale, the Women's Reformatory at Dwight," November 11, 1931, in Emily Washburn Dean Papers, Chicago Historical Society, Chicago.

32. Ibid., 2.

33. Ibid.

34. Mary Lynn McCree, "Louise deKoven Bowen," in *Notable American Women: The Modern Period,* edited by Barbara Sicherman,

Carol Hurd Green with Ilene Kantrov, Harriette Walker (Cambridge, Mass.: Harvard University Press, 1980), 99–101.

35. Bowen, who was born in 1859, a year after Julia Lathrop and a year before Jane Addams, belonged to the same generation as these famous women reformers of Hull House.

36. "Concert for the Benefit of the Juvenile Court," c. February 3, 1904, Louise de Koven Bowen Scrapbooks, vol. 1, Chicago Historical Society, Chicago.

37. Anne Meis Knupfer, "The Chicago Detention Home," in *A Noble Social Experiment? The First Hundred Years of the Cook County Juvenile Court 1899–1999*, edited by Gwen Hoerr McNamee (Chicago: Chicago Bar Association, 1999), 52–53.

38. Thurston, "Ten Years of the Juvenile Court of Chicago," 663.

39. Anne Meis Knupfer, *Reform and Resistance: Gender, Delinquency, and America's First Juvenile Court* (New York: Routledge, 2001), chap. 6.

40. Savilla Millis, *The Juvenile Court Detention Home in Relation to Juvenile Court Policy: A Study of Intake in the Cook County Chicago Juvenile Detention Home* (Chicago: University of Chicago, Graduate School of Social Service Administration, 1927), 19, 22.

41. Lenroot and Lundberg, *Juvenile Courts at Work*, 55.

42. Ibid.

43. Florence M. Warner, *Juvenile Detention in the United States: Report of a Field Survey of the National Probation Association* (Chicago: University of Chicago Press, 1933), 89.

44. Harvey B. Hurd, "Juvenile Court Law: Minimum Principles Which Should Be Stood For," *Charities* (January 7, 1905): 327–328.

45. Andrew J. Polsky, *The Rise of the Therapeutic State* (Princeton, N.J.: Princeton University Press, 1991).

46. Ibid., 16.

47. Lathrop, "The Development of the Probation System in a Large City," 346.

48. Anne Meis Knupfer, *Toward a Tenderer Humanity and a Nobler Womanhood: African American Women's Clubs in Turn-of-the-Century Chicago* (New York: New York University Press, 1996), 71–72.

49. Lenroot and Lundberg, *Juvenile Courts at Work*, 162.

50. Kenneth Cmiel, *A Home of Another Kind: One Chicago Orphanage and the Tangle of Child Welfare* (Chicago: University of Chicago Press, 1995), 126.

51. *The Negro in Chicago: A Study of Race Relations and a Riot in 1919* (Chicago: University of Chicago Press, 1922; reprint, New York: Arno Press, 1968), 333.

52. Ibid., 334.

53. Earl R. Moses, *The Negro Delinquent in Chicago* (Washington, D.C.: Social Science Research Council, 1936), 14.

54. Harry Hill, "Annual Report of the Chief Probation Officer of the Juvenile Court," *Charity Service Reports* (Cook County, Ill., 1927), 364.

55. Moses, *The Negro Delinquent in Chicago*, 16.

56. Ibid., 17.

57. Ibid., 275.

58. Hill, "Annual Report," 364.

59. Ibid.

60. "Juvenile Courts—Probation Officers," *Laws of the State of Illinois* (Springfield: Illinois State Journal, 1905): 151–152.

61. Julian W. Mack, "The Juvenile Court," *Harvard Law Review* 23 (1909–10): 104–122.

62. Franklin E. Zimring, "The Common Thread: Diversion in Juvenile Justice," *California Law Review* 88 (December 2000): 2477–2495.

63. On the concept of social citizenship (i.e., the belief that citizens, at the very least dependent ones, should be provided with a minimum level of shelter, nourishment, education, and medical care) in the context of American history see Linda Gordon, *Pitied but Not Entitled: Single Mothers and the History of Welfare* (Cambridge, Mass.: Harvard University Press, 1994), and Michael B. Katz, *The Price of Citizenship: Redefining the American Welfare State* (New York: Metropolitan, 2001).

64. John McManaman, "The Juvenile Court," in *Eighteenth Biennial Report*, Board of Commissioner of Public Charities (Springfield: Illinois State Journal, 1904): 377.

65. The title of the law was even changed to reflect this new potential. It became "An Act relating to children who are now or may hereafter become dependent, neglected or delinquent, to define these terms, and to provide for the treatment, control, maintenance, adoption and guardianship of the person of such child." The act declared: "that all persons under the age of twenty-one (21) years, shall, for the purpose of the Act only, be considered wards of this State, and their person shall be subject to the care, guardianship and control of the court as hereinafter provided." *Laws of the State of Illinois* (Springfield: Illinois State Journal, 1907), 71.

66. *Charity Service Reports*, Board of Commissioners of Cook County (Chicago: Henry O. Shepard, 1906), 115.

67. Ibid.

68. *Charity Service Reports*, Board of Commissioners of Cook County (Chicago: Henry O. Shepard, 1907), 103.

69. In the first run of extant case files, case numbers 76–176, 39 percent of these "delinquent" children had prior legal experience, and of these children one third had spent time in an institution. Cook County Circuit Court Archives, Richard J. Daley Center, Chicago.

70. *Laws of the State of Illinois* (Springfield: Illinois State Journal, 1905), 153.

71. Helen Jeter, *The Chicago Juvenile Court* (Washington: Government Printing Office, 1922), 14–15. For a discussion of the handling of juvenile homicide cases see David S. Tanenhaus and Steven A. Drizin, "'Owing to the Extreme Youth of the Accused': The Changing Legal Response to Homicide," *Journal of Criminal Law and Criminology* 92 (Spring-Summer, 2002): 641–706.

72. As Joan Gittens has noted about the possible jurisdictional conflict, "at its heart lay the fact that the juvenile court assumed control over children up to age sixteen (later changed to seventeen for boys and eighteen for girls) without ever addressing the issue that the age of criminal responsibility was set at ten years. Instead of trying to change that law, they simply ignored it." *Poor Relations: The Children of the State in Illinois, 1818–1990* (Urbana: University of Illinois Press, 1994), 108–109. The jurisdictional conflict between the juvenile and criminal courts would not be resolved until 1935. See chapter 6.

73. David S. Tanenhaus, "The Evolution of Transfer out of the Juvenile Court," in *The Changing Borders of Juvenile Justice: The Transfer of Adolescents to Criminal Court*, edited by Jeffrey Fagan and Franklin E. Zimring (Chicago: University of Chicago Press, 2000), 13–43. Grace E. Benjamin used the term "gentleman's agreement" to describe this practice. Benjamin, "The Case for the Juvenile Court: Social Aspects of a Simple Legal Problem," *Chicago Bar Record* 16 (May 1935): 233.

74. Tanenhaus, "The Evolution of Transfer," 21.

75. "Testimony of Judge Merritt W. Pinckney," in Breckinridge and Abbott, *The Delinquent Child and the Home*, edited 208–209.

76. Jeter, *The Chicago Juvenile Court*, 89.

77. Case number 108, Cook County Circuit Court Archives, Richard J. Daley Center, Chicago. I have changed the boy's first and last names.

78. *Charity Service Reports*, Board of Commissioners of Cook County (Chicago: Henry O. Shepard, 1907), 115.

79. Ibid.

80. Ibid., 111.

81. David J. Rothman, "The State as Parent: Social Policy in the Progressive Era," in *Doing Good: The Limits of Benevolence*, edited by Willard Gaylin, Ira Glasser, David J. Rothman (New York: Pantheon Books, 1978), 81.

82. Lenroot and Lundberg, *Juvenile Courts at Work*, 171.

83. Breckinridge and Abbott, *The Delinquent Child and the Home*, 23–25.

84. The Illinois law (i.e., "An Act to provide for the punishment or persons responsible for, or directly promoting or contributing to, the conditions that render a child dependent, neglected or delinquent and to provide for suspension of sentence and release on probation in such cases"), unlike Colorado's pioneering legislation, did not give the juvenile court jurisdiction over these cases. In Chicago, the newly created municipal court heard these cases.

85. Breckinridge and Abbott, *The Delinquent Child and the Home*, 207.

86. Clifford R. Shaw and Earl D. Moses, "The Juvenile Delinquent," in *The Illinois Crime Survey* (Springfield: Illinois Association for Criminal Justice, 1929), 647.

87. Lenroot and Lundberg, *Juvenile Courts at Work*, 114.

88. Harvey Humphrey Baker, "Private Hearings: Their Advantages and Disadvantages," *Annals of the Academy of Political and Social Science* 36 (1910): 80.

89. Ibid., 84.

90. Ibid., 80.

91. Knupfer, *Reform and Resistance*, 88–89, 187.

92. Breckinridge and Abbott, *The Delinquent Child and the Home*, 22.

93. Steven L. Schlossman and Stephanie Wallach, "The Crime of Precocious Sexuality: Female Juvenile Delinquency in the Progressive Era," *Harvard Educational Review* 48 (February 1978): 65–94.

94. Mary E. Odem and Steven L. Schlossman, "Guardians of Virtue: The Juvenile Court and Female Delinquency in Early Twentieth-Century Los Angeles," *Crime and Delinquency* 37 (April 1991): 186–203; Odem, "Single Mothers, Delinquent Daughters, and the Juvenile Court in Early Twentieth-Century Los Angeles," *Journal of Social History* 25 (September 1991): 27–43; Odem, *Delinquent Daughters: Protecting and Policing Adolescent Sexuality in the United States, 1885–1920*

(Chapel Hill: University of North Carolina Press, 1995); Anne Meis Knupfter, *Reform and Resistance: Gender, Delinquency and America's First Juvenile Court* (New York: Routledge, 2001).

95. Henry Kitchell Webster, "The Square Deal with Children: Judge Mack and the Work of the Chicago Juvenile Court," *American Illustrated Magazine* (February 1906): 400.

96. Breckinridge and Abbott, *The Delinquent Child and the Home*, 175 (italics added).

97. Ibid.

98. Lenroot and Lundberg, *Juvenile Courts at Work*, 124; Lou, *Juvenile Courts in the United States* (Chapel Hill: University of North Carolina Press, 1927), 132.

99. Lou, *Juvenile Courts in the United States*, 132.

CHAPTER 3

1. Case nos. 45041–45043, Juvenile Cases, Cook County Circuit Court Archives, Richard J. Daley Center, Chicago.

2. The mother's petition, dated May 25, 1914, is in case no. 45041. The mother said that she had $865 in the bank and her attorney was selling some property of hers in Hungary that would approximately double her savings. Verifying all of the mother's account is impossible, but the petition did provide a narrative explaining why the mother had been absent and why she was now a worthy mother.

3. Case nos. 45041–45043.

4. The best historical account of the use of orphanages from the Civil War until the Great Depression is Timothy A. Hacsi, *Second Home: Orphan Asylums and Poor Families in America* (Cambridge, Mass.: Harvard University Press, 1997). For an excellent contemporary source see Hastings H. Hart, *Preventive Treatment of Neglected Children* (New York: Charities Publication Committee, 1910), 57–73.

5. Kenneth Cmiel, *A Home of Another Kind: One Chicago Orphanage and the Tangle of Child Welfare* (Chicago: University of Chicago Press, 1995), 15.

6. For an insightful and provocative account of the revolt against institutionalization, including the leading role played by managers of institutions, see Matthew A. Crenson, *Building the Invisible Orphanage: A Prehistory of the American Welfare System* (Cambridge, Mass.: Harvard University Press, 1998).

7. For good, if somewhat contrasting accounts of the ideological significance of this first White House Conference on the Care of

Dependent Children on the development of the American welfare state, see ibid., especially 258–262; Walter I. Trattner, *From Poor Law to Welfare State: A History of Social Welfare in America*, 5th ed. (New York: Free Press, 1994), 216–217, and Michael B. Katz, *In the Shadow of the Poorhouse: A Social History of Welfare in America* (New York: Basic Books, 1986), 122–124.

8. The best account of the tension between nineteenth-century traditions and public innovations in social policy during the early twentieth century is Morton Keller, *Regulating a New Society: Public Policy and Social Change in America, 1900–1933* (Cambridge, Mass.: Harvard University Press, 1994).

9. Miriam Van Waters, "The Juvenile Court from the Child's Viewpoint: A Glimpse into the Future," in *The Child, the Clinic and the Court*, edited by Jane Addams (New York: New Republic, 1927), 220. Also see Estelle B. Freedman, *Maternal Justice: Miriam Van Waters and the Female Reform Tradition* (Chicago: University of Chicago Press, 1996).

10. As part of the 1930 *White House Conference on Child Health and Protection*, the subcommittee on Mothers' Aid reported: "Since it was in the juvenile court that dependent children appeared, in certain states, to be sent to institutions, it was *natural* that in the inception of the plan its judge should be given the opportunity of ordering payment to the mother instead of an institution" (New York: Appleton-Century, 1933), 224 (italics added).

11. Claims of the law's authorship would actually postdate its enactment. Joanne L. Goodwin, *Gender and the Politics of Welfare Reform: Mothers' pensions in Chicago, 1911–1929* (Chicago: University of Chicago Press, 1997), 104–112.

12. Ibid., 87.

13. Ibid., 104–105.

14. Michael Grossberg, *Governing the Hearth: Law and the Family in Nineteenth-Century America* (Chapel Hill: University of North Carolina Press, 1985), especially chap. 8. On the use of municipal courts in the early twentieth century to police social and moral jurisdictions, see Michael Willrich, *City of Courts: Socializing Justice in Progressive Era Chicago* (New York: Cambridge University Press, 2003).

15. *White House Conference on Child Health and Protection*, 223.

16. For an excellent analysis of the progressive conception of childhood, see Janet E. Ainsworth, "Reimagining Childhood and

Reconstructing the Legal Order: The Case for the Abolition of the Juvenile Court," *North Carolina Law Review* 69 (1991): 1083–1133.

17. Frederic C. Howe and Marie Jenney Howe, "Pensioning the Widow and the Fatherless," *Good Housekeeping* 57 (1913): 291.

18. Twenty state legislatures passed mothers' pension laws between 1911 and 1913. By 1920, forty states had enacted such laws. Theda Skocpol, *Protecting Soldiers and Mothers: The Political Origins of Social Policy in the United States* (Cambridge, Mass.: Harvard University Press, 1992), 424. According to Grace Abbott, "while Judge Pinckney had said that if any other public agency were available the administration of mothers' aid did not belong in the juvenile court, in twenty states it was placed there with the general approval of those interested in dependent children because no other local administrative agency seemed at the time as well qualified. While two of the states adopting the court as the administrative agency were in the East [New Jersey and Vermont] and four in the South [Arkansas, Louisiana, Oklahoma, and Tennessee], the great majority were in the Middle West and Northwest [Colorado, Idaho, Illinois, Iowa, Michigan, Minnesota, Montana, Nebraska, North Dakota, Ohio, Oregon, South Dakota, Washington, and Wisconsin]." *The Child and the State*, vol. 2 (Chicago: University of Chicago Press, 1938), 235–236.

19. Thomas D. Eliot, *The Juvenile Court and the Community* (New York: Macmillan, 1914), 17.

20. Ibid., 17–18.

21. For an accounting of social workers' concerns about judicial administration of welfare programs see *White House Conference on Child Health and Protection*, 224–225. On concerns about socialized justice see Edward F. Waite, "How Far Can Court Procedure Be Socialized without Impairing Individual Rights?" *Journal of Criminal Law and Criminology* 12 (1921): 339–347.

22. Quoted in Martin Bulmer, *The Chicago School of Sociology: Institutionalization, Diversity, and the Rise of Sociological Research* (Chicago: University of Chicago Press, 1984), 13–14.

23. Although it was the first statewide mothers' pensions program, Pinckney was only responsible for its administration in Cook County. Carsten's early findings and conclusions were published in "Public Pensions to Widows with Children," *Survey* (4 January, 1913): 459–466. He also incorporated his analysis of the Chicago program into *Public Pensions to Widows and Children: A Study of Their Administration in Several American Cities* (New York: Russell Sage Foundation, 1913).

24. Amy Dru Stanley, *From Bondage to Contract: Wage Labor, Marriage, and the Market in the Age of Slave Emancipation* (New York: Cambridge University Press, 1998), 112.

25. Although Pinckney shared this concern, the quoted phrase is from Carstens, "Public Pensions," 465.

26. *Youth in Transition: Report of the Panel on Youth to the President's Science Advisory Committee* (Chicago: University of Chicago Press, 1974), 24–26.

27. Grace Abbott quoted in Alan Wolfe, "The Child and the State: A Second Glance," *Contemporary Crisis* 2 (1978): 407.

28. Sylvia Schafer, *Children in Moral Danger and the Problem of Government in Third Republic France* (Princeton, N.J.: Princeton University Press, 1997), 4–5.

29. See, e.g., *Charity Service Reports*, Cook County Board of County Commissioners Chicago: Henry O. Shepard, (1911), 166.

30. According to the 1907 Juvenile Court Act, the definitions of the "dependent" and "neglected" child included: "any male child who while under the age of seventeen years or any female child who while under the age of eighteen years, for any reason, is destitute, homeless or abandoned; or dependent upon the public for support; or has not proper parental care or guardianship; or habitually begs or receives alms; or is found living in any house of ill-fame or with any vicious or disreputable person; or has a home which by reason of neglect, cruelty or depravity, on the part of its parents, guardian or any other person in whose care it may be, is an unfit place for such a child; and any child who while under the age of ten (10) years is found begging, peddling or selling any articles or singing or playing any musical instrument for gain upon the street or giving any public entertainments or accompanies or is used in aid of any person so doing." *Laws of Illinois* (Springfield: State Printers, 1907), 71.

31. According to the Juvenile Court Act, "if the court shall find any male child under the age of seventeen years or any female child under the age of eighteen years to be dependent or neglected within the meaning of this act, the court may allow such a child to remain at its own home subject to the friendly visitation of a probation officer, and if the parent, parents, guardian or custodian of such child are unfit or improper guardians or are unable or unwilling to care for, protect, train, educate or discipline such child, and that it is for the interest of such child and the people of this State that such child be taken from the custody of its parents, custodian or guardian, the court

may make an order appointing as guardian of the person of such child, some reputable citizen of good moral character and order such guardian to place such child in some suitable family home or other suitable place, which such guardian may provide for such child or the court may enter an order committing such child to some suitable State institution, organized for the care of dependent or neglected children, or to some training school or industrial school or to some association embracing in its objects the purpose of caring for or obtaining homes for neglected or dependent children, which association shall have been accredited as hereinafter provided." *Laws of Illinois* (Springfield: State Printers, 1907), 74.

32. Quoted in Ruth Newberry, "Origin and Criticism of Funds to Parents Act" (M.A. thesis, University of Chicago, 1912), 12–12a. See Pinckney, "Public Pensions to Widows: Experiences and Observations Which Lead Me to Favor Such a Law," *Proceedings of the National Conference of Charities and Corrections* (1912): 473–480.

33. Pinckney, "Public Pensions," 142–143. Other notable juvenile court judges, including Julian Mack, constructed similar, narratives about such separations of mother and child. See, e.g., Mark H. Leff, "Consensus for Reform: The Mothers' Pension Movement in the Progressive Era," *Social Service Review* 47 (1972): 400, 410; and Sonya Michel, "The Limits of Maternalism: Policies toward American Wage-Earning Mothers during the Progressive Era," in *Mothers of a New World: Maternalist Politics and the Origins of the Welfare States* edited by Seth Koven and Sonya Michel (New York: Routledge, 1993), 294.

34. *Laws of Illinois* (Springfield: State Printers, 1911), 126.

35. Ben Lindsey, the flamboyant judge of the Denver juvenile court, offered this explanation about the gender-neutral wording of the Illinois and Colorado laws. See Ben B. Lindsey, "The Mothers' Compensation Law of Colorado," *Survey* 29 (February 15, 1913): 714–716.

36. Goodwin, *Gender and the Politics of Welfare Reform*, 117–118.

37. Pinckney, "Public Pensions," 475. Also see Newberry, "Origin and Criticism," 16–17; Joel D. Hunter, "Administration of the Funds to Parents Law in Chicago," *Survey* (January 31, 1914): 516–518; and Carstens, "Public Pensions."

38. Pinckney, "Public Pensions," 474.

39. Ibid.

40. For a good overview of the Charity Organization Movement and its ideology, see Trattner, *From Poor Law to Welfare State*, chap. 5.

41. On the efforts to abolish outdoor relief in the nineteenth century and the rise of scientific charity see Katz, *In the Shadow of the Poorhouse*, 36–84.

42. Pinckney, "Public Pensions," 477, 479. On concerns about male desertion in this period see Micheal Willrich, "Home Slackers: Men, the State, and Welfare in Modern America," *Journal of American History* 87 (September 2002): 460–489.

43. Pinckney, "Public Pensions," 475.

44. The citizens' committee that chose these representatives from its ranks included Jane Addams; Louise de Koven Bowen, the president of the Juvenile Protective Association; Charles Wacker of the United Charities; Sol Sulzberger of the Jewish Aid Societies; Adolph Kurtz of the Jewish Home-Finding Association; Mrs. Arthur T. Aldis of the Visiting Nurse Association; Mary H. Wilmarth of the Woman's City Club; Dr. Henry Favill of the City Club; Gustave Fischer of the Industrial Club; Alexander A. McCormick of the Immigrant's Protective League; and Minnie Low of the Bureau of Personal Service.

45. The following description of the review process draws on Newberry, "Origin and Criticism," and Carstens, "Public Pensions."

46. Carstens, "Public Pensions," 461.

47. See chapter 4.

48. Carstens, "Public Pensions," 461.

49. Pinckney, "Public Pensions," 476.

50. Ibid.

51. On the importance of economic considerations see Joanne Goodwin, "An American Experiment in Paid Motherhood: The Implementation of Mothers' Pensions in early Twentieth-Century Chicago," *Gender and History* 4 (1992): 323–341.

52. Hunter, "Administration of the Funds to Parents Law," 516.

53. Under the common law, the father was always first in the line of responsibility. The principle of extended familial responsibility for poor relations dates back to the Elizabethan poor laws. In Illinois under the Pauper Act of 1874, those liable for support included "the father, grandfather, mother, grandmother, children, grandchildren, [and the] brothers or sisters" of the poor person in question. The lines of responsibility were: "The children shall first be called on to support their parents, if there be children of sufficient ability; and if there be none of sufficient ability, the parents of such poor person shall be next called on if they be of sufficient ability; and if there be no parents or children of sufficient ability, the brothers

and sisters of such poor person shall be next called on if they be of sufficient ability; and if there be no brothers or sisters of sufficient ability, the grandchildren of such poor person shall next be called on if they be of sufficient ability; and next the grandparents, if they be of sufficient ability." *The Revised Statutes of Illinois,* 1874, edited by Harvey B. Hurd (Springfield: State Printers, 1874), chap. 57, 754–759. The Pauper Acts are reprinted in, Sophanison P. Breckinridge, *The Illinois Poor Law* and Its Administration (Chicago: University of Chicago Press, 1939), 243–271.

54. Hunter, "Administration of the Funds to Parents Law," 516.

55. The following section is based on 197 consecutive case files (case nos. 44851–45050) from November 26, 1912, until December 26, 1912. Out of the 197 first-time petitions filed in the juvenile court by family members, probation officers, and the police from November 26 through December 26, 1912, 80 were for a "dependent child." In 1911 this broad category was expanded to include the applications for mothers' pensions. By comparing the twenty-nine applications for financial assistance with the fifty-one "nonpensioned" dependency cases handled by the court, we can see how the court's administration of the new law fundamentally transformed the juvenile justice system.

56. On family violence see Elizabeth Pleck, *Domestic Tyranny: The Making of American Social Policy against Family Violence from Colonial Times to the Present* (New York: Oxford University Press, 1987), and Linda Gordon, *Heroes of Their Own Lives: The Politics and History of Family Violence* (New York: Penguin Books, 1988). Revisionist accounts of orphanages include Nurith Zmora, *Orphanages Reconsidered: Child Care Institutions in Progressive Era Baltimore* (Philadelphia: Temple University Press, 1994); Cmiel, *A Home of Another by Kind;* Hacsi, *Second Home;* and *Rethinking Orphanages for the Twenty-First Century,* edited by Richard B. McKenzie (Thousand Oaks, Calif.: Sage, 1999).

57. Hart, *Preventive Treatment of Neglected Children,* 70.

58. "Report of Chief Probation Officer," *Charity Service Reports, Cook County, Illinois Fiscal Year 1910,* Cook County Board of Commissioners (Chicago: Henry O. Shepard, 1911), 143.

59. Ibid., 144. Witter provided two examples of private charities paying mothers small sums to keep their children at home. He recounted: "An example of this is the case of three children brought to the attention of the Court about three months ago, but for private charity stepping in at least two of these children would have been sent to institutions at a monthly expense to the county of

$7.50 per child; add to this the amount supplemented by the institution, and the amount aggregates $30 per month, making a total of $90 for the three months. The actual amount expended by the Children's Day Association in keeping the children with the mother was $36" (144).

60. Case nos. 45023 and 45037.

61. Case no. 45037. She was paroled to live with her parents on March 31, 1914, and was permanently discharged that December.

62. According to the case files, twenty-one of the thirty-two children committed to an institution were reunited with a family member. See case nos. 44858 (mother), 44859 (aunt), 44860 (parents), 44862 (father), 44863 (aunt), 44865 (aunt), 44895 (father), 44898–44899 (siblings, mother), 44901–44902 (siblings, father), 44948–44951 (siblings, parents), 44962 (mother), 45024 (mother), 45037 (parents), 45041 (mother), 45042–45043 (siblings), and 45044 (parents). The number of reunions was most likely higher, but missing papers from a few case files make it impossible to ascertain to whom children were paroled. See, e.g., case nos. 44952–44956.

63. *In Re Peter for Help* 1918 Juvenile Court, case no. B36877, Cook County Circuit Court Archives, Richard J. Daley Center, Chicago.

64. Case no. 44900.

65. Ibid.

66. Unfortunately, the case file does not tell us what ultimately became of the baby with no name.

67. See case nos. 44857; 44896; 44952–44956 (five siblings); 44963; 44993–44994 (two siblings); 45023; and 45050.

68. An officer of the court and his wife adopted James, a six-month-old African-American baby. It was later discovered, however, that James's mother was a minor at the time of the original adoption and thus could not legally consent to the proceedings. In 1915, a second adoption occurred after the mother reached the age of majority. Case no. 44963.

69. Leff, "Consensus for Reform," 398.

70. There is growing literature on fatherhood, but unfortunately the historical works had little say to say about single fathers in the early twentieth century. See, e.g., Robert L. Griswold, *Fatherhood in America: A History* (New York: Basic Books, 1993). For the history of women and child care in America from colonial to modern times see Sonya Michel, *Children's Interests/Mothers Rights: The Shaping of American Child Care Policy* (New Haven: Yale University Press, 1999).

71. More than one third of the "legitimate" children brought to the court were growing up dependent because they had lost their mothers to death (nine, or 18 percent), desertion (six, or 12 percent), or commitment to an insane asylum (three, or 6 percent). For the following discussion of children growing up without mothers, I am only examining the family situations where the father was still present. I have excluded children born out of wedlock, as well as cases in which both parents either died or deserted their children. The eleven cases of single male-headed families are: 44862, 44895, 44901–44902 (siblings), 44960, 44991, 45041–45043 (siblings; the case of the three sisters), 45044–45045 (siblings). The other motherless children were: 44859 (mother dead, father missing); 44863 (mother dead, father deserted); 44865 (mother dead, father deserted); 44992 (both parents deserted); 45925 (mother deserted, father dead); 45026 (both parents deceased); 45041 (mother deserted, father dead); 45044–45045. There were also a couple of cases in which an illegitimate child's mother had died; see cases 44857 (illegitimate child, mother dead) and 45050 (illegitimate child, mother dead). These children, accordingly, had no legal parents.

72. Case nos. 44862 (reunited with father), 44895 (reunited with father), 44901–44902 (siblings, reunited with father), 44991 (reunited with grandmother), 45041–45043 (siblings, reunited with mother [the case of the three sisters]), 45044 (reunited with parents [mother had been in insane asylum; missing information in sibling's case file 45045 makes it impossible to determine whether he was reunited with family]).

73. Case nos. 44862 (father contributes $10 per month), 44895 (father unable to contribute), 44901–44902 (siblings, father contributes $20 per month), 45041–45043 (siblings, father contributes $15 per month), 45044–45045 (siblings, father unable to contribute).

74. Case nos. 44862 and 44895.

75. See case nos. 44876–44870 (five siblings), 44881–44883 (three siblings), 44884–44885 (two siblings), 44886–44887 (two siblings), 44888–44889 (two siblings), 44890–44892 (three siblings), 44893–44894 (two siblings), 44981–44983 (three siblings), 44984, 44985–44986 (two siblings), and 44987–44990 (four siblings). Hilda is case no. 44985 and Mary is case no. 44877.

The cash payment was part of the probation decree, which read: "And the Court further finds that the defendant ___ parent ___ of said dependent child ___ poor and unable to properly care for the said child, but ___ are otherwise proper guardian. It is therefore ordered that the said ___ be and remain a ward of this Court, and that said ward be permitted to go hence and be and remain in the custody of ___ parent ___ of said child, subject to the friendly visitation of the Chief Probation Officer of this Court or such assistant Probation Officer as may, from time to time be designated by him.

"It is further ordered, adjudged and decreed, that the sum of ___ dollars per month be and hereby is fixed by the Court, as the amount of money necessary to enable the parent ___ to properly care for said child at home, and that the Board of Commissioners of Cook County, Illinois, through its County Agent, or otherwise, be and hereby is directed and ordered to pay to ___ parent ___ the sum of ___ dollars per month, beginning ___ until further order of the Court."

76. The average and median age of the twenty-nine "home-based" track children was seven-and-half years. The average of the fifty-one "institutional" track children was a little over six-and-half years, and their median age was eight years.

77. Edith Abbott and Sophonisba P. Breckinridge, *The Administration of the Aid-to-Mothers Law in Illinois* (Washington, D.C.: Government Printing Office, 1921), 25–27.

78. Ibid., 27.

79. This information comes from a 1914 conference committee report, whose findings are discussed by Abbott and Breckinridge, *The Administration*, 30.

80. Ibid., 31.

81. In 1919 the dietitian was replaced by the written document "Chicago Standard Budget for Dependent Families," which was prepared by the Chicago Council of Social Agencies. *Juvenile Court Annual Reports* (1919), 8.

82. *Charity Service Reports*, Board of Commissioners of Court County (Chicago, 1913), 300.

83. Ibid., 297.

84. Under the 1913 revision of the law, fourteen was set as the upper age limit. In a 1923 revision of the law, the upper age limit for eligibility was raised to sixteen. For a summary of the law's changes, see Goodwin, *Gender and the Politics of Welfare Reform*, 199.

85. For a discussion of both this racial ideology of difference, as well as African-Americans' perspectives on mothers' pensions, see ibid., 31–36, and Mimi Abramovitz, *Regulating the Lives of Women: Social Welfare Policy from Colonial Times to the Present* (Boston, Mass.: South Earl Press, 1988), 318–319.

86. The percentages have been calculated from the statistics in *Charity Service Reports* (1913), 92. Of the 190 cases of dependency involving African-American families, only 6 had received pensions. In contrast, 23 of 48 Austrian, 30 of 54 English, 140 of 311 Irish, and 23 of 69 Russian families received pensions.

87. On concerns about desertion in this period see Willrich, "Home Slackers."

88. Pinckney, "Public Pensions," 479.

89. Ibid.

90. Case nos. 44898–44899.

91. Case nos. 44881–44883 (three siblings) and 44888–44889 (two siblings).

92. According to Goodwin, *Gender and the Politics of Welfare Reform*, "between 1911 and 1927, 13 percent of the pensioned families [in Cook County] included a father who had been either institutionalized or disabled through injury"(161).

93. *Laws of Illinois* (Springfield: State Printers, 1913), 127.

94. Goodwin, *Gender and the Politics of Welfare Reform*, 132.

95. Kathleen D. McCarthy, *Noblesse Oblige: Charity and Cultural Philanthropy in Chicago, 1849–1929* (Chicago: University of Chicago Press, 1982).

96. Abbott and Breckinridge, *The Administration*, 14.

97. Goodwin, *Gender and the Politics of Welfare Reform*, 134.

98. Ibid, 199.

99. Jeter, *The Chicago Juvenile Court*, 18.

100. Annette Marie Garrett, "The Administration of the Aid to Mothers' Law in Illinois 1917 to 1925" (M.A. thesis, School of Social Service Administration, University of Chicago, 1925). Also see Goodwin, *Gender and the Politics of Welfare Reform*, chap. 4. The amount Cook County spent on mothers' pensions also increased from roughly $86,000 in 1912 to over $280,000 in 1919, although the average pension remained fairly constant.

101. Leff, "Consensus for Reform," 413–414.

102. Howard W. Hopkirk, *Institutions Serving Children* (New York: Russell Sage Foundation, 1944), 14.

103. This series includes ninety-nine consecutive case files, case nos. 83301–83400, running from roughly September 1 to 22. There are thirty-two "nonpensioned" dependency cases and thirty-five mothers' pensions among these records.

104. In all but two cases, the mother had died. See case nos. 83319–83320 (siblings, mother insane), 83347–83349 (siblings), 83350–83352 (siblings), 83353–83356 (siblings), 83367–83370 (siblings), 83370, and 83371–83372 (siblings).

105. According to the case files, eleven of the eighteen children committed to an institution were reunited with a family member. See case nos. 83319 (parents), 83350–83352 (father), 83353 (father), 83356 (sister), 83368 (father), 83369 (cousin), 83370 (father), 83371–83372 (father). Two brothers aged out of the system; see case nos. 83348–83349.

106. *Juvenile Court Annual Reports* (1920), 10. On the politics of mothers' pensions in Illinois during the 1920s see Goodwin, *Gender and the Politics of Welfare Reform*, 146–153.

107. Case no. 83325.

108. Case nos. 83399–83400.

109. For the best discussion of the significance of this work requirement see Goodwin, "An American Experiment in Paid Motherhood," 323–341.

110. On the consequences of the devaluing of women's work and the myth that women on welfare did not work, see Goodwin, *Gender and the Politics of Welfare Reform*, 187–197.

111. Abbott and Breckinridge, *The Administration*, 6.

112. On the gradual removal of the administration of mothers' pensions from juvenile courts, see Christopher Howard, "Sowing the Seeds of Welfare: The Transformation of Mothers' Pensions," *Journal of Policy History* 4 (1992): 197.

113. Calvin Coolidge, "Coolidge Urges Home Control Need," *New York Times*, October 25, 1925, pp. 1, 27.

CHAPTER 4

1. *Charity Service Reports*, Board of Commissioners of Cook County, Illinois (Chicago: Ill.: Henry O. Shepard, 1911), 9.

2. *Cook County Appropriation Bill 1912 and Comptroller's Annual Report 1911*, Board of Commissioners of Cook County, Illinois (Chicago, Ill.: 1912), 44.

3. Mary Louise Childs, *Actual Government in Illinois* (New York: Century, 1914), 71–72.

4. Ibid. For the powers of the Civil Service Commission see the amendments to "An Act to Regulate the Civil Service of the State of Illinois," *Laws of Illinois* (Springfield: Illinois State Journal, 1907), 203–207.

5. *Proceedings*, Board of County Commissioners, Cook County, Illinois (December 5, 1910), 2.

6. Joan Gittens, *Poor Relations: The Children of the State in Illinois, 1818–1990* (Urbana: University of Illinois Press, 1994), 191–194.

7. "Probation and Politics," *Survey* 27 (March 30, 1912): 2003–2014.

8. "Blame of Court for Quiz," *Chicago American*, August 11, 1915, n.p., in Louise de Koven Bowen Scrapbooks, vol. 2, Chicago Historical Society, Chicago.

9. "Charge Society Is Enslaving Children," *Chicago Examiner*, July 20, 1910, n.p., box 29, file 9, Children Home and Aid Society of Illinois Papers, University of Illinois—Chicago, Special Collections (hereafter cited as CHASI Papers).

10. "Child Slavery Facts Ready for Officials," *Chicago Record-Herald*, February 17, 1911, p. 18.

11. Ibid.

12. *Fifth Annual Report of the Department of Visitation of Children Placed in Family Homes* (Springfield, Ill.: State Printers, 1911), 9.

13. "Dunn Swells Charge," *Chicago Record-Herald*, February 18, 1911, p. 3.

14. "Says Children Are Sold by Charities by Court Sanction," newspaper clipping, January 11, 1911, p. 1, box 29, file 9, CHASI Papers.

15. *Charity Service Reports*, Board of Commissioners of Cook County (Chicago: Henry O. Shepard, 1908), 186.

16. "Mr. W. H. Dunn Speaks at a Meeting of the D.A.R. in Austin, 3/14/11," p. 4, box 29, folder 9, CHASI Papers.

17. Harriette N. Dunn, *Infamous Juvenile Law: Crimes against Children under the Cloak of Charity* (Chicago: Privately Published, 1912).

18. For a discussion of this case, see David S. Tanenhaus, "Creating the Child, Constructing the State: *People v. Turner*, 1870," in *Children as Equals: Exploring the Rights of the Child*, edited by Kathleen Alaimo and Brian Klug (Lanham, Md. University Press of America, 2002), 127–144.

19. Dunn, *Infamous Juvenile Law*, 20.

20. "Babies Made Slaves," *Chicago Examiner*, April 20, 1911, n.p., clipping in CHASI Papers.

21. Ibid.

22. Timothy Hurley, "Legal Phases of the Juvenile Court Movement," *Juvenile Court Record* 10 (August 1909): 8.

23. Ibid.

24. "Ignores Charges of W. H. Dunn," *Chicago Record-Herald*, March 24, 1911, p. 3; "Ignores Dunn Charges, but Promises Inquiry," *Chicago Evening Post*, March 28, 1911, p. 3.

25. "Child Dependency Quiz," *Chicago Evening Post*, July 19, 1911, p. 3.

26. "Would Halt Court Probe," *Chicago Evening Post*, July 27, 1911, p. 5.

27. Ibid.

28. Ibid.

29. Ibid.

30. "Attacks Juvenile Law," *Chicago Daily News*, July 29, 1911, p. 4; *William H. Dunn v. The County of Cook et al.* (1912), case no. 288,267, Cook County Circuit Court Archives, Chicago.

31. "The Juvenile Court," *Chicago-Record Herald*, August 9, 1911, p. 8.

32. Ibid. These reasons were drawn from section 15 of the revised Juvenile Court Act of 1907. *Laws of Illinois* (Springfield, Ill.: Phillips, 1907), 77.

33. "The Juvenile Court," 8.

34. "Appoints Quiz Board," *Chicago Record-Herald*, August 13, 1911, p. 3: Also see *The Juvenile Court of Cook County, Illinois: Report of a Committee Appointed under Resolution of the Board of Commissioners of Cook County, Bearing Date August 8, 1911* (Chicago: Committee to investigate the operation of Juvenile court, 1912) (hereafter cited as *Hotchkiss Report*), 2.

35. "Now for the Investigation," *Chicago Record-Herald*, August 15, 1911, p. 8.

36. "Juvenile Court Quiz Assumes New Phase," *Chicago Record-Herald*, August 23, 1911, p. 3; "Juvenile Court Probe a Riddle," *Chicago Daily News*, August 22, 1911; p. 4.

37. Ibid. (italics added).

38. "Denies Clash with Bartzen," *Chicago Daily News*, August 23, 1911, p. 14.

39. Ibid.

40. A third investigation also began in October 1911 when the County Judge of Cook County appointed six citizens to a County Board of Visitors to investigate all "the institutions and organizations receiving children through the Cook County Juvenile Court." *Report of the County Board of Visitors* (Chicago: County Board of Visitors, 1912).

41. Harvey B. Hurd, "Juvenile Court Law: Minimum Principles Which Should Be Stood For," *Charities* 13 (January 7, 1905): 327–328. On the importance of the probation officers see Steven L. Schlossman,

Love and the American Delinquent: The Theory and Practice of "Progressive" Juvenile Justice, 1825–1920 (Chicago: University of Chicago Press, 1977), chap. 4.

42. Julia C. Lathrop, "The Development of Probation in a Large City," *Charities* 13 (January 7, 1905): 344–349; Bernard Flexner and Roger N. Baldwin, *Juvenile Courts and Probation* (New York: Century, 1914), 79–172.

43. "Probation Officers Are in a Dilemma," *Chicago Record-Herald*, August 25, 1911, p. 18.

44. "Two Inquiries Sure into Juvenile Court," *Chicago Evening Post*, August 23, 1911, p. 3.

45. Victoria Getis, *The Juvenile Court and the Progressives* (Urbana: University of Illinois Press, 2000).

46. "Lives of Children Menaced," *Chicago Inter-Ocean*, October 18, 1912, n.p., clipping in McCormick Scrapbooks, vol. 1, Newberry Library, Chicago.

47. "Epidemic Perils Wards of County," *Chicago Daily News*, October 18, 1912, n.p., clipping in McCormick Scrapbooks, vol. 1.

48. "Probation Head Out," *Chicago Evening Post*, September 29, 1911, 4.

49. "The Blight of Bartzen," *Chicago Evening Post*, August 2, 1911, p. 6.

50. Ibid.

51. "A. A. M'Cormick Is Advocate and Adherent of Manly Art," *Chicago Inter-Ocean*, October 31, 1912, clipping in McCormick Scrapbooks, vol. 1; "Battling" Peter Avoids Fist Fight with M'Cormick," *Chicago Inter-Ocean*, March 12, 1913, clipping in McCormick Scrapbooks, vol. 2.

52. "Hearst Sheet Misleads Those Who Read It," *Chicago Daily Socialist*, August 25, 1911, clipping in McCormick Scrapbooks, vol. 1.

53. "Club Women Declare War against Bartzen," *Chicago Record-Herald*, October 29, 1912, clipping in McCormick Scrapbooks, vol. 1.

54. "Report of the Meeting Held at the Illinois Theatre, Sunday Afternoon, November 3rd, 1912," typescript in Cook County Board of Commissioners file, Chicago Historical Society, Chicago.

55. Ibid.

56. Ibid.

57. Joanne Lorraine Goodwin, "Gender, Politics, and Welfare Reform: Mothers' Pensions in Chicago, 1900–1930." (Ph.D. dess., University of Michigan, 1991), 198.

58. Elisabeth Parker, "Personnel and Organization in the Probation Department of the Juvenile Court of Cook County, 1899–1933" (M.A. thesis, School of Social Service Administration, University of Chicago, 1934), 23.

59. *Hotchkiss Report*, 16–17: Sophonisba P. Breckinridge and Edith Abbott, *The Delinquent Child and the Home: A Study of the Delinquent Wards of the Juvenile Court of Chicago* (New York: Charities Publication Committee, 1912), 237.

60. Breckinridge and Abbott, *The Delinquent Child and the Home*, 238.

61. *Hotchkiss Report*, 16.

62. *Dunn v. County of Cook et al.* (1912), case no. 288,267, Cook County Circuit Court Archives, Chicago.

63. "Bill for Injunction," case no. 288,267, Cook County Circuit Court Archives, Chicago.

64. "Trying the Juvenile Court Case," *Chicago Record-Herald*, August 1, 1911, p. 10.

65. "Bill for Injunction," 5.

66. Ibid., 6–7.

67. *Witter v. Cook County Commissioners*, 256 Ill. 616 (1912).

68. Julian W. Mack, "The Juvenile Court," *Harvard Law Review* 23 (1909–1910): 104–122.

69. Ibid., 104.

70. Ibid.

71. Ibid.

72. *Bouvier's Law Dictionary and Concise Encyclopedia*, 8th ed., edited by John Bouvier (St. Paul, Minn.: 1914), 1390–1391.

73. *Witter*, 624.

74. Ibid.

75. "Bartzensim Ends in Juvenile Court," *Chicago Inter-Ocean*, January 13, 1912, clipping in McCormick Scrapbooks, vol. 2.

76. See Frank T. Flynn, "Judge Merritt W. Pinckney," *Social Service Review* 28 (March 1954): 26.

77. Grace Abbott, *The Child and the State* (Chicago: University of Chicago Press, 1938), vol. 2: 412–417.

78. Flynn, "Judge Merritt W. Pinckney,"26.

79. Ibid.

80. Ibid.

81. *Lindsay v. Lindsay*, 255 Ill. 442 (1912).

82. *Lindsay*, 444.

83. Ibid.

84. "Lindsay Boy Missing, Judge Raps Sun Cult," *Chicago Daily News,* January 4, 1912, p. 1.

85. *Lindsay,* 443.

86. "Lindsay Boy Missing, Judge Raps Sun Cult," p. 1.

87. Ibid.

88. Ibid.

89. "Grill Hanish in Trial," *Chicago Daily News,* January 6, 1912, p. 3.

90. Ibid.

91. Ibid.

92. "Lindsay Boy Missing, Judge Raps Sun Cult," p. 2.

93. *Lindsay,* 443.

94. Ibid., 443.

95. Ibid., 443.

96. Ibid., 443.

97. Ibid., 445–446.

98. *Lindsay,* 446.

99. *Lindsay,* 446.

100. *Lindsay v. Lindsay,* 257 Ill., 328 (1913) (hereafter cited as *Lindsay II*).

101. *Lindsay II,* 332.

102. *Commonwealth v. Fisher,* 213 Pa. 48 (1905).

103. *Lindsay II,* 332.

104. Ibid., 334. They also cited *Fisher* to support the contention that the juvenile courts was a part of an existing court system.

105. *Lindsay II,* 337.

106. Ibid., 333.

107. Ibid., 338.

108. Ibid., 338.

109. Ibid., 339.

110. Ibid., 339.

111. Ibid., 339–340.

112. Ibid., 339–340.

113. Ibid., 340.

114. Ibid., 340.

115. Ibid., 340.

116. Ibid., 340–341.

117. Ibid., 341.

118. Annette Ruth Appell, "Virtual Mothers and the Meaning of Parenthood," *University of Michigan Journal of Law Reform* 34 (summer 2001): 688.

119. For information about the Juvenile Court's 113 employees and their specific responsibilities see *In Re Peter for Help*, case no. B36877 (1918), Cook County Circuit Court Archives, Chicago.

120. Quoted in a letter from Joel P. Hunter to William C. Graves, April 9, 1917, Julius Rosenwald Papers, box 23, folder 9, Rosenwald Papers. Department of Special Collections, University of Chicago Library.

121. Ibid.

122. Ibid.

123. Rosenwald to Mrs. E. Blaine, 25 July 1912, box 42, folder 14, Rosenwald Papers.

124. William C. Graves to Merritt W. Pinckney, 30 December 1912, box 23, folder 9, Rosenwald Papers.

125. Joel P. Hunter to William C. Graves, 9 April 1917, box 23, folder 9, Rosenwald Papers.

126. W.C. Graves to Julius Rosenwald, March 31, 1917, box 23, folder 9, Rosenwald Papers.

127. Graves to Hunter, April 10, 1917, box 23, folder 9, Rosenwald Papers. Morton D. Hull also loaned $1,900 to the committee. See Graves to Julius Rosenwald, May 21, 1917, box 23, folder 9, Rosenwald Papers.

128. Letter from Committee for the Chicago Bar Association to Julius Rosenwald, May 16, 1917, box 23, folder 9, Rosenwald Papers.

129. *Juvenile Court Annual Reports* (1917), 5–6.

130. Letter from Committee for the Chicago Bar Association to Julius Rosenwald, Rosenwald Papers.

131. The following individuals signed the bond on June 12, 1917: Harrison B. Riley, John P. Wilson, John G. Shedd, Rollin A. Keyes, Frank H. Scott, Charles S. Cutting, John S. Mule, Walter H. Wilson, D. R. McLeman, John V. Farwell, Homer A. Stillwell, Albert D. Dick, Edgar A. Bancroft, Robert Berry Ennis, Jas. R. Forgan, Alfred S. Baker, James A. Patten, Morton D. Hull, Frank H. McCullough, Ethel S. Dummer, Lewis Ferguson, William P. Sidley, Alfred Cowles, Albert A. Sprague II, Thomas D. Jones, Arthur W. Underwood, Harry A. Wheeler, Robert Schaffner, Merritt W. Pinckney, and Victor P. Arnold.

132. "An Act in relation to suits to restrain and enjoin the disbursement of public moneys by officers of the State," *Laws of Illinois* (Springfield, Ill.: State Printers, 1917), 534–535. Also see "An Act to prevent the mere bringing or pendency of any suit from changing the liability of public officers in the disbursement of public funds on

account of notice of any matter contained in the pleadings," *Laws of Illinois* (Springfield, Ill.: State Printers, 1917), 536.

133. *Juvenile Court Annual Reports* (1918), 9.

CHAPTER 5

1. Robert M. Mennel, "Ethel Sturges Dummer," in *Notable American Women: The Modern Period*, edited by Barbara Sicherman and Carol Hurd Green (Cambridge, Mass.: Harvard University Press, 1980), 208–210.

2. Ethel Sturges Dummer, *Why I Think So: The Autobiography of a Hypothesis* (Chicago: Clarke-McElroy, 1937), 35.

3. Ethel Sturges Dummer to Henry Thurston, n.d., c. February 1921, box 37, folder 802, Ethel Sturges Dummer Papers, Schlesinger Library, Radcliffe College, Cambridge, Mass.

4. Dummer, *Why I Think So*, 35.

5. Ethel Sturges Dummer to Henry Thurston, n.d., c. February 1921, box 37, folder 802, Dummer Papers.

6. See Paul Gerard Anderson, "The Good to Be Done: A History of the Juvenile Protective Association of Chicago, 1898–1976" (Ph.D. diss., University of Chicago, 1988), 1:160–161.

7. *Charity Service Report*, Board of Commissioners of Cook County, Illinois (Chicago, Ill.: Henry O. Shepard, 1907), 112, *Charity Service Report*, Board of Commissioners of Cook County, Illinois (1908), 236–243.

8. *Charity Service Report*, Board of Commissioners of Cook County, Illinois (Chicago: Henry O. Shepard, 1908), 238.

9. Ibid., 239.

10. Ibid., 241.

11. Elizabeth Lunbeck, *The Psychiatric Persuasion: Knowledge, Gender, and Power in Modern America* (Princeton, N.J.: Princeton University Press, 1994), 65–71.

12. Ibid., 352 n. 74.

13. Ibid., 65.

14. Lunbeck, *The Psychiatric Persuasion*, 34.

15. Ibid., 3. For a provocative analysis of the concept of "personality" see Warren Susman, *Culture as History: The Transformation of American Society in the Twentieth Century* (New York: Pantheon Books, 1984), 271–285.

16. Jennifer Platt, "'Acting As a Switchboard': Mrs. Ethel Sturges Dummer's Role in Sociology," *American Sociologist* 23 (fall 1992): 28.

17. Ibid., 25.

18. Victoria Getis, *The Juvenile Court and the Progressives* (Urbana: University of Illinois Press, 2000), 1.

19. Letter, January 2, 1909, box 30, folder 578, Dummer Papers.

20. On recapitulation theory see Stephen Jay Gould, *The Mismeasure of Man* (New York: Norton, 1981), 113–122.

21. Dorothy Ross, *G. Stanley Hall: The Psychologist as Prophet* (Chicago: University of Chicago, 1972), 386–394; Peter Gay, *Freud: A Life for Our Time* (New York: Norton, 1988), 206–213.

22. The following biographical information is based on George E. Gardner, "William Healy, 1869–1963," *Journal of American Academy of Child Psychiatry* 11 (January 1972): 1–29, and the transcript of an oral history interview with William Healy and Augusta F. Bronner by John C. Burnham, January 1960, Chicago Historical Society.

23. "Tenney, Horace Kent," in *The Book of Chicagoans: A Biographical Dictionary of Leading Living Men of the City of Chicago* (Chicago: Marquis, 1911), 665.

24. William Healy to Julia Lathrop, April 4, 1908, box 30, folder 578, Dummer Papers. The letter is also reprinted in Robert Bremner, ed., *Children and Youth in America: A Documentary History*, vol. 2 (Cambridge, Mass.: Harvard University Press, 1971), 565.

25. Gould, *The Mismeasure of Man*, 122–145; Ruth Harris, *Murders and Madness: Medicine, Law, and Society in the Fin de Siècle* (New York: Oxford University Press, 1989), 80–87.

26. Copies of these forms are only in the extant files from 1899 until 1906. After this point, the case histories were most likely kept with the probation reports, which were apparently destroyed in the late 1960s.

27. Gardner, "William Healy," 12. For a description of Goddard's work see Gould, *Mismeasure of Man*, 158–174.

28. Gardner, "William Healy," 12.

29. William Healy to Ethel Sturges Dummer, April 29, 1909, box 2, folder 31, Dummer Papers.

30. Mrs. George R. Dean, the institute's secretary, was the third officer. Professor James R. Angell, Judge E. O. Brown, Dr. H. B. Favill, Judge Julian W. Mack, Professor George H. Mead, Dr. Adolf Meyer, Horace K. Tenney, Henry W. Thurston, John H. Wigmore, Judge Merritt W. Pinckney, and Judge Harry Olson served on the advisory council. The executive committee was composed of Jane Addams, Mrs. William F. Dummer, Dr. Frank S. Churchill, Allen T. Burns,

Julia C. Lathrop, Dr. Hugh T. Patrick, Mrs. George R. Dean, and Dr. Graham Taylor.

31. Clipping from the *Chicago Record-Herald*, April 20, 1909, box 23, folder 372, Dummer Papers.

32. Ibid.

33. On the compatibility of eugenics and environmentalism in the Progressive Era, see Michael Willrich, *City of Courts: Socializing Justice in Progressive Era Chicago* (New York: Cambridge University Press, 2003), especially chap. 8.

34. William Healy and Augusta F. Bronner, "The Child Guidance Clinic: Birth and Growth of an Idea," in *Orthopsychiatry, 1923–1948: Retrospect and Prospect*, edited by Lawson G. Lowrey (Menasha, Wis.: American Othropsychiatric Association, 1948), 16; Oral history interview with Healy, 98.

35. Willrich, *City of Courts*.

36. Healy and Bronner, "Child Guidance Clinic," 33.

37. In addition to Healy, the institute also employed a succession of psychologists (Grace M. Fernald, Mary H. S. Hayes, Jean Weidensell, Clara Schmitt, Mary W. Chapin, and finally Augusta F. Bronner, who would later marry Healy); several special researchers (Dr. Anne Burnet, Frances Porter, and Dr. Edith R. Spaulding); and a secretary to the director, Emily Deane Macmillan.

38. William Healy, *The Individual Delinquent: A Text-Book of Diagnosis and Prognosis for all Concerned in Understanding Offenders* (Boston: Little, Brown, 1915), 53–67.

39. Gould, *The Mismeasure of Man*, 148.

40. Healy, *The Individual Delinquent*, 80.

41. William Healy and Grace M. Fernald, *Tests for Practical Mental Classification* (Baltimore: Review Publishing, 1911), 4.

42. Gould, *Mismeasure of Man*, 159.

43. Healy and Fernald, *Tests for Practical Mental Classification*, 11. Healy wrote the text for this monograph. It was also published in *Psychological Review* 13 (March 1911).

44. Healy and Fernald, *Tests for Practical Mental Classification*, 46.

45. Ibid., 47.

46. Ibid.

47. Healy and Fernald, *Tests for Practical Mental Classification*, 47–49.

48. Healy and Bronner, "The Child Guidance Clinic," 27. On Healy's use of the "own story" see James Bennett, *Oral History and*

Delinquency: The Rhetoric of Criminology (Chicago: University of Chicago Press, 1981), 112–122.

49. William Healy, *The Practical Value of Scientific Study of Juvenile Delinquents*, U.S. Department of Labor, Children's Bureau, publication no. 96 (Washington, D.C.: Government Printing Office, 1922), 25.

50. Healy, *The Individual Delinquent*, 21.

51. On the child guidance movement see Margo Horn, *Before It's Too Late: The Child Guidance Movement in the United States, 1922–1945* (Philadelphia: Temple University Press, 1989).

52. Healy, *The Individual Delinquent*, 21.

53. Susman, *Culture as History*, 276.

54. Healy and Fernald, *Tests for Practical Mental Classification*, 7.

55. Ibid., 6.

56. Ibid., 7.

57. William Healy, "The Problem of Causation of Criminality," *Journal of Criminal Law and Criminology* 2 (1912): 853; Healy, "Individual Study of the Young Criminal," *Journal of Criminal Law and Criminology* 1 (1910): 58.

58. Healy, *The Individual Delinquent*, 44.

59. Ibid., 45.

60. *Journal of the American Institute of Criminal Law and Criminology* 1 (May 1910): 2.

61. Ibid., 61.

62. Ibid., 30.

63. Healy, *The Individual Delinquent*, 80.

64. William Healy to Ethel Sturges Dummer, January 24, 1914, box 30, folder 578, Dummer Papers.

65. Ibid.

66. William Healy to Ethel Sturges Dummer, October 4, 1915, box 30, folder 578, Dummer Papers.

67. John H. Laub, "A Century of Delinquency Research and Theory," in *A Century of Juvenile Justice*, edited by Margaret K. Rosenheim, Franklin E. Zimring, David S. Tanenhaus, and Bernardine Dohrn (Chicago: University of Chicago Press, 2002), 196.

68. John H. Wigmore, "Shall Dr. Healy's Work Be Lost to Chicago?" n.d., c. 1916, box 30, folder 578, Dummer Papers.

69. Healy and Bronner, "The Child Guidance Clinic," 34.

70. Kenneth Cmiel, *A Home of Another Kind: One Chicago Orphanage and the Tangle of Child Welfare* (Chicago: University of Chicago Press, 1995), 94.

71. Gardner, "William Healy," 17.

72. *Juvenile Court Annual Reports* (1917), 6.

73. William Healy to Ethel Sturges Dummer, March 8, 1920, box 30, folder 579, Dummer Papers.

74. William Healy to Ethel Sturges Dummer, March 16, 1921, box 30, folder 580, Dummer Papers.

75. Ethel Sturges Dummer to William Healy, November 28, 1921, box 30, folder 580, Dummer Papers; Herbert M. Baker, "Passing of the Juvenile Court," *Survey* 45 (February 12, 1921): 705.

76. Hamilton Cravens, "Child Saving in Modern America 1870s–1990s," in *Children at Risk in America: History, Concepts, and Public Policy*, edited by Roberta Wollons (Albany: State University of New York Press, 1993), 3–31.

77. Evelina Belden, *Courts in the United States Hearing Children's Cases: A Summary of Juvenile-Court Legislation in the United States*, U.S. Department of Labor, Children's Bureau, publication no. 65 (Washington, D.C.: 1920). In 1918, a five-part questionnaire was mailed to 2,391 courts, and 2,034 (85 percent) responded.

78. Ibid., 13.

79. Ibid., 14.

80. Ibid., 15.

81. Ibid.

82. U.S. Department of Labor, Children's Bureau, *Proceedings of the Conference on Juvenile-Court Standards Held under the Auspices of the U.S. Children's Bureau and the National Probation Association*, publication no. 97 (Washington, D.C.: 1922), 5.

83. Ibid., 7–8.

84. Ibid., 8.

85. Ibid., 104.

86. William Healy to Ethel Sturges Dummer, March 16, 1921, box 30, folder 580, Dummer Papers.

87. Horn, *Before It's Too Late*, 4.

88. Quoted in ibid., 30–31.

89. Ibid.

90. Robyn Muncy, *Creating a Female Dominion in American Reform, 1890–1935* (New York: Oxford University Press, 1991), 90–91.

91. U.S. Department of Labor, Children's Bureau, *Juvenile-Court Standards: Report of the Committee Appointed by the Children's Bureau, August, 1921, to Formulate Juvenile-Court Standards, Adopted by a Conference Held under the Auspices of the Children's Bureau and the*

National Probation Association, Washington, D.C., May 18, 1923,
publication no. 121 (Washington, D.C.: 1923), vi; Marguerite
G. Rosenthal, "The Children's Bureau and the Juvenile Court:
Delinquency Policy, 1912–1940," *Social Service Review* 60 (June 1986):
308–310.

92. David J. Rothman, *Conscience and Convenience: The Asylum and
Its Alternatives in Progressive America* (Boston: Little, Brown, 1980),
245–246.

93. Rosenthal, "The Children's Bureau," 308, 317 n. 19.

94. Judge Hugo Pam was the vice-chairman, Mrs. Harry Hart was
the treasurer, and Jessie F. Binford was the secretary. The honorary
chairmen were the Honorable Victor P. Arnold, the presiding judge
of the Cook County Juvenile Court; Dr. William Allen Pusey,
president of the American Medical Association; the Honorable
Mary M. Bartelme, judge of the Juvenile Court; Dr. Herman M. Adler,
the state criminologist and director of the IJR; and John M. Cameron,
president of the Chicago Bar Association. The program chairmen
were Joel D. Hunter and Mrs. William F. Dummer. Mrs. George V.
McIntrye was in charge of arrangements, Mrs. Harry Hart oversaw the
finances, and Joseph L. Moss arranged for exhibits. Anniversary
invitation, box 16, folder 242, Dummer Papers.

95. Hal Higdon, *The Crime of the Century: The Leopold and Loeb
Case* (New York: Putnam, 1975); Paula S. Fass, "Making and Remaking
an Event: The Leopold and Loeb Case in American Culture," *Journal
of American History* 80 (December 1993): 919–951.

96. Maureen McKernan, *The Amazing Trial of Leopold and Loeb*
(Chicago: Plymouth Court Press, 1924), 244.

97. Gay, *Freud*, 453–454.

98. "A Symposium of Comments from the Legal Profession, in the
Loeb-Leopold Murder of Franks in Chicago, May 21, 1924," *Journal of
Criminal Law and Criminology* 15 (November 1924): 395–405.

99. Clipping from W. I. Thomas to Ethel Sturges Dummer, n.d., c.
November 1924, box 36, folder 789, Dummer Papers.

100. Clipping from W. I. Thomas to Ethel Sturges Dummer, n.d., c.
November 1924, box 36, folder 789, Dummer Papers.

101. Ibid.

102. Ethel Sturges Dummer to William Healy, November 1, 1924, box
30, folder 580, Dummer Papers.

103. Ethel Sturges Dummer to W. I. Thomas, December 14,
1924, box 36, folder 789, Dummer Papers.

104. William Healy to Ethel Sturges Dummer, October 27, 1924, box 30, folder 580, Dummer Papers.

105. Ethel Sturges Dummer to William Healy, November 26, 1924, box 30, folder 580, Dummer Papers.

106. Estelle B. Freedman, *Maternal Justice: Miriam Van Waters and the Female Reform Tradition* (Chicago: University of Chicago Press, 1996).

107. Julian W. Mack, "The Chancery Procedure in the Juvenile Court," in *The Child, The Clinic and the Court*, edited by Jane Addams (New York: New Republic, 1925), 298–309, and Miriam Van Waters, "The Juvenile Court from the Child's Viewpoint: A Glimpse into the Future," in Addams, *The Child, The Clinic and the Court*, 217–237.

108. Mack, "The Chancery Procedure," 318.

109. Van Waters, "The Juvenile Court," 221.

110. Ibid., 219.

111. Ibid., 235 (italics in original).

112. Van Waters, "The Juvenile Court," 237.

113. Anniversary invitation, box 16, folder 242, Dummer Papers.

114. William Healy, "The Psychology of the Situation: A Fundamental for Understanding and Treatment of Delinquency and Crime," in Addams, *The Child, the Clinic and the Court*, 52.

115. Kathleen W. Jones, *Taming the Troublesome Child: American Families, Child Guidance, and the Limits of Psychiatric Authority* (Cambridge, Mass.: Harvard University Press, 1999), 91.

116. Ibid., 117.

CHAPTER 6

1. Ernest W. Burgess, Joseph D. Lohman, and Clifford R. Shaw, *"The Chicago Area Project,"* in *Coping with Crime: Yearbook of the National Probation Association* (New York: National Probation Association, 1937), 10. For excellent discussions of how conceptions of community mobilization shaped the "War on Poverty," see Allen J. Matusow, *The Unraveling of America: A History of Liberalism in the 1960s* (New York: Harper and Row, 1984), chap. 4; and Nicholas Lemann, *The Promised Land: The Great Black Migration and How It Changed America* (New York: Knopf), 108–191. For an overview and analysis of community programs in the 1990s, including Communities That Care, see David P. Farrington and Rolf Loeber, "Serious and Violent Juvenile Offenders," in *A Century of Juvenile Justice*, edited by Margaret K. Rosenheim, Franklin E. Zimring, David S. Tanenhaus, and Bernardine Dohrn (Chicago: University of Chicago Press, 2002), 218–223.

2. Paul Gerard Anderson, " 'The Good to Be Done': A History of the Juvenile Protective Association of Chicago, 1898–1976" (Ph.D. diss., University of Chicago, 1988), 1:182.

3. Paul Boyer, *Urban Masses and Moral Order in America, 1820–1920* (Cambridge, Mass.: Harvard University Press, 1978), chaps. 13–16.

4. "Publicity Committee Report," Juvenile Court Committee (c. 1907), Emily Washburn Dean Papers, Chicago Historical Society, Chicago.

5. Louise de Koven Bowen, *Growing Up with the City* (New York: MacMillan, 1926), 121; Bowen, "Our Most Popular Recreation Controlled by the Liquor Interests: A Study of Public Dance Halls" (Chicago: Juvenile Protective Association, 1911); Bowen, "Five and Ten Cent Theaters: Two Investigations by the Juvenile Protective Association of Chicago 1909 and 1911" (Chicago: Juvenile Protective Association, 1911); Edith Abbott, "The One Hundred and One County Jails of Illinois and Why They Ought to be Abolished" (Chicago: Juvenile Protective Association, 1916); and Bowen, "The Colored People of Chicago: An Investigation Made for the Juvenile Protective Association" (Chicago: Rodgers and Hall, 1913).

6. For a detailed examination of the theory and practice of Chicago's municipal court, which served as a national model, see Michael Willrich, *City of Courts: Socializing Justice in Progressive Era Chicago* (New York: Cambridge University Press, 2003).

7. Paul G. Cressey, *The Taxi-Dance Hall: A Sociological Study in Commercialized Recreation and City Life* (Chicago: University of Chicago Press, 1932).

8. Paul G. Cressey, "Report on Summer's Work with the Juvenile Protective Association of Chicago," Ernest W. Burgess Papers, box 129, folder 5, p. 48, Special Collections, Regenstein Library, University of Chicago.

9. On the Chicago school of sociology, which dominated American sociology for more than a generation, see Robert E. L. Farris, *Chicago Sociology, 1920–1932* (San Francisco: Chandler, 1967) and Martin Bulmer, *The Chicago School of Sociology: Institutionalization, Diversity, and the Rise of Sociological Research* (Chicago: University of Chicago Press, 1984).

10. Robert E. Park, "Community Organization and Juvenile Delinquency," in Robert E. Park, Ernest W. Burgess, and Roderick D. McKenzie, *The City* (1925; reprint, Chicago: University of Chicago Press, 1984), 106.

11. Robert E. Park, "The City: Suggestions for the Investigation of Human Behavior in the Urban Environment," in Park, Burgess, and McKenzie, *The City*, 3.

12. Quoted in James Bennett, *Oral History and Delinquency: The Rhetoric of Criminology* (Chicago: University of Chicago Press, 1981).

13. Bulmer, *The Chicago School of Sociology*, 124.

14. Jon Snodgrass, "Clifford R. Shaw and Henry D. McKay: Chicago Criminologists," *British Journal of Criminology* 16 (January 1976): 2.

15. Clifford R. Shaw and Henry D. Mckay, *Social Factors in Juvenile Delinquency*, vol. 2 of *Report on the Causes of Crime of the National Commission on Law Observance and Enforcement* (1931; reprint, Montclair, N.J.: Patterson Smith, 1968), 390.

16. Ibid., 393.

17. Clifford R. Shaw and Ernest W. Burgess, *The Jack-Roller: A Delinquent Boy's Own Story* (Chicago: University of Chicago Press, 1930); Clifford R. Shaw and Maurice E. Moore, *The Natural History of a Delinquent Career* (Chicago: University of Chicago, 1931); and Clifford R. Shaw, Henry D. McKay, J. E. McDonald, Harold B. Hanson, and Ernest W. Burgess, *Brothers in Crime* (Chicago: University of Chicago Press, 1938). For a critical look at how students of crime, including William Healy and Clifford Shaw, have used oral histories, see Bennett, *Oral History and Delinquency*.

18. Clifford R. Shaw and Ernest W. Burgess, *The Jack-Roller: A Delinquent Boy's Own Story* (1930; reprint, Chicago: University of Chicago Press, 1966).

19. Ibid., 34.

20. Ibid., 43

21. Ibid., 183.

22. Ibid., 194.

23. *The Negro in Chicago: A Study of Race Relations* (Chicago: University of Chicago Press, 1922), xiii. Also see William M. Tuttle Jr., *Race Riot: Chicago in the Red Summer of 1919* (New York: Atheneum, 1970), especially chap. 2.

24. *The Negro in Chicago*, 438.

25. Ibid., 623.

26. Ibid., 646.

27. Shaw and McKay, *Social Factors in Juvenile Delinquency*, 388–389.

28. Clifford R. Shaw and Henry D. McKay, *Juvenile Delinquency and Urban Areas: A Study of Rates of Delinquents in Relation to*

Differential Characteristics of Local Communities in American Cities (Chicago: University of Chicago Press, 1942), 156.

29. Anthony Sorrentino, *Organizing against Crime: Redeveloping the Neighborhood* (New York: Human Sciences Press, 1977), 254.

30. Interview by me with Anthony Sorrentino, May 20, 1993.

31. Burgess, Lohman, and Shaw, "The Chicago Area Project," 9–10. For an excellent account of the implementation and operation of one of the Chicago Area Project's pioneering programs, see Steven Schlossman and Michael Sedlak, *The Chicago Area Project Revisited* (Santa Monica, Calif.: Rand, 1984).

32. Sorrentino, *Organizing against Crime*, 87.

33. Ibid., 96.

34. Ibid., 110–112.

35. Ibid., 152.

36. Ibid., 159.

37. Ibid., 159.

38. Ibid., 166.

39. Grace Benjamin, "The Case for the Juvenile Court: Social Aspects of a Simple Legal Problem," *Chicago Bar Record* 16 (May 1935): 233.

40. *People v. Fitzgerald*, 322 Ill. 54, 59–60.

41. Ibid., 59. (italics added).

42. *People v.Bruno*, 346 Ill. 449, 452.

43. Ibid., 452.

44. Ibid., 451.

45. Lauren Beth Lipson, "No Haven for Criminals": The Susie Lattimore Case and the Gradual Decline of Juvenile Justice" (senior thesis, Northwestern University, 2001).

46. Fred Gross, *Detention and Prosecution of Children* (Chicago: Central Howard Association, 1946), 21.

47. "Sullivan Drafts Juvenile Court Act Amendment," *Chicago Tribune*, April 17, 1935, p. 18.

48. *People v. Lattimore*, 362 Ill. 206, 207.

49. Ibid., 209.

50. Benedict S. Alper, "Forty Years of the Juvenile Court," *American Sociological Review* 6 (1941): 230.

51. *People v. Malec*, 362 Ill. 229, 230.

52. John Dickinson, "Juvenile Court: Statute Giving It Discretion," *Illinois Bar Journal* 25 (1936): 78.

53. Ibid., 79.

54. Mara L. Dodge, "'Our Juvenile Court Has Become More Like a Criminal Court': A Century of Reform at the Cook County (Chicago) Juvenile Court," *Michigan Historical Review* 26 (fall 2000): 62.

55. Charles W. Hoffman, "Next Steps in Juvenile Courts and Probation," in *The Yearbook of the National Probation Association* (New York: National Probation Association, 1934), 44.

56. Ibid., 51.

57. Sorrentino, *Organizing against Crime*, 90.

58. Interview with Anthony Sorrentino.

59. Quoted by James R. Bennett, Introduction to Anthony Sorrentino, *Organizing against Crime*, 23.

60. Farrington and Loeber, "Serious and Violent Juvenile Offenders," 222.

61. Ibid., 229.

CONCLUSION

1. Judge Eugene A. Moore, "Sentencing Opinion: People of the State of Michigan v. Nathaniel Abraham," *Juvenile and Family Court Journal* 51 (spring 2000): 9.

2. Ibid., 5.

3. Ibid., 5.

4. Ibid., 8.

5. Ibid., 8.

6. Ibid., 11.

7. Ibid., 9.

8. Ibid., 9.

9. Ibid., 9.

10. Ibid., 10 (italics in original).

11. Ibid., 11.

12. Ibid.

13. David Goodman, *Judge Spares Eleven-Year-Old Killer from Life in Prison*, APWIRES 00:45:00, January 14, 2000. See also Mitch Albom, "We Can't Afford the Death of Hope," *Times Union (Albany)*, January 19, 2000, A15.

14. *Young Murderer Quotes*, APWIRES 15:53:00, January 13, 2000.

15. Goodman, *Judge Spares Eleven-Year-Old Killer*.

16. L. L. Brasier, "Young Killer Admits Reality," *Detroit Free Press*, November 20, 2002, at 1B and 4B.

17. Jane Addams, *My Friend Julia Lathrop* (New York: Macmillan, 1935), 137.

18. The most comprehensive critique of the modern juvenile court and call for its abolition is Barry C. Feld, *Bad Kids: Race and the Transformation of the Juvenile Court* (New York: Oxford University Press, 1999).

19. For an overview of how juvenile offenders have been characterized in the twentieth century, see John H. Laub, "A Century of Delinquency Research and Delinquency Theory," in *A Century of Juvenile Justice*, edited by Margaret K. Rosenheim, Franklin E. Zimring, David S. Tanenhaus, and Bernardine Dohrn (Chicago: University of Chicago Press, 2002), 179–205.

20. See, e.g., Franklin E. Zimring, *The Changing Legal World of Adolescence* (New York: Free Press, 1985); Thomas Grisso and Robert G. Schwartz, eds., *Youth on Trial: A Developmental Perspective on Juvenile Justice* (Chicago: University of Chicago Press, 2000); Elizabeth S. Scott, "The Legal Construction of Childhood," in Rosenheim, Zimring, Tanenhaus, and Dohrn *A Century of Juvenile Justice*, 113–141; and Peter Edelman, "American Government and the Politics of Youth," in Rosenheim, Zimring, Tanenhaus, and Dohrn, *A Century of Juvenile Justice*, 310–338.

21. For an overview of juvenile justice reforms since the 1950s, see Margaret K. Rosenheim, "The Modern Juvenile Court," in Rosenheim, Zimring, Tanenhaus, and Dohrn, *A Century of Juvenile Justice*, 341–359. The demands to abolish the court include Harriette N. Dunn, *Infamous Juvenile Law: Crimes against Children under the Cloak of Charity* (Chicago: Privately published, 1912); Thomas D. Eliot, *The Juvenile Court and the Community* (New York: Macmillan, 1914); Jesse Olney, "The Juvenile Courts—Abolish Them," *State Bar Journal of the State Bar of California* 13 (1938): 1; Marvin E. Wolfgang, "Abolish the Juvenile Court System," *California Lawyer* (November 12, 1982): 12–13; Janet E. Ainsworth, "Reimagining Childhood and Reconstructing the Legal Order: The Case for Abolishing the Juvenile Court," *North Carolina Law Review* 69 (1991): 1083–1133; and Barry C. Feld, "Abolish the Juvenile Court: Youthfulness, Criminal Responsibility, and Sentencing Policy," *Journal of Criminal Law and Criminology* 88 (1997): 68–136.

[BIBLIOGRAPHIC ESSAY]

There have been three distinct traditions in the literature on the history of juvenile justice: the progressive mythmakers, the skeptics, and the neoprogressive preservationists. All three traditions have focused their historical inquiries primarily on the rise of the juvenile court. This bibliographic essay highlights the key works that this book engages from each tradition. It also directs the reader to selected works on children, the family, public policy, and American political and legal development that help to place these three traditions into a historiographic context.

The progressive mythmakers, writing in the early twentieth century, characterized the juvenile court movement as a revolutionary, humanitarian advancement in child protection and, through their reminiscences published in the 1920s and 1930s, helped to establish the myth of its immaculate construction. Classic works in this tradition include Timothy D. Hurley, *Origins of the Illinois Juvenile Court Act: Juvenile Courts and What They Have Accomplished* (Chicago: Visitation and Aid Society, 1907; reprint, New York: AMS Press, 1977); Julian W. Mack, "The Juvenile Court," *Harvard Law Review* 23 (1909–1910): 104–122; Sophonisba Preston Breckinridge and Edith Abbott, *The Delinquent Child and the Home* (New York: Charities Publication Committee, 1912); Helen Jeter, *The Chicago Juvenile Court* (Washington, D.C.: Government Printing Office, 1922); Harriet S. Farwell, *Lucy Louisa Flower, 1837–1920: Her Contributions to Education and Child Welfare in Chicago* (Chicago: Private printing, 1924); Jane Addams, ed., *The Child, the Clinic, and the Court* (New York: New

Republic, 1925); Herbert Lou, *Juvenile Courts in the United States* (Chapel Hill: University of North Carolina Press, 1927); Jane Addams and Alice Hamilton, *My Friend, Julia Lathrop* (New York: Macmillan, 1935); and Grace Abbott, *The Child and the State*, 2 vols. (Chicago: University of Chicago Press, 1938).

For examinations of the role of progressive experts in state building and reform generally see Richard Hofstadter, *The Age of Reform: From Bryan to FDR* (New York: Knopf, 1955), Robert H. Wiebe, *The Search for Order: 1877–1920* (New York: Hill and Wang, 1967); David Garland, *Punishment and Welfare: A History of Penal Strategies* (Brookfield, Vt.: Gower, 1985); Morton Keller, *Regulating a New Society, 1900–1933* (Cambridge, Mass.: Harvard University Press, 1994); Daniel T. Rodgers, *Atlantic Crossings: Social Politics in a Progressive Age* (Cambridge, Mass.: Harvard University Press, 1998); and Michael Willrich, *City of Courts: Socializing Justice in Progressive Era Chicago* (New York: Cambridge University Press, 2003).

For the development of child welfare policy in this era see Susan Tiffin, *In Whose Best Interest? Child Welfare Reform in the Progressive Era* (Westport, Conn.: Greenwood Press, 1982); LeRoy Ashby, *Saving the Waifs: Reformers and Dependent Children, 1890–1917* (Philadelphia: Temple University Press, 1984); Michael Grossberg, *Governing the Hearth: Law and the Family in Nineteenth-Century America* (Chapel Hill: University of North Carolina Press, 1985); Michael B. Katz, *In the Shadow of the Poorhouse: A Social History of Welfare in America* (New York: Basic Books, 1986); Margo Horn, *Before It's Too Late: The Child Guidance Movement in the United States, 1922–1945* (Philadelphia: Temple University Press, 1989); Martha Minow, *Making All the Difference: Inclusion, Exclusion, and American Law* (Ithaca, N.Y.: Cornell University Press, 1990); Robyn Muncy, *Creating a Female Dominion in American Reform, 1900–1935* (New York: Oxford University Press, 1991); Theda Skocpol, *Protecting Soldiers and Mothers: The Political Origins of Social Policy in the United States* (Cambridge, Mass.: Harvard University Press, 1992); Joan Gittens, *Poor Relations: The Children of the State in Illinois, 1818–1990* (Urbana: University of Illinois Press, 1994); Linda Gordon, *Pitied But Not Entitled: Single Mothers and the History of Welfare, 1890–1935* (New York: Free Press, 1994); Molly Ladd-Taylor, *Mother-Work: Women, Child Welfare, and the State, 1890–1930* (Urbana: University of Illinois Press, 1994); Mary Ann Mason, *From Father's Property to Children's Rights: The History of Child Custody in the United States* (New York: Columbia University Press, 1994); Kenneth Cmiel, *A Home of Another Kind: One*

Chicago Orphanage and the Tangle of Child Welfare (Chicago: University of Chicago Press, 1995); Kathryn Kish Sklar, *Florence Kelley and the Nation's Work* (New Haven: Yale University Press, 1995); Estelle B. Freedman, *Maternal Justice: Miriam Van Waters and the Female Reform Tradition* (Chicago: University of Chicago Press, 1996); LeRoy Ashby, *Endangered Children: Dependency, Neglect, and Abuse in American History* (New York: Twayne, 1997); Joanne L. Goodwin, *Gender and the Politics of Welfare Reform: Mothers' Pensions in Chicago, 1911–1929* (Chicago: University of Chicago Press, 1997); Timothy A. Hacsi, *Second Homes: Orphan Asylums and Poor Families in America* (Cambridge, Mass.: Harvard University Press, 1997); Kriste Lindenmeyer, *A Right to Childhood: The U.S. Children's Bureau and Child Welfare, 1912–1946* (Urbana: University of Illinois Press, 1997); Elizabeth J. Clapp, *Mothers of All Children: Women Reformers and the Rise of Juvenile Courts in Progressive Era America* (University Park, Pa.: Pennsylvania State University Press, 1998); Matthew A. Crenson, *Building the Invisible Orphanage: A Prehistory of the American Welfare System* (Cambridge, Mass.: Harvard University Press, 1998); Walter I. Trattner, *From Poor Law to Welfare State: A History of Social Welfare in the United States,* 6th ed. (New York: Free Press, 1999); Sonya Michel, *Children's Interests/Mothers' Rights: The Shaping of America's Child Care Policy* (New Haven: Yale University Press, 1999); Jeffrey P. Moran, *Teaching Sex: The Shaping of Adolescence in the twentieth Century* (Cambridge, Mass.: Harvard University Press, 2000); Michael Grossberg, "Changing Conceptions of Child Welfare in the United States, 1820–1935," in *A Century of Juvenile Justice,* edited by Margaret K. Rosenheim, Franklin E. Zimring, David S. Tanenhaus, and Bernardine Dohrn (Chicago: University of Chicago Press, 2002); and Maureen A. Flanagan, *Seeing with Their Hearts: Chicago Women and the Vision of the Good City, 1871–1933* (Princeton, N.J.: Princeton University Press, 2002).

For historical studies that downplay the revolutionary nature of the juvenile court and instead emphasize its continuities with nineteenth-century youth corrections and policing see Joseph M. Hawes, *Children in Urban Society: Juvenile Delinquency in Nineteenth-Century America* (New York: Oxford University Press, 1971); Robert M. Mennel, *Thorns and Thistles: Juvenile Delinquents in the United States, 1825–1940* (Hanover, N.H.: University Press of New England, 1973); Steven L. Schlossman, *Love and the American Delinquent: The Theory and Practice of "Progressive" Juvenile Justice* (Chicago: University of Chicago Press, 1977); Peter C. Holloran, *Boston's Wayward Children: Social Services for Homeless*

Children, 1830–1930 (Rutherford, N.J.: Fairleigh Dickinson University Press, 1989); Eric C. Schneider, *In the Web of Class: Delinquents and Reformers in Boston, 1810s–1930s* (New York: New York University Press, 1992); and David Wolcott, "Juvenile Justice before Juvenile Court: Cops, Courts, and Kids in Turn-of-the-Century Detroit," *Social Science History* 27 (2003): 109–136.

Although the skeptical tradition dates back to the early twentieth century, it did not blossom until after the U.S. Supreme Court's landmark decision in *In Re Gault* (1967). Its proponents have used the concept of social control to explain the ideological origins of the juvenile court and to call into question the benevolent motives of its architects. Many have also criticized the juvenile justice system for denying due process protections to children and their families and its limited success in rehabilitating juvenile offenders. Early works from this tradition include Harriette N. Dunn, *Infamous Juvenile Law: Crimes against Children under the Cloak of Charity* (Chicago: Privately published, 1912); Thomas D. Eliot, *The Juvenile Court and the Community* (New York: MacMillan, 1914); and Edward F. Waite, "How Far Can Court Procedure Be Socialized without Impairing Individual Rights?" *Journal of Criminal Law and Criminology* 12 (1921): 339–347.

The post-*Gault* studies include Anthony M. Platt, *The Child Savers: The Invention of Delinquency* (Chicago: University of Chicago Press, 1969); Sanford Fox, "Juvenile Justice Reform: An Historical Perspective," *Stanford Law Review* 22 (1970): 1187–1239; Ellen Ryerson, *The Best-Laid Plans: America's Juvenile Court Experiment* (New York: Hill and Wang, 1978); David J. Rothman, *Conscience and Convenience: The Asylum and Its Alternatives in Progressive America* (Boston: Little, Brown, 1980); Lawrence Meir Friedman and Robert V. Percival, *The Roots of Justice: Crime and Punishment in Alameda County, California, 1870–1910* (Chapel Hill: University of North Carolina Press, 1981); Andrew J. Polsky, *The Rise of the Therapeutic State* (Princeton, N.J.: Princeton University Press, 1991); Janet E. Ainsworth, "Reimagining Childhood and Reconstructing the Legal Order: The Case for Abolishing the Juvenile Court," *North Carolina Law Review* 69 (1991): 1083–1133; Thomas Bernard, *The Cycle of Juvenile Justice* (New York: Oxford University Press, 1992); Mary E. Odem, *Delinquent Daughters: Protecting and Policing Adolescent Female Sexuality in the United States, 1885–1920* (Chapel Hill: University of North Carolina, 1995); Christopher P. Manfredi, *The Supreme Court and Juvenile Justice* (Lawrence: University of Kansas Press, 1998); Barry C. Feld, *Bad Kids: Race and the Transformation of the Juvenile Court* (New

York: Oxford University Press, 1999); Victoria L. Getis, *The Juvenile Court and the Progressives* (Urbana: University of Illinois Press, 2000); and Anne Meis Knupfer, *Reform and Resistance: Gender, Delinquency, and America's First Juvenile Court* (New York: Routledge, 2001).

For important historical and theoretical studies about social control and power, broadly conceived, see Michel Foucault, *Discipline and Punish: The Birth of the Prison* (New York: Pantheon Books, 1977); Christopher Lasch, *Haven in a Heartless World: The Family Besieged* (New York: Basic Books, 1977); Jacques Donzelot, *The Policing of Families* (New York: Pantheon Books, 1979); Linda Gordon, *Heroes of Their Own Lives: The Politics and History of Family Violence: Boston, 1880–1960* (New York: Viking, 1988); Regina G. Kunzel, *Fallen Women, Problem Girls: Unmarried Mothers and the Professionalization of Social Work* (New Haven: Yale University Press, 1993); George Chauncey, *Gay New York: Gender, Urban Culture, and the Making of the Gay Male World, 1890–1940* (New York: Basic Books, 1994); Elizabeth Lunbeck, *The Psychiatric Persuasion: Knowledge, Gender, and Power in Modern America* (Princeton, N.J.: Princeton University Press, 1994); and Kathleen W. Jones, *Taming the Troublesome Child: American Families, Child Guidance, and the Limits of Psychiatric Authority* (Cambridge, MA.: Harvard University Press, 1999).

Legal scholars and historians have also begun to reexamine the history of individual rights and state power in American history, see Robert Kaczorowski, "Revolutionary Constitutionalism in the Era of the Civil War and Reconstruction," *New York University Law Review* 61 (November 1986): 863–940; Hendrik Hartog, "The Constitution of Aspiration" and "The Rights that Belong to All of Us," *Journal of American History* 74 (1987): 1013–1034; Eric Foner, *Reconstruction: America's Unfinished Revolution* (New York: Harper and Row, 1988); William J. Novak, *The People's Welfare: Law and Regulation in Nineteenth-Century America* (Chapel Hill: University of North Carolina Press, 1996); Akhil Reed Amar, *The Bill of Rights: Construction and Reconstruction* (New Haven: Yale University Press, 1998); Amy Dru Stanley, *From Bondage to Contract: Wage Labor, Marriage, and the Market in the Age of Slave Emancipation* (New York: Cambridge University Press, 1998); William E. Nelson, *The Legalist Reformation: Law, Politics, and Ideology in New York, 1920–1980* (Chapel Hill: University of North Carolina Press, 2001); and Barbara Young Welke, *Recasting American Liberty: Gender, Race, Law, and the Railroad Revolution, 1865–1920* (New York: Cambridge University Press, 2001).

The neoprogressive preservationists view the history of juvenile justice, especially its beginnings, as a valuable site for excavating a usable past. They generally accept that the founders of the juvenile court were well intentioned but that the concerns of the skeptics about the rights of children and families must also be incorporated into the juvenile justice system. Among these studies are Margaret K. Rosenheim, ed., *Justice for the Child: The Juvenile Court in Transition* (New York: Free Press of Glencoe, 1962); Margaret K. Rosenheim, ed., *Pursuing Justice for the Child* (Chicago: University of Chicago Press, 1976); Franklin E. Zimring, *The Changing Legal World of Adolescence* (New York: Free Press, 1982); Robert J. Sampson and John H. Laub, *Crime in the Making: Pathways and Turning Points through Life* (Cambridge, Mass.: Harvard University Press, 1993); Simon I. Singer, *Recriminalizing Delinquency: Violent Juvenile Crime and Juvenile Justice Reform* (New York: Cambridge University Press, 1996); William Ayers, *A Kind and Just Parent: The Children of Juvenile Court* (Boston: Beacon Press, 1997); Howard Snyder and Melissa Sickmund, *Juvenile Offenders and Victims: 1999 National Report* (Washington, D.C.: U.S. Department of Justice, 1999); Jeffrey Fagan and Franklin E. Zimring, eds., *The Changing Borders of Juvenile Justice: Transfer of Adolescents to the Criminal Court* (Chicago: University of Chicago Press, 2000); Thomas Grisso and Robert G. Schwartz, eds., *Youth on Trial: A Developmental Perspective on Juvenile Justice* (Chicago: University of Chicago Press, 2000); and Margaret K. Rosenheim, Franklin E. Zimring, David S. Tanenhaus and Bernardine Dohrn, *A Century of Juvenile Justice* (Chicago: University of Chicago Press, 2002).

For an excellent introduction to the trends in criminology since the 1970s, see David Garland, *The Culture of Control: Crime and Social Order in Contemporary Society* (Chicago: University of Chicago Press, 2001).

[INDEX]